Historical Problems:
Studies and Documents

Edited by
PROFESSOR G. R. ELTON
University of Cambridge

20
BRITAIN AT BAY

In the same series

BRITAIN AT BAY

Defence against Bonaparte, 1803-14

Richard Glover
Professor of History, Carleton University, Ottawa, Ontario

LONDON: GEORGE ALLEN & UNWIN LTD
BARNES AND NOBLE BOOKS - NEW YORK
(a division of Harper & Row Publishers, Inc.)

British ISBN 0 04 940043 6 hardback
          0 04 940044 4 paperback

Published in USA 1973 by
HARPER & ROW PUBLISHERS, INC.
BARNES & NOBLE IMPORT DIVISION

American ISBN 06-492445-9

Printed in Great Britain
in 10 point Plantin type by
The Aldine Press · Letchworth · Hertfordshire

CONTENTS

The purpose of this book is to describe how England was defended against invasion during the eleven years of the Napoleonic War from 1803 to 1814. Its first chapter sketches the background, beginning with the nature of the threat the island faced and explaining why 1814 should be chosen as the final date. It also reviews the various stages through which the war passed. The next chapter discusses that highly complicated subject, the organisation of British defence from the office of the Prime Minister downwards, with special attention to the land forces. Third, the navy receives, as it deserves, a chapter to itself. I have avoided going into details on any particular operations at sea. These have been well described by others; and naval battles were in any case infrequent. The great task of the navy through all those eleven years of war was controlling the seas from week to week and month to month by blockading the enemy's fleets and being at all times ready to fight them. This task required ships, men, rations and discipline, and these accordingly are the subjects of my third chapter. I have not ventured into such technical questions as medical services and naval hospitals. Sound criticism of the health measures adopted in any period requires more professional medical knowledge than I can call to my aid. But my readers will lose little by this omission, thanks to the solid work of J. J. Keevil, Christopher Lloyd and J. L. S. Coulter to which those who are specially interested in this subject may be referred.[1] The fourth and fifth chapters are on those two very closely related topics – the great Boulogne flotilla of 1803–5, and the fortification of the English coast which had made it obsolete for other purposes than bluff by 1807. The sixth and last chapter deals with raising men both for the home defence of Britain and for that essential corollary to defence, counter-attack. Documents chosen to illustrate these topics follow.

My subject is limited to the defence of England itself. I do not deal with Ireland, mainly for lack of space, but also because I have been led to the view that the dangers threatening England from Ireland were less than is sometimes supposed. Ireland in the Napoleonic era is still an interesting subject to which I hope to return.

An author's final, and pleasantest, task in writing a preface is to thank those who have made his work possible. My thanks are due, first, to Her Majesty the Queen, for gracious permission to work in the archives of Windsor Castle; also, to successive librarians at the War

[1] *Medicine and the Navy, 1200–1900*, 4 vols. (Edinburgh, 1957–63).

Office, Mr White and Mr King, for much assistance and guidance in their collections; to the always helpful and obliging staff of the Public Record Office on Chancery Lane; and to Professor Hugh Trevor-Roper for permission to quote, from his *The Philby Affair*, the passage on pp. 48–9 n. 42 below.

I regret that two interesting books appeared too late for me to use them when writing on the fortification of the English coast. They are Sheila Sutcliffe, *Martello Towers* (London, 1972) and P. A. L. Vine, *The Royal Military Canal* (London, 1972).

INTRODUCTION

Background

How Napoleon Bonaparte, the First Consul (and after 1804 Emperor)[1] of the French, planned to invade and conquer Britain in 1803–5 is one of the abiding folk memories of the English people. As children, in our school days, we heard about his great 'Army of England' drilling on the cliffs of France, all ready and waiting to cross the Channel. We heard, too, of the vast flotilla of invasion barges which 'Boney' assembled in his Channel ports to ferry this army over to England. The climax of the story was how Nelson met a hero's death in his victory at Trafalgar; and from then on, it was inferred, everybody in England lived happily ever after, because the danger of invasion was over.

Those well-known episodes in British history are part of the subject of this book. The present chapter will examine, first, the nature of the dangers confronting Britain throughout the Napoleonic War. Secondly, it will review the changing stages of that war, from its start when Britain fought alone to its end in which Britain contributed much to the final victory that freed Europe from French domination.

DANGERS CONFRONTING BRITAIN

The first thing to be said about the danger of invasion is that it was real; and the second is that we were misinformed when we were led to suppose that the victory of Trafalgar put an end to it.

It is necessary to insist that England's danger was real, because today some make light of it. Among them are certain British naval historians who are perhaps over-impressed by Admiral Lord St Vincent's remark to his fellow peers, 'I do not say, my Lords, that the French will not come. I only say they will not come by sea'; and a more positive remark than that could hardly be made. But before one accepts it at face value,

---

[1] The British never recognised this latter title which Bonaparte assumed after England went to war with France in 1803 and had lost before peace was made in 1814. To them he remained, officially, General Bonaparte throughout the war.

it is proper to ask whether, in the circumstances, St Vincent could have said anything less positive. For St Vincent was not only a distinguished seaman; he was also First Lord of the Admiralty in Addington's cabinet; his preparations for defence were under bitter attack; this much quoted statement was part of his reply; and on such an occasion no politician can be expected to confess any doubts he may privately feel about his own handiwork. But St Vincent's fellow admirals did not all share his publicly expressed confidence. Among those who differed was Admiral Lord Keith, whose command of the squadron charged with guarding the invasion coasts compelled him to examine carefully all possibilities open to the enemy; and in October 1803 he was at pains to give the Commander-in-Chief of the Army a confidential warning that the French fleet might 'get out of Brest unperceived' and run up to 'the Downs or Margate Roads, in which case it might be superior to our squadron long enough to cover the landing of any extent of Force' on the English coast (Doc. 2). And in this statement Lord Keith endorses the practicality of something very like Bonaparte's actual plan for 1805.

Across the Channel the question of how seriously Bonaparte really intended to invade England was raised by no less a man than Col. Edouard Desbrière, who made so exhaustive study of French projects for attacking Britain. Desbrière noted that in July 1805, Bonaparte had landing craft enough to carry over 151,940 men across the Channel (a total of which had grown to 167,000 by 8 August), but no more than 93,000 at his Channel ports ready to sail nor any reinforcements nearer than Paris; and Paris was four days' march away. These facts led Desbrière to suggest that the Boulogne flotilla was a mere bluff, designed partly to scare the British, and partly to enable Bonaparte to keep a great army ready for service at any moment against Austria; and Sir Julian Corbett was emphatically of the same opinion.[2]

But these authors had evidently not made some rather particular calculations which must be made before Bonaparte's situation can be properly assessed; and when they are made it appears that he should have had ample time to complete his concentration.

The data are as follows. First, the fleet, with which Bonaparte intended to protect his voyage, was to reach the Channel from the East, after going north-about round Ireland and Scotland and stopping off the Texel to pick up the Dutch battle squadron (Doc. 14c). Second, the distance from the Texel to Boulogne is nearly 300 miles; and 100 miles

[2] Edouard Desbrière, *Projets et Tentatives de Débarquement aux Isles Britanniques* (Paris, 1902) IV, 830. Corbett was even more downright, declaring, 'Nothing, not even the army itself, was ever ready'. *The Campaign of Trafalgar* (new edition, London, 1919) I, 17.

a day was a good average for ships under sail[3]; also the Dutch might have to wait at least half a day for a tide to get them out of Texel. Hence a space of three days must be reckoned to elapse between the fleet's arrival at the Texel and the start of the invasion. But, third, Texel was linked with Paris by the semaphore telegraph, and the fleet's arrival there should be known to Bonaparte within an hour, and his marching orders to the army should be promptly issued. This means that additional troops should begin reaching Boulogne only some twenty-four hours after the fleet. Then, fourth, the Boulogne flotilla was so large that it needed six tides, or three days, to get to sea. So reinforcements ordered to march after the fleet's arrival at the Texel was signalled should reach Boulogne in time probably for the third, certainly for the fourth, tide after the operation began. The only troops needed at the coast earlier than that were those who would go off on the first two or three tides; and for that some 93,000, or well over half the force the boats could carry, would seem ample.

The fact, then, that Bonaparte never concentrated on the coast more than two thirds of the men his invasion craft could carry is not evidence that he never seriously intended to invade England. It is nothing more than another example of how he applied his own maxim 'Disperse to feed, concentrate to fight' – and in these days, when trains, lorries and aircraft enable us so speedily to deliver any amount of tinned foods at a given point, it is important to remember how hard it then was to feed great masses of men in an age when our modern means of transport, and even the art of preserving tinned foods, were still undreamt of.

There should, then, be no doubts about the reality of the danger England faced in 1803–5. The British admiral commanding in the Straits of Dover believed it possible that the French might gain command of the narrow seas for long enough to land 'any extent of Force' on the English coast; and a study of the time factor leaves no grounds for the supposition that Bonaparte was only bluffing. Then add that Bonaparte devoted two years to building and assembling his vast flotilla of specially designed landing craft; that he created four new harbours to shelter it; also that on 14 March 1805 – the very year in which it is suggested his proposed invasion of England was a mere

---

[3] So I was first informed by my friend Mr B. Sivertz, recently Commissioner for the North West Territories and a former officer in the Royal Canadian Navy during the Hitler War, who in his youth twice crossed the Pacific under sail. I find his recollections supported by the record of Captain William Bligh, who averaged 108 miles per day on his voyage from Britain to Tahiti in the *Bounty*. It is proper to stress that we are here dealing in averages, taking good days with bad; and that on good days ships might do more than 100; but it is also proper to recall that the prevailing winds in the Channel are from the West, i.e. head winds for a fleet proceeding from the Texel to Boulogne.

front to conceal preparations against Austria – he ordered an additional 20,000,000 francs to be spent on improving his roads from Paris to his naval bases, Brest, Cherbourg and Boulogne, but not a cent for the roads leading from Calais and Boulogne to Austrian territory;[4] and it becomes impossible not to believe that in 1803–5 Bonaparte had every intention of landing in England and crushing his enemies there on their own soil.

But when the reality of the menace in 1803–5 is accepted, curious doubts remain about the years after 1805; and some serious historians, who do not belittle the threat from Boulogne, allege that Nelson's victory at Trafalgar made 'any revival of the [invasion] threat impossible' – an allegation which poses as baffling a riddle as any in historiography today. How can that assertion be made by authors who also describe the Copenhagen campaign of 1807 and the Walcheren Expedition of 1809 ? For it is made by such authors; and yet the British attacks on both Copenhagen and the Scheldt were essentially defensive. Neither had a chance of weakening Bonaparte's landpower, but each was a blow against the seapower with which he threatened England; and, with their kindred operations, Sir Sidney Smith's threat to bombard Lisbon in November 1807 and Admiral Gambier's very effective night attack on the Aix Roads in April 1809,[5] they betoken a change in the nature of the war.

That change in the nature of the war came in 1806. Until 1806 was well advanced, there were no regular fortifications to protect the

---

[4] J. Holland Rose, *Pitt and Napoleon: Essays and Letters* (London, 1912) 137.

[5] I say 'Gambier's . . . night attack' because the attack with fire ships was his idea, proposed before the Admiralty inflicted Captain Lord Cochrane on him as its executant. I say 'very effective' because it resulted in the complete destruction of one 50-gun ship and 3 ships of the line and put the other 7 French line of battle ships out of action by damaging them so severely that it took years, rather than months, to repair them. After carefully reading the evidence given at Gambier's court martial I am left, first, with a conviction that nothing more could have been done in the action and, second, with a total contempt for Cochrane as a man of honour. His *Autobiography of a Seaman* is not only highly selective in the evidence it chooses to present; it also contains falsehoods which the age of its author at the time of writing cannot excuse. Errors of memory one may pardon; deliberate lies one may not; and Cochrane is just a plain and shameless liar who, in describing Gambier's trial, presents, with all the paraphernalia of quotation marks and page references, texts that purport to be the actual words of the witnesses, but are in fact Cochrane's own rewriting of their evidence with substantial modifications – all duly quoted and italicised beside the original by Lady Chatterton in her *Memorials . . . of Admiral Lord Gambier*, vol. II. Before one complains that after the Aix Roads Cochrane 'was slighted in every possible way [by the Admiralty] and never employed again' one should ask what commander would consent to accept him as a subordinate after seeing how he had treated Gambier. See also E. Chevalier, *Histoire de la marine française* (Paris, 1886), 341.

beaches of Kent and Sussex; instead the enemy's handiest landing places were guarded by nothing better than guns in earthen entrenchments. Against such defences an assault landing had unpleasantly good prospects of success; and, while this was the case, Bonaparte could continue to plan an invasion of England with only a local and temporary command of the sea and with a flotilla designed for no more than a ten or twelve hour voyage in good weather. But this favourable situation ended in the autumn of 1806 when those new coast defences, the Martello Towers and the Royal Military Canal, were finished and ready for use. As we shall see, these formidable new fortifications made it fruitless to attempt an assault on those beaches which could be reached with a short voyage and only a local command of the sea. Henceforth, if Bonaparte was to subdue Britain, he must first defeat the Royal Navy on the seas.

To this task he now turned, and there was nothing in the results of Trafalgar to make it impossible for him to succeed. That great battle was indeed a crowning mercy for England. One way or another, none of the eighteen French line of battle ships which took part in it ever fought for France again; and this loss, followed, as it was, by Sir John Duckworth's destruction of all five ships in Leissegue's squadron off St Domingo in February 1806, and the losses suffered by Willaumez, dealt a heavy blow to Bonaparte's seapower.[6] But it could not destroy his seapower. France still had the dockyards, timber and seamen, which are the foundations of naval power; she still had substantial squadrons – in Rochefort and Brest – which had not suffered at Trafalgar. She still had her old allies, the Spaniards and Dutch, whose fleets Bonaparte counted as his own; and in 1807 she gained another ally – Russia. Out of these resources Bonaparte hatched a new plan.

At Tilsit, in July 1807 he and the Tsar, Alexander I, between them agreed to unite all the navies of Europe in one grand confederate fleet to overwhelm the British by sheer weight of numbers; and the attack on Copenhagen was part of Britain's counterstroke to that plan. It was a very successful counterstroke too; Admiral Gambier and General Cathcart captured the whole of Denmark's navy of twenty-one line of battle ships[7] and emptied her arsenals of ship-building stores – losses

---

[6] To the 14 French ships either captured, sunk or blockaded (and in 1808 surrendered) in Cadiz after Trafalgar must be added Dumanoir's squadron of 4, which Sir Richard Strachan destroyed on 4 November 1805; Leissegues' squadron of 5, which Sir John Duckworth destroyed off San Domingo on 6 February 1806; and Willaumez's squadron of 6 of which one was wrecked and burnt on the U.S. coast, 4 interned in U.S. harbours and only one, the *Veteran*, commanded by Jerome Bonaparte, got back to France.

[7] Twenty-one was Denmark's total, of which the British found 3 unfit to sail and burnt them; whether these could have been made ready for the sea after a winter's work is a question I cannot answer.

which the Danes were never able to make good while the war lasted. This blow shattered Bonaparte's hopes in the North. Without the aid of the Danes, the Russians could not take on the combined squadrons of Sweden and Britain in the Baltic, let alone overcome the Swedes and seize their fleet.

In a bare eight months two more events destroyed Bonaparte's hopes in the South. The first, at Lisbon, robbed him of Portugal's fleet, which General Junot had been ordered to secure when he invaded that country in November 1807. Sir Sidney Smith foiled that plan. As the French advanced on Lisbon, and the Portuguese prince regent, knowing not what to do, dithered in helpless indecision, Smith assisted him to make up his mind with an ultimatum requiring him to sail with his fleet to Brazil or see his capital bombarded. The prince chose to sail; and Bonaparte lost another eight line of battle ships. Then, of course, in the next spring the Spaniards rose in revolt against their French masters, thus starting the Peninsular War, Bonaparte's 'Spanish ulcer' which over the next six years was to drain away so much French blood and French gold; and its immediate result was to rob Bonaparte of the whole Spanish navy.

So, thanks to two bold strokes by the British and the unforeseen revolt of the Spaniards, the whole scheme of crushing England with the grand armada of the continent in 1808 crumbled. But had there been hesitations in London, and the expected degree of submissiveness in Madrid, God alone knows what would have happened that year. Various calculations have been made of the naval force Bonaparte might have assembled and their totals do not all agree; but this at least seems clear – that the combined fleets of Europe would have considerably outnumbered the grand total of line of battle ships which the British admiralty could have equipped and manned and which she no longer had Nelson to command. And England's lucky star has surely never shone more brightly than in the timing of the Spanish revolt. It relieved her from fear of the Spanish fleet in the very hour when she had to begin to take Russia's fleet seriously. She was lucky too in the fact that Alexander I's enthusiasm for France as an ally soon cooled, and his hostility to England became more nominal than real.

But even these great events did not end Britain's danger nor break Bonaparte's determination to destroy her. He still possessed those indispensable foundations of seapower – men, drawn from all the subject nations of his empire, materials and bases; and among the last one must note the rise of Antwerp. When the French conquered Belgium and Holland in the autumn and winter of 1794-5, they put an end to one of their ancient weaknesses at sea. Hitherto France had possessed no naval base, where a fleet might shelter, north and east of Brest. But from 1749 to 1814 she had Antwerp, of which Bonaparte made a great

naval base than Brest itself; and between the two he created yet another
base, capable of building, as well as sheltering and repairing ships of
the line, at Cherbourg. With these new resources, added to those of
France's old bases, at Brest, Rochefort and Toulon, and those of his
other new bases, at Genoa, Naples and Venice, Bonaparte flung himself
into the task of out-building the Royal Navy from the means his own
empire provided. His publicly declared target was a fleet of 150 line of
battle ships; even the Russian disaster did not end his ship-building
programme; he continued to plan for the defeat of Britain. (Docs. 19, 20.)

The great renaissance of French seapower which followed attracts
strangely little attention today. Our ancestors, Bonaparte's contemporaries, were very much aware of it and explicit in describing it. So
Captain Edward Brenton, who was both a historian and veteran of the
war at sea, records that, after Trafalgar, 'another French navy, as if by
magic sprang forth from the forests to the seashore, manned by a
maritime conscription exactly similar in principle to that edict by which
the trees were appropriated to the building of ships'.[8] How that fleet
grew is a story I have told elsewhere[9] and need not repeat here. It will
be enough to say that in six years Bonaparte's fleets increased from the
mere 34 line of battle ships counted in French and Dutch harbours in
1807 to over 80 ready for the sea with another 35 building in 1813.[10]
When one notes that through the whole war Britain was never able to
equip and man in any year more than the 113 ships of the line achieved
in 1808-9 and that from then on the totals she reached declined to
107 in 1811, 102 in 1813 and 99 in 1814, one sees the events of 1805-6,
which lopped over 30 ships off the French fleet, in a new light. One
can appreciate, too, the fact that Britain's danger did not end in 1805
or even in 1808. It lasted as long as the war lasted, a point which the
First Lord of the Admiralty, Lord Melville, frankly confessed to the
diarist Greville, over the dinner table, after Bonaparte's fall. Then at
last Melville could admit that, given time, Bonaparte would 'have sent
forth such powerful fleets that our navy must eventually have been
destroyed, since we could never have kept pace with him in building
ships nor equipped numbers sufficient to cope with the tremendous
power he could have brought against us.'[11]

[8] Edward Brenton, *The Naval History of Great Britain from 1793 to 1822*
(London, 1823-5), IV, 3.

[9] Glover, 'The French Fleet, 1807-1814: Britain's Problem; and Madison's
Opportunity,' *Journal of Modern History*, Vol. 39 (1967), 233-52.

[10] France's total in 1814 is commonly given as 103; but this total includes old
vessels fit only to serve as guard ships or store ships; the important number is the
total of those 'fit for the sea' – with crews, stores and weapons, and structurally
sound.

[11] L. Strachey and R. Fulford (eds.), *The Greville Memoirs* (London, 1938), I,
14.

But Bonaparte was not given time. He was denied it by the epoch-making events of the campaigns waged on land in 1812–14; and at this point then we must turn to look at the successive stages of the war through which Britain struggled from 1803 to Bonaparte's fall.

THE STAGES OF THE WAR

The whole period of Britain's war against Bonaparte breaks down into five stages. The first is from 1803 to 1805 when she fought alone. The second is the period of disastrous continental alliances from 1805 to 1807. The third is the brief interlude from July 1807 to May 1808, when the Spanish revolt began. The fourth is the period of offensive defence which runs from 1808, when the British army returned to the continent, down to 1812. The fifth and last is the stage of effective counter-attack in 1813–14 when British forces were the first troops of the final alliance against Bonaparte to invade France.

Henry Addington was Prime Minister when the war began. He had few admirers then, and perhaps not too many now. As a speaker he had the misfortune, in an age of oratorical giants, to be at best second-rate and to be too easily rattled by a hostile audience. His pompous manner invited ridicule and so did the fact that his father was only a physician; hence he was nicknamed 'the Doctor', and, to illustrate how his prestige as premier fell, one need only quote Wellington's recollection, 'At that time the word "Doctor" was enough to convulse the House with laughter.'[12] Our day has hardly been kinder, and most of us were brought up to accept Holland Rose's sweeping dismissal of his government: 'Over against Addington set Bonaparte; with Hawkesbury compare Talleyrand; with Hobart, Berthier. The weighing need go no further. The British Ministry kicks the beam'.[13] Yet Addington was nobody's fool.[14] His declaration of war was admirably timed, at a moment when Bonaparte had made his hostility clear and still was unready to fight. He kept Britain strong even after he had made the peace of 1802; he did a very respectable job of making her still stronger as soon as war began again; and the way he raised money for the war is now recognised as first class.[15]

In April 1804, Addington fell and was replaced by Pitt. Great credit, as we shall see, is due to Pitt for at least one thing, approving the Duke

---

[12] Stanhope, *Conversations with the Duke of Wellington* (Oxford, 1947), 130.
[13] *William Pitt and the Great War* (London, 1911), 487.
[14] So I was led to conclude when writing *Peninsular Preparation; the Reform of the British Army* (Cambridge, 1963), 30–2. Mr Philip Ziegler comes to the same conclusion in his excellent biography, *Addington* (London, 1965).
[15] See A. Farnsworth, *Addington, Author of the Modern Income Tax* (London, 1951); and Ziegler, op. cit., 189–94.

of York's expensive plans for fortifying the south coast. But his cabinet was not very noticeably stronger than Addington's – indeed, it contained many of the same people; and his foreign policy led directly to the second stage of the war, the stage of disastrous alliances of 1805–7.

For Pitt's alliances were indeed most disastrous, as well as expensive. Yet it would be unjust to blame him for making them. The task of any statesman involved in a life and death struggle is to bring the war to a victorious end, and sheer lack of manpower to raise sufficient armies made it impossible for Britain alone to defeat France. It was, then, natural for Pitt to seek allies, and Bonaparte's insensitive disregard for others helped him gain them. Out of the well-meant exertions of the one and the reckless provocations of the other came the ill-coordinated alliance of the Third Coalition, in which Pitt was reduced to financing the war effort of allies who rejected his war aims. Ruin swiftly followed as the battles of Ulm and Austerlitz and the treaty of Pressburg knocked Austria out of the war by Christmas 1805.[16] Then, on 23 January 1806, Pitt died of 'a typhus fever, caught by some accidental infection',[17] and his government fell. His cousin, Lord Grenville, next formed, mainly out of Whigs, the government of All-the-Talents, which lasted from February 1806 to March 1807. This ministry began by attempting to make peace with France and ended by financing Prussia and Russia in their fight against Bonaparte. The next ministry, the Duke of Portland's, was in power when the peace of Tilsit between France and Russia ended this phase in July 1807.

The situation which Britain faced after the Treaty of Tilsit can only be compared with that in which she found herself in 1940; indeed, it was in some ways worse than 1940; and that is the yardstick by which to measure the results of Pitt's disastrous alliances. Of the world's powers America was still neutral, but far from friendly; Sweden and the helpless Bourbon king of Naples, who now ruled no more than Sicily, were Britain's only allies. The rest of Europe, from the Atlantic Ocean to the Urals and beyond, was united in the enemy's camp.

The bitterest thing about it all is that Britain had so little right to complain at the way the world turned against her; for her own efforts in the War of the Third Coalition had been despicable. Though Pitt had begun negotiating with Russia before 1804 was over, not a single step toward preparing a British expeditionary force to support his allies in northern Europe seems to have been taken till Lord Castlereagh

[16] The date of the actual signature of the Treaty of Pressburg was Boxing Day, 26 December 1805.

[17] Lord Brougham, *Historical Sketches of Statesmen in the Time of George III* (London, 1839), III, 312. As Brougham got the diagnosis from Lord Wellesley, who had visited Pitt during his last illness, it seems sounder than the story that the news of Austerlitz killed him, a legend perhaps derived from Wilberforce (*Life of Wilberforce*, by his Sons (London, 1838), IV, 245).

became Minister for War in July 1805. Castlereagh, to be sure, spared
no pains; but it was then too late for his hastily contrived invasion of
Germany to accomplish anything. Pitt's attempt at a second front in
Italy was equally futile. Trafalgar was indeed a superb triumph for
Britain. To measure what Nelson's victory meant to her, one need
only recall that every one of the 18 French ships of the line which
Villeneuve led into that battle was ultimately lost to France;[18] and then
consider what they would have done to the balance of power at sea if
they had still been Bonaparte's in 1812–13. But, one must add, only
Britain benefited from Trafalgar. Though the shattering of French
ships, and slaughter of French seamen, in the Atlantic did much for her
safety, it did nothing to reduce the odds against which her Russian and
Austrian allies were to struggle so vainly at Austerlitz.

But at least Pitt tried. His successors did not even do that. At this very
day it is still painful for an Englishman to read in the Foreign Office
archives the repeated and fruitless requests of the Russians in 1806 that
Britain should make 'partial expeditions on the Coasts of France and
Holland for the purpose of distracting the attention of the Enemy and
impeding the march of the French Reserves which have received orders
to follow the Army under the personal command of Napoleon'.[19] Such
a policy of commando raids had been part and parcel of the strategy of
the great elder Pitt in the Seven Years War. His expeditions were
indeed nothing more than raids; they secured no lasting gains; but they
did draw off French troops from the East; and that was what the
Russians now wanted. In 1806 the Prime Minister, Lord Grenville,
was the great Pitt's own nephew, but he never lifted a finger to copy the
example of his incomparable uncle. The ministry of All-the-Talents
made but three serious attempts at an offensive strategy – at Constantinople, Alexandria and Buenos Aires. All were fiascos; only one –
Constantinople – offered any prospect of helping the Russians, who
were at war with the Turks as well as the French; and the attempt at
Buenos Aires to conquer the Spanish colony which has become Argen-
tina was actually made when Spain was negotiating to join the allies
against Bonaparte. It is true, indeed, that in this year one small British
force under General Sir John Stuart did land in Europe and win one
nice little victory – at Maida in southern Italy on 3 July 1806. But as
this incursion was made, without London's knowledge, on the local

---

[18] To those sunk or captured during the actual battle must be added the
squadron of four (*Formidable, Mont-Blanc, Scipion* and *Duguay-Trouin*) which
Sir Richard Strachan intercepted and captured on 4 November; and the five
(*Neptune, Algeciras, Pluton, Argonaute* and *Heros*) which escaped to Cadiz, but
had to surrender to the Spaniards there in 1808.

[19] Stuart to Howick, St Petersburg, 28 November 1806, reporting the request
of General Budberg, the Russian foreign minister; and on 18 December, he
wrote again reporting a similar request from the Tsar himself. FO/65/65.

initiative of the commander of the British garrison in Sicily, the government can claim little credit for it. Yet the exaggerated hopes aroused by both the achievement and the example of General Sir John Stuart's raid into Calabria and disappointment at the collapse of these inflated expectations, undoubtedly increased the Russian's disgust at their ally. It is really a little hard to blame Alexander I if he greeted Bonaparte at Tilsit with an outstretched right hand and the words 'I hate the English as much as you do'.

Yet when Alexander used these words, the English had a new government that was eager to help him – a government of brave young men under an elderly and inept, but amiable, figure head. It may be true that the Prime Minister, the Duke of Portland, brought nothing to the council board except a rather specially pompous indecision, as Sir John Fortescue put it in one of his vivid phrases; but under Portland were the men of the future – Spencer Perceval, the eldest, aged 45; Lord Liverpool, aged 37; Lord Castlereagh, aged 38; George Canning, aged 37. This government opened the third phase of the war by utterly disconcerting Bonaparte with its vigorous attack on Copenhagen and seizure of the Danish fleet in August and September 1807, as has been described. It thwarted him again by taking steps to persuade Dom John, the Regent of Portugal, in November 1807, to remove both his court and his fleet to Rio de Janeiro before General Junot's French forces seized Lisbon.

The Portland government was still in power when the Spanish revolt of May 1808 opened the fourth period of the war and offered them the chance to send the British army overseas to fight the French on the continent. They seized their chance and a topsy turvy four years followed.

We today look back to the years 1808–12 as one of the heroic periods of English history, a period of stubborn fighting which set the stage for decisive victory. But contemporaries were, of course, denied this retrospective view of a glorious end to years of persistent effort. For them these were years of unsurpassed difficulty and danger. In this period they saw successive governments destroyed, literally, by pistol shots. For Portland's fell apart when two of his Secretaries of State, Canning and Castlereagh, carried cabinet dissension to the point of fighting a duel on 21 September 1809; and Spencer Perceval's ended when the Prime Minister himself was murdered in the lobby of the House of Commons on 11 May 1812. The first month of 1809, when Sir John Moore's advance into Spain became a retreat followed by his death at Corunna, saw a campaign that looked like a military disaster;[20] it also

[20] The extent to which Moore's foray into Spain had in fact unhinged Bonaparte's plans for reconquering the country could not be known at the time in England; on which, see the short final chapter to Christopher Hibbert's *Corunna* (London, 1961).

saw what really was a military disaster, the enquiry into the conduct of
the very able Commander-in-Chief of the Army, the Duke of York,
which caused his resignation, just as the Peninsular War was beginning
in earnest. Worse still, the enquiry into the Duke's conduct took up
nearly the whole time of the House of Commons from 20 January to
18 March. Rather naturally, no active military planning was done while
this business absorbed the government's attention; and this in turn
contributed to another disaster – the long delay in launching the Walcheren expedition which aimed at both helping Austria and destroying
the French fleet in the Scheldt. It failed in both objects. The Austrians,
Bonaparte's most stubborn opponents of the continent, were ready in
1809 to strike another blow for the freedom of Europe from France,
but they wanted aid in the spring. It was the end of July before the
Walcheren expedition sailed. By then the two-day battle of Wagram on
5–6 July had ended Austria's single-handed struggle. The expedition
never seriously threatened Antwerp's dockyards either; and the
government had to face another damaging Parliamentary investigation
into their management of this campaign. Simultaneously, money, in the
form of gold, was never more needed or harder to come by than in these
lean years when so much had been so recently and so recklessly lavished
on the hungry Spanish juntas of 1808.[21] October 1810 brought the final
madness of 'the good old King',[22] George III. In his place came that
unpredictable political hazard and long-time friend of the opposition
leaders, the Prince Regent; none could foresee what policy he would
follow, but all admitted his right to change his ministers, if he so chose.

Meanwhile the early months of the old king's madness and the first
winter of the Regency ushered in the most depressing period of the
Peninsular War. In September 1810 Massena had swept into Portugal
with what seemed overwhelming force. Wellington's one battle –
Busaco – was an excellently handled rearguard action; but, as it ended
in retreat, it was not easily represented as a British victory. Many of the
civilian public deplored continental campaigns as 'dreadfully expensive',[23] but few indeed were qualified to comprehend the enemy's

[21] In six months in 1808, writes John Sherwig, 'Britain had sent money and
arms to the Peninsula valued at more than £2,500,000. Never had so much been
spent in such a short time only to yield a bitter return', in *Guineas and Gunpowder: British Foreign Aid in the Wars with France, 1793–1815* (Cambridge,
Mass., 1969), 203. One result of this disastrous generosity was that lack of cash
to finance a campaign anywhere else dictated the choice of the Scheldt for
England's attempted diversion in Austria's favour in 1809.

[22] As many of his subjects regarded him in the later years of his reign.

[23] So Wilberforce, who was far from being an embittered partisan in politics,
is found writing on 26 July 1809, 'Whether and for what purpose is our large
army going [i.e. the Walcheren expedition]? . . . We really do not enough
remember that our proper arms are not military but naval, and that these
military expeditions are dreadfully expensive.' *Life of Wilberforce*, IV, 414–15.

difficulties as he faced Wellington's fortifications at Torres Vedras that winter. Even before this crisis was reached, the parliamentary opposition and much of the press were eloquently opposing continued operations in the Peninsula.[24] The government itself was moved to enquire whether Wellington's army could be safely re-embarked and brought home; and Britain's participation in the Peninsular War continued chiefly because Wellington was too cool and clear-headed to lose hope, and because the ministers trusted a soldier who had so recently been one of their political colleagues.[25]

In short, these years of trial show little of that united determination of the whole country which sustained Churchill through the darkest days of the Hitler War. Instead the nation was ruled by a succession of weak governments which were unsure of the support of either the House of Commons or the throne. But through these years of uncertainty one thing stood firm. That was the conviction of successive cabinets – Portland's, Perceval's and Liverpool's – that a nation at war must fight; and that the place where England must fight was the Peninsula. So the Spaniards continued to receive support; the Portuguese army, paid, equipped, drilled and largely officered by the British, became as effective a force as any of its size in Europe; 30,000–40,000 British troops were committed to the struggle; and the French never became the masters of the Peninsula. 'The Spanish ulcer killed me', said Bonaparte in later years. Much credit should go to this succession of weak British governments for the obstinacy with which they kept the Spanish ulcer open, and did so in defiance of prophets of doom in and out of the House of Commons.

How long the Spaniards could have struggled alone and how many French troops they would have tied up if the British had not evicted the French from Portugal for the first time in 1808, then garrisoned, successively, Lisbon and Cadiz, and latterly made Lisbon a base from which to wage an offensive against the French in Spain, one cannot say. But by doing all these things England accomplished more than merely making things harder for Bonaparte. She set the stage for the knock-out blow of 1813–14 which ended her years of danger.

[24] See Spencer Walpole, *Life of Rt Hon. Spencer Perceval* (London, 1874), II, 113. 'It is certainly true', Lord Liverpool confessed to Wellington in September 1810, 'that in the House of Commons the Portuguese subsidy was carried by a small and unwilling majority; and I believe that if the House had been left free to act upon their own feelings, they would in the month of February, when the subsidy was voted, have decided upon withdrawing the army from Portugal.' C. D. Yonge, *Life and Administration of the 2nd Earl of Liverpool* (London, 1868), I, 335.

[25] In view of the common opinion that Wellington was 'too much of a soldier to be a good politician', it is worth recalling that he made his mark as a politician, in the very difficult position of Chief Secretary for Ireland, before he had won any reputation in European warfare.

So much we all know now. But at the time 1812 was another year which seemed to promise nothing but trouble. It brought first the sordid murder of the Prime Minister by a lunatic. Then came President Madison's declaration of war and mortal peril for a slimly garrisoned Canada. Worst of all was Bonaparte's assault on a Russia which had barely 200,000 men to oppose the half-million and more whom he brought against her. In that summer none could foresee the ruin in which the French would recoil from Moscow through the winter's snow; rather, all had to fear another Napoleonic conquest which would unite French and Russian resources against England. But it is one of the happier of history's lessons that our worst fears do not always come true. Instead of being a year of disaster, 1812 was a prelude to triumph.

In Britain Perceval was succeeded by Lord Liverpool, a man made great by his genius for inducing colleagues of diverse opinions to work loyally together in one cabinet and his talent for putting first things first. Concentrating on victory in Europe he left Canada to its fate, so far as land forces went.[26] Thanks to the skill and daring of Sir Isaac Brock, the fighting quality of the handful of British regulars there and the gallantry of the colonial militia, that fate was not the slick and easy conquest on which Americans were counting. To the Foreign Office Liverpool brought Castlereagh, who was to knit together and sustain the grand alliance which at long last destroyed Bonaparte's empire. He poured money into the continent, financing the Russians (for whom the 1812 campaign was economically crippling), buying the aid of the Swedes with another massive subsidy, and then financing the Prussians and latterly Austrians as well. Arms as well as money flowed to the continent from a Britain which had now become the arsenal, as well as the banker, of the grand alliance – nearly 1,000,000 muskets in 1813 alone, besides cannon, flints and powder.[27] British troops were found for northern Europe as well as Spain; and in the latter country, on 21 June 1813, Wellington won at Vitoria what must rank as one of the decisive battles of the war.

Here, as always, one must be careful not to attribute too much to a single cause; and certainly Wellington's campaign of 1813 was made far easier by Bonaparte's losses in Russia in the previous winter. But the

[26] Though British troops could not be spared for the American war before 1814, British seamen and shipwrights were. After the British North Sea fleet had been handsomely reinforced by 15 Russian line of battle ships in December 1812, some 1,500–2,000 volunteers from British dockyards were sent out to Kingston in Upper Canada. There they built with remarkable dispatch the fleet which controlled Lake Ontario in 1814 whose principal ships were the *Princess Charlotte* of 42 guns, the *Prince Regent*, 56 and the *St Lawrence*, 102. Control of the lake by British ships made it possible to supply and maintain the army defending the Niagara peninsula at its western end.

[27] John M. Sherwig, *Guineas & Gunpowder*, 288. Britain had also sent upwards of 190 artillery pieces to the Northern powers (ibid., 277, 287).

facts remain that France made an astonishing recovery from the Russian disaster; that, in spite of Prussia's joining the Russians, Bonaparte started the campaign with the larger armies; that before 21 June the victories were all French, as battered Russians and Prussians went reeling back first from Lutzen, then from Bautzen; and that after Bautzen these powers accepted an armistice, while Austria, far from joining the common cause for the liberation of Europe, endeavoured to restore peace on terms that ignored Britain's war aims. But then came Wellington's success at Vitoria, with the utter rout of Joseph Bonaparte's army and the capture of every last gun of his artillery; and it was well said by a man on the spot at the Prussian headquarters that Vitoria 'produced as great a change in the atmosphere of Dresden and the North as it could have effected in southern Europe'.[28] It brought the Tsar to his knees in the first *Te deum* the Russians ever celebrated for a foreign victory; it inspired Beethoven to give us his so-called Battle Symphony (Op. 91); still more to the point, at the Austrian headquarters it sent Count Stadion hurrying down the corridors to rouse the Chancellor, Metternich, from his bed with the news; and then and there, by the candle light, the two men swore to enter the struggle and continue it till Bonaparte's fall was accomplished. That decision, bringing 200,000 Austrians into the war, upset the superiority in numbers which had won Lutzen and Bautzen for France; and the news of his brother's crushing defeat made it all the more impossible for Bonaparte, a conqueror whose power was built on victory, to accept the proposed terms of peace which would in fact have preserved his dynasty and much of his empire.

So events moved toward their end, with the British, as the first of all the allies, invading France on 14 October, before Leipzig was fought; with a Bourbon prince, the Duc d'Angoulême, following them to proclaim his uncle as King Louis XVIII of France on 14 March 1814, in a Bordeaux bedecked with the white cockades of his family, before ever Napoleon had fallen or the allies had accepted the principle of legitimacy; and with Wellington's armies holding a broad expanse of southern France before the Northern allies closed in on Paris.

These, then, were the stages of a war which brands as a stupid lie the clap-trap phrase that 'wars never settle anything'. This war began with Britain in danger of conquest and Europe threatened with the overlordship of the single power of France. It ended with Britain secure, and Europe restored to a balance of power which preserved a general international peace for longer than any previous settlement.

---

[28] The verdict of Castlereagh's brother, General Sir Charles Stewart (later Lord Londonderry), the British envoy at the Prussian headquarters in 1813. Lord Londonderry, *The War in Germany and France in the Years 1813 and 1814* (London, 1830), 81.

END NOTE

The size of the confederate fleet which Bonaparte hoped to mass against England after Tilsit is an important question. On the answer depends his chance of victory; the answer is likewise the only yardstick by which to measure the threat that Portland's cabinet faced, and the wisdom of those neutrals who concluded that, once peace was made between France and Russia, England's days were numbered. One must therefore attempt to arrive at some approximation of what the probable strengths of both sides would have been if Bonaparte's hopes had come true.

The first point to be made in any 'numbers game' of this kind is that the number of ships which counts in a naval campaign is not the total which a nation possesses but the number that are 'ready for the sea' at any one given time; and to be 'ready for the sea' ships should be structurally sound, fully manned, armed and provisioned. Second, dockyards exist in order to do the repairs that will make unsound ships ready for the sea again; (and that, of course, is why, after capturing Copenhagen in September 1807, the British destroyed those Danish ships which were not then fit for a voyage to England). Third, the earliest date for the naval campaign envisaged by Bonaparte's agreement with the Tsar in July 1807 was the summer of 1808; and that allowed a very useful number of months for getting French, Spanish, Russian, Danish and Portuguese ships 'ready for the sea'.

Now for the figures. On the English side the 'Annual Abstracts' printed in the appendices to William James, *Naval History of Great Britain from 1793 to the Accession of George IV*, ed. Captain Chamier, R.N. (London, 1837), show that Britain had 103 line of battle ships in commission during 1807 and 113 during 1808. But these totals are not to be taken at face value. They do not give us what we want to know, namely, the number of ships 'ready for the sea' at any one time. The reason is the need of repairs. Britain's fleets at sea constantly had more ships in need of repair than her bases could handle; and as soon as one ship was ready to come out of dry-dock, another was waiting to come in. Both these ships would be commissioned for some part of the same year; so both appear in the annual total. But obviously both could not be at sea at the same time. On the other hand the British would hardly have hesitated to send unsound and undermanned ships to sea in a crisis, so I do not know what deduction to make from James's totals. I doubt, however, if Britain could have got much more than 113 ships to sea at one time, even in a crisis, as this was the largest number she was ever able to commission in the full course of a single year; and she reached this figure twice only, in the years 1808 and 1809.

On the enemy side William Clowes, *The Royal Navy; a History from the Earliest Times to the Present* (London, 1900), V, 208–9, gives the following figures:

French and Spanish in Europe	'upwards of 45'
French in the West Indies and America	3
Russians in the Mediterranean	5
In the Scheldt, 3 Dutch, 8 French	11
Dutch in the Texel	3
Sweden	11
Denmark	16
Russians in the Baltic	19 or 20

GRAND TOTAL   'upwards of' 123 or 124

But Clowes' figures are incomplete. They ignore Admiral Siniavin's Russian squadron of 9 in the Tagus; and the Portuguese fleet of 10. It also appears from contemporary Admiralty intelligence reports that the Russians had 7, not 5, in the Mediterranean; and that there were 20 line of battle ships in French harbours, excluding Antwerp, to add to the 6 French and 24 Spanish ships in Spanish ports. These reports also put the whole Russian Baltic fleet definitely at 20, not 19; the Danish total, including ships which the British destroyed, should be 21, not 16; and A. Alison (*The Lives of Castlereagh and Sir Charles Stewart* (Edinburgh and London, 1861), I, 273, credits the Swedes with 12, not 11. So British ministers, looking to the summer of 1808, had to reckon on Bonaparte then massing up to 155 ships against 113.

I should add that Sir William Clowes was led to believe that James underestimated England's total of line of battle ships commissioned in 1808; but he does not specify what particular ships he would add to James's total; nor, in fact, would he add any very significant number to that total; and I suspect that James, working with a contemporary's knowledge of the events of his own day, would be better able to interpret the data in *Steel's List* than an early twentieth-century author. For these reasons I accept James's figure of 113 for the British as close enough for the sort of comparison which one can attempt today. It should also be noted that Jomini reckoned that Tilsit should have given Bonaparte a confederate fleet of 180 line of battle ships, or nearly half again as many as Clowes allowed; but this seems excessive.

English historians emphasise the advantage of superior seamanship which British crews acquired during their constant service afloat. This point is valid within limits, but must not be exaggerated; skill can be overwhelmed by sufficiently superior force.

2

The Organisation of British Defence

WHETHER, like Winston Churchill, he formally takes the title or not, Britain's Prime Minister is inevitably her chief Minister of Defence in wartime. He must bear the final responsibility for the success or failure of the nation's war effort; he must select the various members of his cabinet team who perform particular defence duties; and he must coordinate their work. His job is always vast and it has rarely been less enviable than in the age of Bonaparte. Then the stakes were as high and the nation's defence organisation as intricately complicated as they had ever been. No fewer than four cabinet ministers had specific defence jobs to do – the First Lord of the Admiralty, the Secretary of State for War and Colonies, the Home Secretary and the Master General of the Ordnance; also one minister outside the cabinet – the Secretary-at-War; and a Commander-in-Chief, whose authority could be embarrassing to the cabinet because so much of it stemmed from the facts that he was a royal duke and that his strongest supporter was his father, the King. To the above we must add the Secretary of State for Foreign Affairs and the Chancellor of the Exchequer. Until 1794, when Pitt created the office of the Secretary of State for War and Colonies, the Foreign Minister had been personally responsible for the planning of the army's campaigns in Europe (while the Colonial Secretary commonly planned its operations in his sphere of interest). Even after 1794, however, the Foreign Minister could not help being interested in the army's, and the navy's, operations. His diplomacy was made easier by their successes or harder by their failures. It was his duty, also, to coordinate, if he could, the operations of Britain's allies with her own and to gain secret intelligence about the enemy. The Chancellor of the Exchequer had, of course, to find money for the war; and, if he had no positive voice in deciding the nation's strategy, he at least had a negative one. For the army and navy could only attempt operations which he could find money to pay for; and when he could find no money, there could be no operations. Often, however, as in the cases of Addington,

Pitt and Spencer Perceval, the Prime Minister and Chancellor of the
Exchequer were the same man. Finally, the land forces of Britain may
be described as consisting, in effect, of four separate and ill-coordinated
armies. So, all told, the Prime Minister had a very complicated team to
handle; and he had besides a number of particular jobs of his own to do.
In this chapter I shall deal in order, first, with all above-mentioned
parts of the defence organisation which were directly concerned with
war on land, and last with that very important matter, intelligence.
The Admiralty and its duties are so large a subject as to require a
separate chapter.

Taking first the defence duties of the Prime Minister, it will be
obvious that his job made large demands on his good judgement. To
begin with, he had to pick the right men for very responsible posts; and
politics rarely made that easy. As the captain of the team he had also to
know when to urge men on, when to direct them and when to leave them
alone. Not the least difficult of his problems was his relationship with
the Commander-in-Chief. In theory, the principles which should rule
a premier's relations with his chosen professional soldier are as simple
as those of a householder with his plumber; pick a man you can trust;
tell him what you want done; strain every nerve to give him what he
needs to do it; and then leave him to get on with the job as long as he
retains your confidence. Theory and practice, however, are two different
things. Telling a soldier what you want done means first and foremost
defining the objects of your strategy. But strategy itself cannot be
soundly decided without military knowledge of the kind which civilians
very pardonably lack and which modern general staffs exist to supply.
So there one immediately encounters a debatable zone, part civilian and
part military. Nor is there any really clear-cut dividing line between
strategy and tactics (or military theorists would never have had to
invent the phrase 'Grand Tactics'). Hence the degree to which the
Commander-in-Chief would have had a free hand in fighting his own
battle once the enemy had landed in England is very uncertain. Addington probably knew enough of his own limitations to leave the commander alone. Of Pitt one cannot be half so sure. His besetting sin as a
war minister was plunging headlong into tasks which he had no qualifications for performing; and the list of dangers connected with the
invasion which England escaped in 1804-5 should include the possibility
of this eminent amateur overturning the best laid plans of the Commander-in-Chief with his own spirited interventions.

To turn now to the other responsibilities of premiers, Addington
deserves credit for reviving and improving the very unpopular income
tax which Pitt had first introduced in 1797; and it was to last as long as
the war. In finance, however, Addington was surpassed by Pitt, whose
bold approval of costly plans for fortifying the south coast was to

transform the whole business of defending England against invasion. The finest work of all in the field of finance, however, was surely that done by Spencer Perceval from 1807 to his death in 1812. In the worst years of bullion scarcity, trade depression and Bonaparte's Continental System, Perceval still somehow found money enough to support Wellington in the Peninsula – a task dismissed as impossible by many able contemporaries.[1]

Before 1806 the prime ministers also framed the nation's recruiting policies. Addington, as we shall see, managed this very well, Pitt much less so. The best work in this field was done by Lord Castlereagh, Minister for War in the Duke of Portland's cabinet from 1807–9; and the worst by William Windham, Minister for War in the All-the-Talents ministry in 1806–7.

Not least the Prime Minister, as First Lord of the Treasury, was ultimately responsible for the Commissariat. Britain had no rationally organised Royal Army Service Corps in those days (though for a while it had looked as if she might develop one in the last campaigns of the Seven Years War). Instead the whole business of supplying an army in the field was left to civilian commissionaries who were 'only employed in time of War and sought for at the moment of active operations'.[2] These men worked under the Commissary General or after 1808 under a Commissary-in-Chief, who received 'his Instructions direct from the Treasury'.[3] It was their job to buy all the meat, cheese, bread and beer or wine needed by the men and all the oats and hay needed by the horses of the army; to lay in magazines where these things were stored; to hire waggons, horses and waggoners – usually all civilians engaged in the actual theatre of war – to move them; to move, too, tents and hospital stores, all the tonnage of spare roundshot, grape, canister, shrapnel and powder (in 90 lbs. barrels) needed by the artillery, all the engineers' stores, from picks, shovels and demolition charges to bridging equipment, and the reserve small arms ammunition for the muskets, rifles, carbines and pistols of the infantry and cavalry. It is one of the grimmer facts of British history that in war after war these immensely responsible and varied jobs were given to inexperienced civilians over whom the commander of the troops they served had no direct authority. For it is indeed true that the Commissariat had only a

[1] 'Lord Grenville left office in 1807 convinced that we were capable of waging only a defensive war; any major continental campaign, he told his closest associates, was financially beyond our means.' Denis Gray, *Spencer Perceval: the Evangelical Prime Minister* (Manchester, 1963), 323, citing Buckingham, *Court and Cabinets of George III*, IV, 206.

[2] On the organisation of the Commissariat, see Havilland Le Mesurier's 'A System for the British Commissariat', printed as Appendix B to my *Peninsular Preparation*, 267–305. This quotation is from p. 267.

[3] Ibid., p. 268.

skeleton staff in peace. When it expanded in war, it had little time to
pick and choose good men; instead it had to take those who were
available. The too frequent quality of these is sufficiently indicated by
Wellington's remark 'the prejudices of society against a Commissary
almost prevent him from receiving the common respect due to the
character of a gentleman'.[4] Yet the system lasted until the sufferings of
the troops in the Crimean winter of 1854–5 compelled a thorough
reform.

The odd combination of duties performed by the Secretary of State
for War and Colonies is explained by the fact that the British army
spent so much of every war in conquering the enemy's colonies and had
then to garrison the empire in peace. The chief military task of the
department, however, was planning the strategy of the army and co-
ordinating the work of the other departments responsible for equipping
an expeditionary force. Addington gave this office to Lord Hobart, a
professional soldier and a former governor of Madras. The commonsense
which distinguishes Addington's military policy may owe much to him.
On the change of government in April 1804 that ineffectual creature,
Lord Camden, held the job until Castlereagh took over in July 1805,
and had time to show something of his quality before Pitt died and the
government fell in January 1806. For the next eighteen months England
was in no immediate danger of invasion because Bonaparte was too
busy with his continental war against Russia and, latterly, Prussia.
This was fortunate since for so much of that time the war department
was ruled by William Windham, one of the most charming, scholarly
and eloquent, but also least competent, of all men who have held that
office. The best thing that the All-the-Talents ministry did in this
period was to complete the fortification of the south coast which Pitt
had begun. Under the Duke of Portland, Castlereagh, as noted above,
returned to the war ministry until Portland's government fell in
September 1809.

The cause of its fall was the quarrel between two Secretaries of State,
Canning at the Foreign Office and Castlereagh at the war ministry;
for Canning had claimed, in a most reactionary manner, that the
Foreign Office should decide Britain's European strategy. When Perceval learnt of Canning's intrigue late in June 1809, he wrote to that
minister:

'I think . . . that if your office is to have the management of the war
in any part of the world, it should have it in every part; and that the

[4] To Colonel Gurwood, 19 December 1810. Colonel Gurwood (ed.), *The
Despatches of the Duke of Wellington in the Peninsula* (London, 1837–8), VII.
And society's prejudices were often too well justified; on which, see Denis
Gray's discussion of Spencer Perceval's problems with the Commissariat:
Spencer Perceval, 325–8 (especially 327–8).

direction of the whole force of the country should be with the
Minister who is to direct any part of it.'[5]

This was the principle which Pitt had followed when he created the
Secretaryship of State for War and Colonies in 1794. As premier
Perceval upheld Pitt's principle, and he chose for this post the same
Lord Liverpool who, as Lord Hawkesbury, had held the foreign office
under Addington. No one could challenge the authority of such a
Secretary for War. Finally, Liverpool, when he succeeded Perceval in
May 1812, chose Lord Bathurst for the War Ministry. Of these men
Castlereagh unquestionably deserves the accolade of Fortescue who
described him as 'the ablest man that ever controlled the war office
[sic]'.[6] In spite of the prejudices of Napier, the historian of the Peninsular War, Liverpool's fairness, tolerance, industry and commonsense
made him also a very good minister. Bathurst, a less commanding
figure, was at least equal to carrying on a going concern. So Britain's
War Ministry was in the hands of competent men for the last eight of
the twenty-two years she spent fighting revolutionary and Napoleonic
France.

In the above paragraphs I have used the phrase 'war ministry' to
describe the office over which the Secretary of State for War and
Colonies presided. It must be carefully distinguished from the 'War
Office' which was another thing altogether. This was the office of the
Secretary-at-War, who handled military finance and law, directed the
issue of arms to troops from the Ordnance and gave the actual marching
orders for all troop movements in Britain.

The Home Secretary was responsible for raising the Militia and the
Volunteers (of whom we shall say more shortly). He also required the
Regular Army for what was called 'Internal Defence' – a polite phrase
which meant using troops to do duties which we now entrust to the
police. Inevitably, these duties affected Britain's strategy. If only the
country had provided itself with competent police forces, it could
have used more troops on foreign service. But competent police work
in Britain hardly began until Sir Robert Peel made his great reform
of the London constabulary in 1829; and the use of troops as
police at times even thwarted the Commander-in-Chief's plans for
training.

The fifth minister who shared responsibility for defending Britain
was actually a soldier, the Master General of the Ordnance. He was
normally a General and in the cabinet whom he was nominally supposed to advise on strategy. His department manufactured artillery

[5] Spencer Walpole, *The Life of the Rt Hon. Spencer Perceval* (London, 1874),
I, 335.
[6] *County Lieutenancies and the Army* (London, 1909), 234.

and ammunition and provided small arms for both the army and the navy. It had besides 'to defray the expense of the Corps of Artillery, the Corps of Engineers and other Military Corps attached to the Ordnance Service; and also the charge of repairing and building Fortifications at home and abroad; excepting Field Works abroad and excepting also those Fortifications which Commanders-in-Chief [abroad] may deem it expedient to erect without instructions from home' (Doc. 3). By 1803 one change had been made in this list of duties. Then the task of erecting 'Field Works', or temporary fortifications of entrenchments and palisades, had been transferred to the army. But the erection of permanent fortifications was still left to the Ordnance Department; and this was unfortunate for it was a most inefficient department.

It was nominally ruled by its Master General who, as a soldier, was 'Commander-in-Chief of the artillery and engineers' and, as a member of the cabinet, had 'the entire management of, and control over, the Ordnance Department', if he chose to exercise it.[7] But under the Master General was a committee of permanent officials called the Board of Ordnance; and if the Master General did 'not interfere' the Board were 'competent of themselves to carry on all official business' (Doc. 3). Perhaps as a result of this arrangement the Master Generalship of the Ordnance became a job for men whom it was felt necessary to retain in the cabinet but impossible to trust with serious responsibilities. This was plainly stated by Perceval as his reason for giving Lord Mulgrave the job in 1810. Mulgrave was growing old and ill; 'he had given me notice for some months,' wrote Perceval, 'of his utter inability to stay much longer [at the Admiralty]. His removal to the Ordnance necessarily would make a vacancy for an efficient man.'[8] But, however inadequate he may have found himself at the Admiralty, Mulgrave can hardly have been a less 'efficient man' at the Ordnance than his predecessor there, Lord Chatham. With the brief interlude of the All-the-Talents ministry Chatham was Master General of the Ordnance from 1801 to 1810. Like Mulgrave he had also been First Lord of the Admiralty until his own brother, the younger Pitt, had had to replace him in December 1794. Chatham certainly did not lack ability; when he chose, as Fortescue has said, he could both think and write; his contemporaries were impressed by the sense and wisdom of his conversation; and he could be stubborn; but he could not act. Indeed, he was surely the laziest man ever to hold a British cabinet office. His unfitness for any administrative job is demonstrated by the fact that when he left the Admiralty 'many hundred packets' of public correspondence which he had carried home to his own house 'were found there

[7] *Thirteenth Report of the Commissioners of Military Enquiry* (1810–11), 4.
[8] Walpole, *Spencer Perceval*, II, 79.

unopened'.[9] It was most unfortunate that such a man should have such a job in years of peril; and the dilatoriness of the Master General can only have increased the almost inevitable friction between the Army and the Ordnance.

Finally, there was the Commander-in-Chief of the Regular Army. What has been said already will reveal much of the limitations and nature of his duties. Since the Artillery and Royal Engineers were two separate corps of specialists under the Master General of the Ordnance, he commanded only the Cavalry and Infantry; and he had to rely on the Master General to provide gunners and engineers for the forces he might have to lead in the field. Likewise, he had to rely on the Treasury for duties now done by the Royal Army Service Corps. He had no authority over the Militia and the Volunteers until they were called out on active service. Unlike the Master General of the Ordnance, he was not a member of the cabinet. Strategy and recruiting policies were decided, often on purely political grounds, by civilians who rarely wanted his advice. He had to find troops for overseas operations which he had not planned, or to keep order in manufacturing towns which had no competent police. He could not even order troop movements on his own authority, since marching orders to regiments in England always came from the Secretary at War. If the enemy landed, he would have to defend a country where he had no power to build, or even repair, any permanent fortifications. Prior to an invasion, the powers his office gave him were merely to direct the training and discipline of the regular Cavalry and Infantry, the appointment and promotion of their officers and building 'Field Works'.

No doubt the modern citizen of a democracy will see little to criticise in some of these limitations. Certainly we do not expect the command of the army to be a political appointment, as it would have to be if its holder were in the cabinet. We believe, fervently, that civilians must have the last word in deciding the military policies of a free country. Nevertheless the land forces of Britain – ordnance corps, army, commissariat and the auxiliary forces – could certainly have been much more efficiently managed if the prejudices of the time had allowed them the unity of command which they enjoy today or even that degree of unity which had prevailed at the end of the Seven Years' War.[10] Moreover,

[9] The authority for this statement is William Marsden, who became second Secretary at the Admiralty in 1795, the year after Chatham ceased being First Lord. *A Brief Memoir of the Life of William Marsden, by himself; with Notes from his Correspondence* (London, 1838), 115n.

[10] Then the two jobs of Commander-in-Chief and Master General of the Ordnance had been combined in the person of that grand old soldier, Field Marshal Lord Ligonier. In 1760 the Commissariat had been made a military department under Ligonier, who appointed Colonel Pierson as its head (Rex Whitworth, *Field Marshal Lord Ligonier; a Story of the British Army, 1702–1770*,

none of the limitations imposed on the British Commander-in-Chief applied across the Channel. There Bonaparte was both master of an autocratic state and commander-in-chief of all its armed forces. He was free to conscript as many young men for the army each year as he saw fit and to spend the nation's money wherever he chose. No civilian prescribed his strategy or could meddle with his tactics. He directed the fleets as well as the armies of his empire. In short, he enjoyed all the advantages of a dictator. Dictatorship must always be abhorrent to a free people; yet realism requires one to observe how handicapped a British Commander-in-Chief was in comparison with an opponent enjoying such powers as these.

The man who held this post of Commander-in-Chief through nearly the whole of our period was George III's second son, Frederick, Duke of York. He is a well remembered prince but usually for the wrong reason. His fame, or ill-fame, rests so largely on the fact that he was man enough to resist blackmail and so was hounded from office in 1809, at the insistence of Wilberforce, after the unforgettable and unforgotten scandal of a Parliamentary investigation into charges of corruption levelled at him by his ex-mistress, the famous Mary Ann Clarke. 'No apparent sense in the House of the guilt of adultery, only of political offence'[11] wrote the saintly Wilberforce as the investigation went its sordid way through the Commons. But of political offence, of personally making a profit out of promotions, the House found York innocent. There can be no denial of his adultery, but neither should too much be made of misconduct which others in responsible positions have been known to commit. Kindness has drawn a veil over the peccadilloes that led to Castlereagh's suicide; Dilke's infidelities are not unduly stressed in our histories; Gladstone himself turned a blind eye to Parnell's adultery until Captain O'Shea exposed it; and little was heard of Lloyd George's promiscuity until his son wrote a book which is perhaps most kindly regarded as a sort of catharsis for a wretched family life. The best comment on the Mary Ann Clarke scandal was surely that made at the time by Lord Grey, the future author of the great Reform Bill of 1832. 'It is impossible to believe that anything more can be imputable to the Duke than might have happened to any man who has the misfortune to keep a mistress. It is shocking to see the House of Commons' time and the attention of the public occupied by such matters at the present moment,'[12] wrote Grey (whose own later

---

[Oxford, 1958] 324). Finally, in 1762, the government scrapped the happy-go-lucky old system of relying for army transport on the waggons of hired contractors and bought its own waggon train (so writes Havilland Le Mesurier, *A System for the British Commissariat* (1796), printed in my *Peninsular Preparation*, 273).

[11] *Life of Wilberforce*, III, 402.   [12] *Auckland Papers*, IV, 318.

liaison with the Duchess of Devonshire is, by the bye, not mentioned in his standard biography).

In 1803 the Duke of York was probably the best trained, and by no means the least experienced, soldier in Britain. He had received his training in Germany, where he made a favourable impression on Frederick the Great and the Duke of Brunswick, another very highly regarded soldier of the time;[13] and he had attended annual manœuvres in both Prussia and Austria. In 1793-4 and 1799 he had commanded British forces in the Netherlands and Holland; and for long he was supposed to have done it very badly. But Lt Col. Alfred Burne's study of his campaigns compels one to revise that opinion. Indeed one doubts whether even a Marlborough could have succeeded in the circumstances in which York failed. Thus at the siege of Dunkirk everything that York could do was done brilliantly; but he was atrociously let down by his own government (whose failings he most magnanimously covered up) and he was ill-supported by his Hanoverian subordinate Field Marshal Freytag.[14] In the five-pronged attack which his Austrian allies directed against the French at Turcoing in 1794, York carried out his orders to the letter. But only one other allied commander did so. As a result the British received the punishment that comes all too naturally to detachments thrust unsupported into exposed positions; and but for the Duke's skilful leadership they would have been still worse handled. His attempted defence of Holland in the autumn of 1794 was frustrated by the incredible ineptness of his Dutch ally.[15] These failures, little as he deserves blame for them, have eclipsed his remarkable successes in lesser actions where he was in full command – at Linselles on 16 August 1793, at Vaux on 17 April, Beaumont on 26 April and Willems on 10 May 1794. Again in 1799, his plan for the

[13] Brunswick's reputation is not high now; instead we remember him as the vanquished leader of Prussian troops at Auerstadt. This is not wholly fair. In 1806 Brunswick was already seventy-one; with Frederick William III at his headquarters, his command was more nominal than real; and he was himself mortally wounded in the action. But he had distinguished himself in his youth, serving under his uncle, Ferdinand of Brunswick, in the Seven Years' War; and at Pirmasens and Kaiserslautern in 1793 he won creditable successes over the armies of revolutionary France.

[14] See my *Peninsular Preparation*, 98–100.

[15] The fullest account of the Duke's difficulties with the Dutch Stadholder that I have read is his own, written to William Windham on 24 November 1794 (B. M. Addit. MS. 37,842). It is an astonishing chronicle of procrastination and broken promises. The reader may object that it is an *ex parte* statement. That is true; but it is also precise, detailed and contemporary, and Windham, who had recently been on the continent and was a member of the cabinet, was in a position to check its accuracy. Nothing, it appears, could induce the Stadholder either to garrison or provision his fortresses or to carry out promised troop movements.

battle of Bergen was praised by the French as 'a bold, but also a just, extensive and skilful application of the principles and rules of the art of war'.[16] To achieve success, however, a general must do more than make skilful plans. He must also be able to ensure that his plans are carried out. In the event the Duke's plan for Bergen was to be wrecked by the insubordination and the rout of his Russian allies. But almost no one has heard of the Russian General Hermann or of the fact that in 1799 the Duke's hands were tied by orders to do nothing without the approval of a council of war.[17] It may be fair enough if the evil that men really do lives after them; it is not fair that a soldier should be damned forever by evils he had no power to control. Rather it is reasonable to believe that the defence of England against an invader would have been handled with all the boldness and skill to be expected of the victor of Linselles, Vaux, Beaumont and Willems if only the Duke of York had been left free to follow his own good judgement.

The important question about all of what I have called Britain's four separate and ill-coordinated armies is their fitness for war. These armies were the Ordnance Corps, the Regular Army, the Militia and the Volunteers.

The Ordnance Corps were the Royal Artillery, the Royal Artillery Drivers and the Royal Engineers. Of these the Royal Artillery Drivers was a new force, raised in 1794 by the Duke of Richmond to end the old and inept system of hiring civilians and their horses to draw the army's guns. The idea was excellent, a notable reform; but unfortunately the corps was neglected by Richmond's successors at the Ordnance and its discipline was poor. The Royal Engineers was a body of officers only; but these officers, and those of the Royal Artillery, were excellently trained, for all were graduates of the progressive and well-staffed Royal Military Academy at Woolwich. There were, however, too few of both, for the very reason that they were required to be graduates of Woolwich. But the greatest defect of these corps was that their officers,

---

[16] Cited by Lt Col. Alfred Burne, *The Noble Duke of York* (London, 1949), 266.

[17] The authority for the statement that the Duke's hands were tied by orders imposing a council of war on him comes from Sir Henry Bunbury, *The Great War with France*, ed. by Sir John Fortescue (London, 1927), 29. Bunbury, as Lt Col. Alfred Burne notes, 'is almost invariably quoted in accounts of "the Helder campaign", and "has done much damage" to the Duke's reputation as a commander in the field' (*The Noble Duke of York*, 286). Burne gives his own reasons for dissenting from parts of Bunbury's assessment. I will give my own for another. 'It too often happened that [the Duke] could not say No when he ought to have said No', writes Bunbury. But in Holland his orders forbade him to say No to his council of war; and on other occasions I have found the Duke saying No very firmly, though politely, to persons in very high places. He could never have reformed the army as he did if he had been incapable of uttering this decisive monosyllable.

unlike those of the army, did not gain promotion by the sale and purchase of commissions. Instead all promotion in these corps went by
seniority. In theory certainly nothing could seem more fair than the
Ordnance system or more iniquitous than the army's system which, to
all appearance, so blatantly favoured the wealthy at the expense of the
poor. But judged by results the army's method was easily the better.
A system by which commissions could be sold ensured every officer the
equivalent of a pension whenever he wished to retire. Many retired
early and so made room for keen, young men to reach high rank while
still in the prime of their health and vigour. There can be much worse
systems than the one which enabled men of the calibre of Moore,
Wellington, Beresford, Rowland Hill, Stapleton Cotton, Crauford and
Picton to become colonels in their twenties and generals in their forties
or earlier.[18] By contrast the Ordnance officer, who could not 'sell out',
had no way of gaining a pension; so, in order to live, he clung
to his commission and his pay to the death. The result was stagnation in the lower and senility in the higher ranks; and one of the
paradoxes of Wellington's peninsular campaigns is the humble rank
of men who carried very high responsibilities in the Artillery and
Engineers.

The British Regular Army's reputation at home and abroad was never
worse than in the French revolutionary war, and no bad reputation was
ever better earned. The degree to which the younger Pitt had let the
British army rot in the decade of peace from 1783 to 1793 is almost
unbelievable. He left it without any Commander-in-Chief from 1783
till the war with France began in 1793. Then he gave the job to Lord
Amherst, a time-worn veteran who at the age of 76 was no longer equal
to making reforms; indeed, to its existing abuses he added new and
disastrous muddles of his own. Prior to Amherst's appointment Pitt
left all army patronage to the secretary at war, Sir George Yonge, who
abused it atrociously. Commissions were so frankly treated as pensions
as to be given to 'boys ... whilst they were yet acquiring the first
elements of education', or even while still in their cradles.[19] It was

[18] The system of purchase is too commonly judged and condemned on the
authority of its enemies who wished to abolish it. No one has yet published a
thorough study of how it actually worked in practice. My cousin, Michael
Glover, is engaged in such a study now. His preliminary findings suggest that
we have to change our views on purchase a good deal, and are to appear in *The
Army Quarterly* in 1973.

[19] My quotation is from Lord Londonderry, *Narrative of the Peninsular War
from 1808 to 1813*, I, 4. I add the cradles on the authority of Sir Walter Scott's
obituary of the Duke of York ('Memoir of H.R.H. the Duke of York' in *The
Naval and Military Magazine*, 1827, 2ff.) Scott (here called 'the Author of
Waverly') adds that 'commissions were in some cases bestowed on *young ladies*,
when pensions were not to be had', and cites a case he knew personally.

hardly to be expected that 'officers' barely old enough for prep school would do duty with their regiments; and in this period a shocking number of officers went absent without leave and with impunity.[20] Once in the service, too, they were permitted to buy their promotion up to the rank of lieutenant colonel with no check of any kind on their qualifications for their duties.[21] With no Commander-in-Chief in control, indiscipline ranged so high that colonels of regiments blandly ignored the General Order of June 1792, which prescribed General David Dundas's *Rules and Regulations for the Movements of His Majesty's Infantry* as the standard drill manual for the whole army. Instead 'every commanding officer manœuvred his own regiment in his own fashion'. The result was that 'if a brigade of troops was brought together, it was very doubtful whether they could execute any one combined movement and almost certain they could not execute the various parts of it on the same principle';[22] and while such confusion reigned, it was 'absolutely impossible' for a general 'to attempt the most simple manœuvres before an enemy, much less such complicated ones as the circumstances . . . may point out and require'.[23] Too many regimental officers found in this confusion an excuse for not learning any drill at all; and on parade 'an intelligent sergeant whispered from time to time the word of command which his captain would have been ashamed to have known without prompting'.[24] As for training staff officers in the higher duties of their profession, this was undreamt of in an army where even proper battalion training was neglected. There is, therefore, some real cause for surprise that the Duke of York should have done as well as he did with the British troops in the Netherlands in 1793–4. But these campaigns ended in the ghastly, if forgotten, disaster of the winter of 1794–5 – the long, grim retreat through Holland, on which the army, to its immortal shame, lost its men while it preserved its baggage.[25]

This summary of the state of the army when Britain started her greatest war will give some idea of what had to be done before that army was fit to repel an invader. To his infinite credit the Duke of York was equal to making the necessary reforms. He began almost as soon as he took over the Command-in-Chief at home in February 1795. A swift

[20] *Peninsular Preparation*, 163, 167–8.
[21] Ibid., 149, 150.
[22] 'Memoir of H.R.H. the Duke of York.'
[23] David Dundas, *Principles of Military Movements* (London, 1788), 17.
[24] 'Memoir of H.R.H. the Duke of York.'
[25] The authority for this statement is the Hanoverian, General Walmoden, who took over when York was recalled in 1794. The British army, wrote Walmoden in February, 1795, was '*detruite . . . les officiers, les equipages, les trains immenses, cela est rest pendant que la misère et les malades ont detruites les individus combattans*'. W.O. Original Correspondence: Entry Book No. 11.

series of tours and inspections, north, east, south and west, familiarised him with his problems. By imposing a vigorous training programme in the summer of 1795 he restored uniformity of manœuvre among Britain's chaotic regiments.[26] With his Adjutant General, the elderly, but excellent, Sir William Fawcett, he launched a ruthless campaign against absent officers. Some returned to duty; some hastened to sell out; and some were dismissed the service. All learnt that the old laxness was a thing of the past.[27] By new rules, imposing stated periods of service in the lower ranks before men bought promotions, by requiring applications for promotion to be approved by men's commanding officers and by a new (and in some quarters, hated) system of confidential reports on officers, he found a means of denying promotion to unqualified persons.[28] Lastly he tackled the matter of staff training. In 1798 a distinguished French émigré, of wide European experience, offered to set up a staff school in Britain. This was General Francis Jarry, who had received his own staff training from no less a soldier than Frederick the Great and whom the Duke of York may well have known personally in Berlin in earlier days. The Duke lost no time in seizing this opportunity. The new school opened at High Wycombe in May 1799,[29] and its first graduates proved their quality in the campaign of 1801–2 against the French in Egypt.

That now almost forgotten campaign revealed how much the Duke had accomplished in five years of vigorous reform; and Jomini was to write of the British army that '*la campagne d'Egypt a marquée l'époque de sa régénération*'.[30] So whether he realised it or not (and his rude remark to Soult at Waterloo suggests he did not)[31] Bonaparte would have faced in England a far more dangerous British army than the one he had driven out of Toulon in 1793.

He would also have faced a much larger British army than existed in 1793; and for this the utmost credit is due to that underrated premier, Henry Addington. In military matters British politicians from generation to generation too often prove as incapable as the restored Bourbons of learning or forgetting anything. So frequently the very first thing they do when peace is made is to hustle as many soldiers as they possibly can back into civil life without a thought for the future. So in

---

[26] *Peninsular Preparation*, 121–2.

[27] Ibid., 167–8.

[28] Ibid., 152–4, 194.

[29] Ibid., 199.

[30] H. Jomini, *Histoire critique et militaire des Guerres de la Révolution*, Book I, Chap. X.

[31] 'Because you have been beaten by Wellington you think him a great general. And I tell you that Wellington is a bad general, that the English are bad troops, and that this will be the affair of a *dejeuner*.' Cited by Holland Rose, *Life of Napoleon I*, II, 490.

1697 they cut the army down to a mere 7,000; and in 1701 found themselves needing more soldiers than ever to meet Louis XIV again. After the peace of Aix-la-Chapelle in 1748 they so sweepingly cut down the great army they had raised for the War of the Austrian Succession that in 1756 they were reduced to hiring Hessians to defend Kent and Sussex. They scrapped after 1763 the light infantry regiments they had raised to fight the French and Indians in America; and a dozen years later found themselves at war again on the same continent. How they let the army rot after the American War of Independence has already been described. In 1919, Lloyd George swept hundreds of thousands of men from the ranks of the army into the ranks of the unemployed, only to find himself in 1922 needing troops whom he could not supply to hold the line against the insurgent Turks at Chanak. To all these examples the wisdom of Addington provides a shining contrast. He retained after the peace of Amiens a regular army of 132,000.[32] Of these nearly half were stationed overseas, and as more than garrisons. There were enough in the West Indies for a prompt reconquest from France of the colonies of St Lucia, Tobago, Demerara and Essequibo when war broke out again in 1803. The 81,000 odd left in Britain, with 50,000 Militia added, provided a garrison far larger than any force Bonaparte could hope to land with the shipping he then possessed, when war began again in 1803.

This brings us to the Militia, which must not be confused with the Regular Army. Soldiers in the Army were all volunteers, enlisted usually for life. In Britain (but not Ireland where enlistment was voluntary) militiamen were conscripts, selected by ballot and required to serve only for five years. Soldiers in the Army were enlisted for overseas service, militiamen only for home defence. Army officers were professionals who chose soldiering as a career, in peace as well as war; militia officers were amateurs of good family who came forward to help defend their country in wartime. The Army was administered by the Commander-in-Chief and his staff, with aid from other departments, as described above; the Militia was raised by the Home Secretary working through the Lords Lieutenant of the counties. The Army included both cavalry and infantry; the Militia provided infantry only.

Addington in 1802 had revised the Militia Acts, and in March 1803, before the new war began, he was able to call out for service 50,000 men of the 'Old Militia', to be followed shortly after by 25,000 of the Supplementary Militia. But here again comes the important question; what was the fighting value of these 75,000 men suddenly haled from farm and factory to be drilled and disciplined, not by regular officers, but by well-intentioned gentlemen of respectable county families?

---

[32] Sir John W. Fortescue, *A History of the British Army*, V, 168.

It should not be underrated. As for their officers, I do not know how to evaluate a contemporary French report that nearly all the officers who commanded the Militia were drawn from the Regulars;[33] but certainly very many of the Militia officers of 1803 would have had up to nine years' experience in that force in the previous war and would be no novices at soldiering. One can hardly doubt that many of those serving in the ranks as substitutes were also old hands from the previous war. Once they were called out the Militia came under the authority of the Commander-in-Chief. Their discipline and training like those of the Regulars were then supervised by the General Officers commanding Districts; and in not too many months they should have become nearly as formidable as ordinary regular battalions.

The last of Britain's armies was the Volunteers. They included both infantry and cavalry (the last being called Yeomanry). Of the organisation of this part-time army it will be enough to say here that it, like the Militia, came under the Home Secretary and the Lords Lieutenant of the counties; that it was composed, as its name implies, of men who voluntarily offered their services in locally organised units; and that the Yeomanry provided their own horses too. In return the government provided arms, pay, freedom from Militia service and required varying periods of serious training.

Again the serious question is what the Volunteers were worth as a fighting force. Here the first very important fact is that Addington brought a united nation into the new war with the French. There were no more British Jacobins looking to France as the apostle of liberty, equality and fraternity. 'Boney' was everywhere accepted as the deadliest enemy the island had yet faced; the island prepared to fight him; that was that, and there was much patriotic enthusiasm. But for victory more than mere untutored enthusiasm is necessary; and the next important fact is the patience and wisdom with which the Duke of York laboured to help this vast amateur force, numbering over 300,000, to become fit to fight. He was allowed no authority over the internal management of Volunteer units, and no professional soldier could give them an order until they were called out on 'permanent duty'. But the Duke won approval for an advisory body of Inspecting Field Officers for the Volunteers. These men were to attend the parades of the Volunteer units assigned to them; to be ready whenever asked to help

[33] 'Les officiers qui commandent la milice sont presque tous tirés de l'armée de la ligne', says the French, agent Dupont Derval, Mémoire sur l'Angleterre,' (Edouard Desbrière, 1793–1805, Projets et Tentatives de Debarquements aux Iles Britanniques [Paris, 1902], III, 326). If the writer means that former regulars had been found to serve as commanding officers of Militia battalions he is likely to be right. He cannot be right if he means that nearly the whole officer corps of the Militia, from platoon commanders up, were regulars.

the captains of Volunteer companies; and to send regular reports on their progress to the Horse Guards. In many cases their improvement was rapid; from areas as far apart as Devon, Sussex, Kent and the home counties, from the midlands and the manufacturing cities of the North reports of Volunteers being 'fit to be joined to Regular Troops' were flowing in to the Horse Guards early in 1804 (Docs. 26 a and b). Indeed already in December, 1803, that most experienced soldier, Lord Cornwallis, had written that 'no man, whether civil or military, will persuade me that 300,000 men, trained as the volunteers at present are, do not add very materially to the confidence and to the actual security of this country'.[34]

Much besides training, of course, was wanted to make the Volunteers effective in the field. They needed weapons, transport and a staff. The weapons were the hardest to supply. At the beginning of the new war the Ordnance had in its stores a reserve of some 150,000 muskets and bayonets. Out of these the department had first to equip men raised to reinforce the Regular Army and to make good any shortages among the Militia. The Volunteers came last, and as the offers of some 70,000 in Ireland and well over 300,000 in England had been accepted by the government, it was obviously impossible to arm them all at once. Early in 1804 complaints from companies of unarmed Volunteers grew frequent and bitter; and from April of that year comes a report of 103,572 pikes having been issued to Volunteers.[35] But the officials of the Ordnance did what they could, by hastening the production of new muskets in Birmingham whence they received 208,358 stands of arms between April 1803 and the end of December 1804,[36] and buying some 293,000, of varying quality, from abroad.[37]

Farm carts provided the transport for 'camp kettles and necessaries' for the Volunteers, one cart for each company. They were rented, not purchased; they were required to be on parade at the regular inspections of the Volunteers (which occurred every two months); and the farm cart of each company had to be painted with its name and number. But the Duke insisted on more than this to make the Volunteers a mobile force. Wherever possible he sought to have their places of assembly located in places handy to canals, the forerunners of the railway for inland transport. Elsewhere he ordered arrangements to be made for what can only be described as a system of 'horse buses' – recalling nothing so much, perhaps, in modern war as the use of the

---

[34] C. Ross (ed.), *The Correspondence of Marquis Cornwallis* (London, 1859), III, 509.

[35] Hadden to Pole Carew, 6 April 1804 (HO/50/397).

[36] 40,609 in the last nine months of 1803; 167,749 in 1804. *Fifteenth Report of the Commissioners of Military Enquiry*, Appendix 9.

[37] *Peninsular Preparation*, 58.

taxis of Paris to carry that city's garrison to the front for the battle of the Marne in 1914. The Duke's 'buses' were not luxurious; they were in fact no more than impressed country waggons fitted with planks for seats; the planks, and the planks only, being purchased by the nation. Yet with relays of horses they should have at least doubled the number of miles a unit could cover in a day; and they would ensure that the men arrived fresh as well as fast.

The staff was most easily provided of all. As we have seen, the Duke had appointed a body of Inspecting Field Officers to supervise the training of the Volunteers; and he organised those same Inspecting Field Officers to serve as staffs for brigades of Volunteers when the invader landed and battles had to be fought on English soil.

Now to sum up on the value of the Volunteers. In 1803 they might have released some regular troops from the police duties required of the Army. By 1804 a considerable number of them were ready for active service; and if Bonaparte had landed in 1805 he would have found in the Volunteers about as formidable a citizen army of part-time soldiers as any nation has ever raised. They are part of the justification for the Duke's writing to Pitt, of a particular scare of that summer, that invasion 'certainly would have been one of the rashest attempts, in my opinion, that Bonaparte ever made'.[38] Unfortunately, this very respectable force was to be as good as thrown away within a matter of months of Pitt's death in January 1806, by that reckless theorist whom the All-the-Talents placed at the War Ministry, William Windham; but, as we have seen, Bonaparte was too busy elsewhere to threaten England while this government was in office. By the time the two great autocrats, Bonaparte and Alexander I of Russia, had made their peace at Tilsit in July 1807, and had agreed on joint hostilities against Britain, Castlereagh had had nearly four months in which to set about repairing the damage. The fact remains that the Volunteers were at their best in the period of greatest danger, the period when Bonaparte was waiting and hoping to see the united fleets of Ganteaume and Villeneuve sail up the Channel together to a total of some fifty line of battle ships to cover his crossing.

Yet the observant reader will have noticed certain weaknesses in Britain's garrison even in its heyday in 1805. The number of mounted troops among the Volunteers was not scientifically arranged to provide a properly thought out proportion of cavalry to infantry; it was simply the number who offered to serve with their own horses. Among the 75,000 Militia there were no mounted troops at all. The vast army of defence was therefore very short of cavalry; and this weakness was the more serious because the Regular Army itself had a much smaller percentage of cavalry than continental armies considered necessary.

[38] Cited by Burne, *The Noble Duke of York*, 255.

The defending forces were even weaker in field artillery. None of the Militia or Volunteers were gunners. For gunners, the whole force, Regular, Militia and Volunteers, had to rely on the limited number of artillery units which the Ordnance could supply. This was almost inevitable because it took so much longer to train a recruit in the complicated duties of a gunner that artillerymen were necessarily professionals. But it was unfortunate that the peace time establishment of the Royal Artillery was calculated, so far as it was calculated at all, on the strength of the Regular Army only, without thought of the great auxiliary forces which Britain might raise in wartime (Doc. 25).

It would be childish to suppose that these weaknesses were not perfectly well known to the great artillery officer who commanded the legions of the enemy across the Channel. 'Nothing was too great or small for his proboscis', said Wellington of Bonaparte; and certainly his information from England was excellent.

That point leads us to the vital matter of military 'intelligence'; for intelligence is indeed vital, even if it is too often neglected. The simple fact is that without accurate information on the enemy there can be no sound planning in war; and without sound planning there can be no success, except from the chance effects of mere luck. The duties of military intelligence are two-fold – to conceal one's own strength and intentions and to discover those of the enemy. The excellence of Bonaparte's intelligence was, in fact, such a serious matter for England that it is worth examining one of his successes before turning to British methods.

Shortly after becoming Britain's Minister for War in July 1805, Castlereagh had instructed the Duke of York to prepare a 'disposable force' ready at any moment to strike a blow against the French. It was to be composed of 30,000–35,000 infantry and 8,000–10,000 cavalry. The troops were to be stationed near Cork, Portsmouth and in East Kent. To move them across the water Castlereagh undertook to hold ready 'a fleet of transports perfectly equipped and victualled for foreign service' and capable of carrying 'about 10,000 men' in one lift. The letter in which he proposed this to the Duke was dated '26 July' and marked 'most secret'.[39] But the secret was very soon known in Paris. On 28 August Bonaparte was writing that the British had ready a striking force of some 40,000 men;[40] and his knowledge of it led him to take certain very particular steps before he marched eastwards against Austria that autumn.

Here one hardly knows which to admire most, the accuracy of Bonaparte's information or the speed with which it reached him; and

[39] Lord Londonderry, *Letters and Correspondence of Lord Castlereagh*, VIII, 6–7.
[40] *Correspondence de Napoléon I*^{er}, IX, nos. 9155, 9159, 9164, 9228, 9248, 9252.

the question is, how did he get it? Some may ask whether he had a well-placed spy in London, like Lord North's famous agent, Dr Edward Bancroft, whom Benjamin Franklin so trustingly employed as secretary to the American embassy in Paris throughout the War of Independence. If, however, there was such a French spy in London in 1805, historians have still to discover him; and in fact Bonaparte knew nothing on this occasion which he could not have learned through ways regularly used for espionage at the time.

First, there was the matter of the ships. Even if these had not been hired by public tender, a favourite method of thrifty governments, the preparation of a fleet of transports could not help being widely known in the British harbours where they were provisioned and prepared.[41] The next step was for news of them to cross the water. And here we touch the role of smugglers in the Napoleonic wars. The British regularly used these men to bring information from across the Channel; so did the French; and evading wartime restrictions was hardly a problem for men whose peacetime lives were devoted to evading, or corrupting, customs officers. Of course, it was realised that smugglers could be double-agents; but they went to and fro anyway and were too useful to ignore (Doc. 5). They were a natural source of information on England's shipping.

Once he knew transports were being prepared, Bonaparte had only to learn what troops they might carry; and this also does not seem unduly difficult. Castlereagh had asked the Duke of York to concentrate these troops in places where they could be handily embarked – near Cork, Portsmouth and the Downs, areas well within the range of smugglers. But one fears that once the troops had arrived in their new quarters, all that French agents needed do to inform Paris was that routine job of good intelligence – sending home the English local newspapers.[42] For troop movements were nowhere harder to conceal

[41] The number of steps involved in preparing such a fleet make this inevitable. Among those steps were:
  (a) hiring the ships; and this, which required no more than making contracts between the Transport Board and the ship-owners, could readily be kept secret. But then
  (b) the ships would have to be provisioned with food and water, on a far larger scale than necessary for its crew alone, unless for a very long voyage. This would be known to every stevedore who helped load them. Next
  (c) crews would have to be hired; and they too might talk. Fourth,
  (d) 8,000–10,000 of the troops were to be cavalry. That meant that a number of ships would have to be refitted as horse-transports – a job for many dockyard workers.
By the time all these jobs were done, too many people would have known about the fleet of transports for its existence to remain a secret.
[42] Newspapers are at no time to be despised. Professor Trevor-Roper,

than in a country which boasted the freedom of its press. In fact the irresponsible way in which British newspapers then abused their freedom seems quite astonishing today,[43] and they were regularly studied across the Channel. So one by one the various pieces of the jigsaw puzzle would filter back to Paris. There they would be assembled in the card indexes kept under the eye of an incomparable master of the art of war (Doc. 4). As the picture revealed the arrival of new troops in embarkation areas, and a fleet to carry them, the right conclusion would not be hard to draw.[44]

So far then Bonaparte's information on Castlereagh's planning was excellent; but it was also limited. Its limits appear in the use he made of it when he marched eastwards in September against the Austrians. Then his first thought was to protect Boulogne and its precious flotilla. 30,000 regulars under Marshal Brune were left to guard this port against an English attack. Next on his list was Antwerp, an ideal base for a British expeditionary force if they could but secure it; two French divisions were left to protect this city and its dockyards. Third came Holland, which the British had invaded in 1799; two more divisions stood on guard there. So all told, Castlereagh's failure to hide the secret of his expeditionary force very usefully cut down the size of the armies Bonaparte was to lead against Austria. Yet Bonaparte's guesses as to where that force would be used were all wrong. The British attacked none of the points where he expected them. Instead they landed in North Germany where, they vainly hoped, the Prussians might be induced to join the coalition against France. One concludes, then, that

---

writing from his own experience in dealing with intelligence, correctly states that 'secret intelligence is the continuation of open intelligence by other means. . . . Intelligence, in fact, is indivisible. The greater part of it must always be acquired by open or official methods. Only a relatively small area requires secret penetration, or espionage. Nevertheless this small area may be vital. . . . The date of a surprise military operation; the details of a vital technical process; the *arcana imperii* of any political system; the identity of an agent who can supply such facts; the list of secret codes which are read – these are all secrets which are rightly protected by one side, and rightly sought out by the other.' (Quoted by permission from *The Philby Affair* [London, 1968], 66–67. This is an excellent summary of the duties of any secret service; and newspapers are a necessary source of 'open intelligence'.)

[43] For the anxieties which the British press caused Wellington in the Peninsula, *see* Colonel Gurwood (ed.) *The Despatches of the Duke of Wellington in the Peninsula* (London, 1837–38), X, 101, 106, 247, 544, 555; and C. D. Yonge (ed.), *The Life and Administration of Robert Banks, second Earl of Liverpool* (London, 1868), I, 362–3.

[44] Let me make it perfectly clear that this reconstruction of how Bonaparte might have acquired this particular piece of intelligence is conjectural. I have not managed to trace the channels through which the news reached him. My aim is to show how easily it could have reached him by methods of espionage which were used at the time.

Bonaparte had no spy in the Horse Guards or the ministry for war to report the secret intentions of the British government. But his knowledge of what took place along the coastline he threatened was first-class. That fact must be numbered among the dangers Britain faced.

On the English side the business of gaining information about the enemy was far less well managed. The Commander-in-Chief of the army had no intelligence organisation at all. Instead an act of 1782 prescribed that money 'for Foreign Secret Service . . . shall be issued and paid to one of his Majesty's Principal Secretaries of State or to the first Commissioner of the Admiralty'.[45] So the Duke of York is found writing in 1804 that 'The Knowledge which I have acquired of the Enemy's Preparation [is] derived from His Majesty's Confidential Servants'; and the officers at the Horse Guards whose advice Castlereagh sought on the Scheldt expedition of 1809 had to warn him that they could give no information even on the number of militia locally available for the defence of Antwerp. To those who have been taught the importance of knowing the enemy's order of battle this will seem a shocking piece of ignorance. Yet it is hardly surprising in a country where the secret service was so very civilian and where no professional military staff was provided to assess all the reports which came in or to provide particular questions for agents to answer.

Yet the English were still by no means so ignorant in 1803–5 as in 1940.[46] They used, of course, 'the interceptions', a discreet phrase meaning the dirty business of opening other people's mail in the post office, copying it and then resealing and sending it on. Neutral diplomats were common victims of this practice.[47]

Second, they had the agents hired by the Secretaries of State and the Admiralty. Agents need careful handling. They have to earn their

---

[45] Cited by Alfred Cobban, 'The British Secret Service in France, 1784–1792,' English Historical Review, 69 (1954), 232–3.

[46] On which point, see Peter Fleming, Invasion 1940 (London, 1957), Chapter 11.

[47] This practice was of course general and used by all nations. 'At Vienna,' records Lord Stanhope quoting Wellington, 'they scarcely made a secret of their system of opening the Foreign Minister's letters. "Once," said the Duke, "Burghersh said boldly at the Chancellerie, I beg you will make haste and let me have my letters as soon as you have read them," and they without showing any displeasure, answered quietly that he should have his letters immediately.' (Conversations with the Duke of Wellington [Oxford, 1947], 226). For more on the interesting office which did this work in Britain, see Kenneth Ellis, The British Post Office in the Eighteenth Century (London, 1958), 60–77, 127–31 and Sir Lewis Namier, The Structure of Politics at the Accession of George III (London, 1957), 192–4. Its small but select staff included translators, forgers of counterfeit seals and code-crackers. One of the latter, Edward Willes, was in 1743 actually made Bishop of Bath and Wells in part payment for his services, as unlikely a reward for a 'cloak-and-dagger' specialist as could well be imagined.

living; to do so, they must send reports to their paymasters; and the value of their reports varies greatly. Some men serve as spies because they are idealists who believe their duty to mankind requires them to risk their lives by betraying their own government; and, if they are well placed to get information, like Richard Sorge, the Rosenbergs, Kim Philby or Oleg Penkovskiy, they are invaluable. Others spy because their personal hopes are bound up with the success of the enemy – notably in our period Irish malcontents who worked for France and French émigrés in neutral countries who worked for England. Such men may be able to get 'hard' intelligence, but their reports are too liable to be coloured by their own wishful thinking. Then there are men of no loyalties at all who just want money. Sometimes they are in positions where they can get good information, but often they are mere peddlers of worthless gossip. The surest criterion for sifting good spies from bad is the record of their past performance; and he who receives undercover information must be forever checking it and eliminating sources which prove untrustworthy (Doc. 8). How far the constantly changing civilian secretaries of state, whom politics placed, and re-placed, in the ministry for war, were equal to this task is a question more easily asked than answered. That much secret service money was wasted on rogues seems certain. There were also reliable men on the British payroll who from time to time sent accurate reports of French troop movements.[48] But British agents were no more successful than those of any other power in penetrating Bonaparte's deeper secrets.[49]

Then, as we have seen, there were the smugglers – a dubious crew of professional lawbreakers (Doc. 5). They were hardly experts on military affairs; and it may be significant of their incompetence that, though Antwerp is a great port close to England, Castlereagh's only information on its fortifications in 1809 seems to have come from army officers who had not seen it since 1794. That smugglers could be double spies has already been mentioned. Indeed one may doubt if they would have survived very long unless they had been willing to serve both sides; and some seem to have been employed for a remarkably long time.[50] But they did at least go ashore on enemy soil; they could question their

[48] Notably the agent whose report in August 1805 that the French Imperial Guard had been ordered from Paris to Boulogne was correct, though soon countermanded. Burne, *The Noble Duke of York*, 255.

[49] 'No leakage of Napoleon's plans is known to have occurred... until the confusion of "The Hundred Days". Then information that the Emperor was moving on Brussels was sent to Wellington from a person in the *Ministère de la Guerre*. That the messenger was detained at the British outpost line is another story.' Brigadier-General Sir James Edmonds, 'Leakages', *The Army Quarterly*, (October 1953), 84.

[50] One would like to know more of a character called Johnstone. There was a smuggler of this name employed by Pitt to gain information from Holland

confederates across the water; and no doubt they contributed to the arrangements by which the *Moniteur* was read in London four days after it was printed in Paris.

Besides smugglers there was the Navy; and at an early stage in the war the Duke of York was put in direct touch with Admiral Lord Keith, the commander of the North Sea squadron whose duties included watching the French channel ports. It must be said at once that naval officers were often very poor judges of what troops could do ashore. But they were assiduous in questioning neutral merchantmen and the fishermen who, like smugglers, continued in war to follow their peace-time trade. They sometimes picked up enemy deserters and escaped prisoners of war (Docs 6 and 7). They, too, acquired French news-papers. They kept a close watch on the enemy's ports, and especially on his naval bases (Docs 10 and 11). As we shall see, their information on the state of the enemy's fleets was consistently excellent; and since the enemy would have to do his best to protect his invasion flotilla, this information was of first class importance.

It is proverbial that stale intelligence is too often worthless intelli-gence, and that news must travel fast if it is to be useful. So one finds the Duke of York requesting in the summer of 1803 that the telegraph be re-established. 'Telegraph' is a word suggestive of the Morse code and the latest twentieth century devices. The telegraph of 1803 was nothing of the kind. It was an adaptation of naval methods of signalling for use on land, a semaphore system somewhat recalling its much simplified descendant, the signals employed on our railroads today. Both sides used it, and, given clear weather and good signallers, it was most efficient – so efficient that the message 'The French are landing near Hythe' could be passed from the Sussex coast to London in a mere eleven minutes.[51] But if the French had really come, London might very possibly have known their intentions before ever they landed; for the telegraph also linked London with Admiral Keith's station at the Downs, and the news that the French army was putting to sea might well have reached the English capital before the invaders reached the English coast.

In all these ways the British kept watch on their enemy across the water. But probably the greatest asset to British intelligence in these years was the strength of the country's defending forces by land and sea. In 1908 the Committee of Imperial Defence recommended that 'our

before the Alkmaar expedition of 1799. A smuggler of the same name reappears in Castlereagh's correspondence ten years later, when he was promised great rewards if he served Lord Chatham well on the Scheldt expedition. I suspect it was the same man on both occasions. I have no clue to the real value of his services, how much he was paid or how long he continued to receive secret service money.

[51] Major Charles James, *Military Dictionary* (London, 1810), *sub* 'Telegraph'.

army for home defence ought to be sufficient in number and organisation not only to repel small raids, but to compel the enemy who contemplates invasion to come with so substantial a force as will make it impossible for him to evade our fleets'.[52] Addington's government was ready in 1803 with forces on the scale called for by this recommendation. Consequently Bonaparte faced a far tougher problem than any which had earlier confronted Louis XV and Louis XVI. If the French in 1759 had managed to carry out their plan of landing 15,000–20,000 men in Scotland followed by 48,000 in the south of England, these forces should have been 'able to overrun the British Army [at home] without reinforcement or resupply,' writes Rex Whitworth. Also in 1759 the French had 'in Toulon, Rochefort and Brest . . . sufficient warships [both to] disperse the British battle fleets and protect the crossing of [their] armada from them'.[53] It took the great naval victories of Boscawen off Lagos and Hawke in Quiberon Bay to bring that threat to a happy ending. Again in August 1779, Lord Amherst had 'hardly 20,000 effective regulars in Britain' with whom to meet the French invasion force of 31,000 that lay waiting and ready at Le Havre and St Malo;[54] and England has never been luckier than on this occasion when her enemies' own bungling squandered their temporary command of the Channel. But, as we have seen, in 1803 the Duke of York had 132,000 Regulars and Militia in Britain (not counting the Volunteers). Bonaparte's fleet was then inferior even to Louis XV's in 1756 (when it foiled Admiral Byng's relief of Minorca successfully enough) and it was not comparable at all to Louis XVI's. Therefore he was compelled to choose the shortest, quickest crossing. The force he hoped to land in 1804 was 120,000 men[55] – enough for but a local superiority in England, even if all got ashore in decent order. But to lift as large a force as this he had to mass so much shipping in his Channel ports that his opponents were left in no doubt of the general area he threatened. So from the start he had no chance of scoring strategic surprise. Yet it is typical of the man that in spite of every difficulty he still pursued his purpose; and the fact that he never revived the threat from Boulogne after his peace with Russia in 1807 does not mean that he had by then dismissed his earlier plans of 1797, 1801 and 1803–5 as vain hopes which had never been practical. It is

[52] Cited by R. Wheatley, *Operation Sea Lion* (Oxford, 1962), 2.

[53] Whitworth, *Ligonier*, 298.

[54] A. Temple Patterson, *The Other Armada* (Manchester, 1960), 108, 151. Besides the 20,000 regulars Britain also had another 30,000 English militia and in Scotland some 3,500 Fencibles (or home defence troops), and the Irish garrison of 10,000 regulars. But a garrison in Ireland was of no use in England; and the value of the militia was then very doubtful. Too many of its regiments were newly raised and too many of its officers were amateurs.

[55] Rose, *Pitt and Napoleon*, 129.

simply added evidence of the accuracy of his information; for (as will be shown below) by 1807 the English had fortified their south coast in a way which left him no other road to victory than winning the command of the sea.

END NOTE

In this chapter I have said nothing about the too familiar proposals for 'driving the country' so as to leave a 'scorched earth' before the French. There is, in fact, very little to say. The first reference to the idea that I have found dates from 1779, when it was proposed by General William Roy. But as the French failed to land that year, no attempt was then made to drive the country. The idea came up again in 1801, perhaps as a conscious revival of the earlier proposal for the Duke of York had studied his predecessors' plans for defence. This time the proposal was fairly torpedoed by the Duke of Richmond, himself a soldier, a former (and excellent) Master General of the Ordnance and still Lord Lieutenant of the county of Sussex. In 1803, one can only suppose by some error, similar orders were sent out again by the Secretary of State and a similar blast came from Richmond. Very cogently Richmond argued that if it were possible to destroy all supplies in an invaded country, the result would be famine among all those of the inhabitants, notably the elderly and infirm poor, who could not flee; but in fact the job was so vast that it was not possible; and Richmond carried his enumeration of the food supplies of Sussex even to the point of giving the numbers of deer in noblemen's parks in the county. The Duke of York's comments are contained in a letter to Charles Yorke of 20 October 1803. There he explained that since 1801 officers employed on defence planning had moved from doubts about the value of driving the country to a universal 'distrust of the *possibility* and *expediency* of this measure'. He himself perfectly coincided 'in the opinion that Horses and draft Cattle alone ought to be removed in the event of Invasion'. In other words, the enemy was to be denied mounts for his cavalry and teams for his guns and his baggage. As for 'the destruction of dead Stock . . . nothing more can be done than generally to recommend its being done when the danger is evident of its falling into the hands of the Enemy'. But the destruction of valuable stores when they can no longer be denied to the enemy in any other way is a normal and proper operation of war, far more limited than were the early and extravagant ideas of 'driving the country'.

3

The Admiralty's Tasks

THIS chapter will describe no naval battles. It is enough to remember that, as Lord Barham wrote, thanks to 'Sir Robert Calder's action, the splendid victory off Trafalgar, the valiant achievement of Sir Robert Strachan [and] Sir John Duckworth's brilliant action off San Domingo . . . the enemy lost in the short space of six months 31 sail of the line, 5 frigates and 5 corvettes', in 1805–6 [1]; that in 1806 he lost most of Missiessy's squadron of 6 sail of the line; that in 1807 the British made sure that the Danish and Portuguese fleets would never fall into Bonaparte's hands; that the Spanish revolt of 1808 robbed him of the remains of the Spanish fleet too, and half a dozen more of his own ships; and that in 1809 Admiral Lord Gambier destroyed 3 and crippled 7 of the 10 French ships of the line which he attacked with fire-ships in the Basque Roads. Besides these another half-dozen French ships of the line were captured in minor actions between 1807 and the end of the war; and every line of battle ship lost to the enemy was a gain to the defence of Britain. There were no more major naval battles, although important French squadrons did from time to time put to sea; and the reason why they were not brought to book will appear in due course. Instead of describing battles our purpose here is to deal with the tasks of the British sailors and the problems of the handful of men at the Admiralty who directed the world-wide employment of the Royal Navy.

At the top was a member of the cabinet, the First Lord of the Admiralty, who was assisted by the Admiralty Board composed of the first, second and third sea lords, the civil lords and the secretaries. Appointments to this Board were political and hence liable to change when governments changed. But various shades of Tories were in power for most of the war, and some members of the Board held their posts for long periods. They were often able – for example, among the Board's secretaries (of whom there were two) were John Wilson Croker, Wellesley Pole (Wellington's brother) and Sir John Barrow, who was later to take so much interest in Arctic exploration. The fact

[1] Laughton, *Barham Papers*, III, 274.

that appointments to the Board were political did not prevent naval officers from receiving them; and the Board had a useful blend of administrative experience and professional knowledge.

Under the Admiralty Board were the Navy Board which was responsible for building and repairing ships and the Victualling Board which provisioned them. The navy, like the army, received weapons and ammunitition from the Ordnance Department.

When the war began the First Lord of the Admiralty was that great, gruff, no-nonsense character, Admiral Lord St Vincent; and he was the planner of Britain's defensive strategy in the first year of the war. In 1804 he was succeeded by Henry Dundas, first Viscount Melville. Lord Melville is credited by his biographer with an unusually good grasp of naval affairs.[2] Unfortunately he was also a very lax administrator; and his political career ended when the Commission of Naval Enquiry, which St Vincent had set on foot, found that his carelessness as Treasurer of the Navy in the previous war had enabled his Deputy Treasurer to use the navy's money for private speculation. So Melville perforce resigned in June 1805, and Sir Charles Middleton (later Lord Barham) succeeded him; Barham, though in his eightieth year, was one of the outstanding First Lords of the Admiralty whom none of his successors equalled in professional knowledge or strategical insight. He directed the strategy of the Trafalgar campaign. After him came Lord Howick (the future Lord Grey of the Reform Bill) from February to September 1806, Thomas Grenville from September 1806 till 6 April 1807, then Lord Mulgrave until May 1810, Charles Yorke till May 1812, and Robert Dundas, the second Lord Melville, from then on until after war ended.

The job of these men, as we said above, was directing 'the world-wide employment of the Royal Navy' and there was hardly an ocean in which its ships did not serve at one time or another. The Baltic, the North Sea, the Channel, the Mediterranean and West Indian waters all had to be kept open to British merchantmen. In the Pacific the Admiralty had to maintain communications with the colony of New South Wales and to protect British trade, of which there was much with the Spanish colonies after 1808. This ocean also saw one sharp action when the *Phoebe* and the *Cupid* ended the depredations of the U.S. frigate *Essex* by sinking her off the Chile coast in April 1814. In Indonesia the Navy had to support the landing operations which made Britain for a short space the ruler of much of the Dutch East Indies. Nearer home Mauritius and the Ile de Bourbon in the Indian Ocean and the Cape of Good Hope had to be captured. To the south Atlantic the Navy had to convoy the troops of General Whitelocke who there crowned the

---

[2] Holden Furber, *Henry Dundas, First Viscount Melville* (Oxford, 1931), 148.

feckless strategy of his masters, the Ministry of All-the-Talents, by bungling his attack on Buenos Aires in 1807.[3] In the North Atlantic a squadron based on Halifax kept guard over the sea lanes of British merchantmen. In the heart of North America itself Captain Robert Barclay, R.N., was to suffer in the Battle of Lake Erie, of July 1813, one of the completest disasters ever inflicted on a British commander when the Americans sank every ship which the Provincial Marine of Upper Canada possessed on that Lake. In Kingston, on the other hand, shipwrights sent out from Plymouth and Portsmouth built the squadron which by the end of the War of 1812 held the command of Lake Ontario, with, as its flagship, the great *St Lawrence*, of 102 guns.[4]

Such was the scope of the Admiralty's responsibilities. But the heart of its problem lay nearer home, in the European ports where the enemies' main fleets were massing.

The four major commands were the North Sea, the Channel, the Mediterranean and, latterly, the Baltic. The North Sea squadron was based on the Thames and its task was to keep watch on the Dutch fleet at the Texel and the new navy which Bonaparte was building in Antwerp. The Channel squadron was so named because it was based on Plymouth and, in a lesser degree Portsmouth, but its duties were mainly in the Atlantic, guarding against French and Spanish bases from Brest to Vigo and Ferrol. The Spanish base of Cadiz and all that lay east of it were in the sphere of the commander of the Mediterranean squadron.

The Baltic merits a short section to itself as the scene of one of Britain's strangest and least known naval wars. It was a war waged only in summer, because in those days ice was liable to close so much of this inland sea in winter;[5] a war in which all the Baltic powers were in due course to be arrayed against Britain; yet also a war whose decisive battle was fought before either Russia or Sweden entered it; and for the most part a war in which neither side wished to take the fighting too seriously. The decisive battle was, of course, the British attack on Copenhagen and the seizure of the Danish fleet in September 1807. The Russians still declared war that winter, as they had promised at

[3] This was not the first, but it was the biggest, British attack on Spain's South American colonies.

[4] She has sometimes been credited with more than 102 guns, but this is how I find her rated in a statement of the force of the Lake Ontario squadron of the Royal Navy, dated 14 October 1814, and catalogued in the Public Record Office under 'Dockyards, Canada' (ADM/106/1997).

[5] A change in the world's climate needs to be remembered here. What ecologists call 'the Little Ice Age' lasted from about 1250 to 1850 A.D. In the Baltic this period produced winter of the sort which enabled Charles X of Sweden to invade Denmark by marching an army over the frozen sea. Further south it produced so much ice in the Scheldt that Bonaparte's fleet there was hauled ashore every winter.

Tilsit. But Sweden remained an ally and in 1808 British and Swedish ships together controlled the Baltic. The revolt of the Spaniards that spring naturally affected the Baltic war. Their naval bases no longer needed blockading and more ships were available for the north. This relief was most welcome in 1809 when the Swedes overthrew Gustavus IV, took Charles XIII for king and made peace with Russia, leaving Britain to patrol the Baltic alone that summer. In the following winter Sweden took the further step of declaring war on Britain. But she was a most unwilling adversary and the Russian and Swedish fleets never joined together against Admiral Sir James Saumarez's British squadron. Finally, Russia herself became an ally when Bonaparte attacked her in 1812. The role of Turkey during this contest should not be forgotten either. She was, of course, at war with Russia until 1812, and, thanks to her control of the Straits, the Russian Black Sea fleet could never threaten the British in the Mediterranean.

With that we may turn to the main enemy fleets which Britain confronted from the Texel westwards past the Scheldt to Brest, southwards past L'Orient and Rochefort to Cadiz, and eastwards past Toulon and Genoa to Naples and Venice.

The enemy might go to sea at any time for a variety of reasons. He might seek to put Britain at Bonaparte's mercy with the kind of naval victory for which Villeneuve had hoped on his luckless excursion from Cadiz which ended at Trafalgar. Again, the enemy might wish to convoy troops to occupy or conquer new territory – like the Ionian Islands which Bonaparte took over from Russia after Tilsit, or Sicily which the French was repeatedly scheming to attack. Another aim was to slip supplies and reinforcements through to French dependencies across the water, for which Ganteaume was sent to Corfu in 1808 and Leisségues and Missiessy to the West Indies in 1806. On other occasions moves were made to concentrate two separate squadrons – like Allemand's voyage to join Ganteaume in the Mediterranean in 1808, or that of the Brest fleet to the Aix Roads where Gambier crippled it in April 1809.

Whatever the enemy might attempt, it was the duty of British commanders to thwart him; and the chief of all their duties was, of course, to win safety for England by destroying his fleets in battle. But that could not be done while enemy warships lay secure in well-defended harbours or came out only under conditions in which they were safe from attack. These were the things which the French very sensibly did for most of the time, as they waited, while their fleets grew, for that day which never came – the day when they would be ready to challenge the Royal Navy's command of the sea. As long as the enemy stayed in port, British commanders had to blockade him there, through month after weary month of beating to and fro outside his bases. This job began against France as soon as war began in 1803; and the Navy's watch over Spanish ports had started even before Spain declared war in December 1804. No blockade could ever be perfect, and weather which drove British squadrons away gave the French their opportunities to slip out which, as we have seen, they occasionally took. But year in, year out, a very close watch was still kept on French bases.

Next, English commanders had to collect all the information they could about the particular foe they were blockading. They gained this in a number of ways. They questioned deserters, prisoners of war, fishermen (Docs. 6 and 7) and such neutrals as still came and went from enemy's harbours. When they could, they introduced their own agents or suborned disaffected persons in key places ashore. Somehow they managed to acquire the enemy's newspapers pretty frequently; and they studied his signal code in order to read the messages he passed over his semaphore telegraph (Doc. 9). Occasionally, too, they had the luck to intercept secret letters of the enemy's high command. Wherever possible one of their most important tasks was to make regular and direct inspections of what was going on inside the enemy's harbours. This, of course, was not possible at a place like Antwerp which lay far up a well-defended river, and no clear view could be had of the dock-yards in Venice either. But Brest, Rochefort, Toulon, Genoa and Naples were all regularly examined by sloop or frigate commanders who climbed to the masthead with telescopes after sailing as close in as possible (Doc. 11d).

These inspections were not the healthiest of jobs for they were commonly made under the crossfire of shore batteries designed expressly to prevent them. But still they were made; and British captains carefully observed both what ships were building on the stocks and what size they were – information the Admiralty needed to estimate how fast the enemy's seapower was growing. These observers reported, too, what training the enemy was carrying out in harbour; how his ships were painted – an obvious aid to recognising them if they came out to sea; how they were rigged; and finally – a most important point – how deep they were in the water. A ship riding light and high was clearly pretty empty; but one that floated deep could be presumed to be fully laden, with all the ammunition, stores, food and water needed to make her ready for the sea. From all these sources British admirals compiled the reports on the enemy's progress which they were required to send the Admiralty each month (Docs. 10 and 11); and when the end of the war in April 1814 enabled them to visit the harbours they had guarded so long, they had the satisfaction of discovering that their reports had been, on the whole, exceedingly accurate. So, one way and another, the Admiralty had excellent information on which to base its strategy.

Finally, British sailors had to destroy the enemy's seaborne trade. This was the happiest of all their tasks, for every ship and cargo they took meant prize money for its captors.[6] Yet it was also a job that was never properly accomplished. The high seas were indeed swept pretty clear of the enemy's shipping, but to the end of the war the French kept up an immense coastal trade. This was natural, because coastal shipping was never so important as in the days before railroads gave nations a swift and relatively cheap means of moving goods by land. The importance the French attached to this coastal trade is made evident by the immense pains they took to protect it. All along his shorelines Bonaparte developed a vast chain of fortified posts with sea batteries to defend bays where convoys could find sanctuary from British cruisers. To these fortified posts he added the semaphore telegraph which passed warning of the movements of British ships along the coast. These measures had much success, in spite of the efforts of such artists in destruction as the famous Lord Cochrane – a real master of minor operations at sea;[7] and Bonaparte's success in protecting his coastal trade was a grave matter for Britain. For these carefully shepherded convoys of little ships carried more than just the innocent cargoes of civilian merchants. They brought to Bonaparte's main naval bases timber for building his new fleets and stores for provisioning them. Likewise, their crews, constantly employed at sea, provided him with a 'nursery of seamen' from which to man those fleets when they were ready to attempt the final overthrow of Britain (Docs. 12 and 13). The failure of the British to stop this coastal trade was therefore serious; and its cause will be noted shortly.

The first things an admiral needed to perform all his duties were, of course, ships; and of these the most important were those called line of battle ships, or more simply, ships of the line. Both names describe generally ships designed to exchange fire in line of battle against the strongest ships of the enemy. But ships of the line were themselves divided into several classes, according to their size and the

[6] Gilbert White, the famous naturalist of Selborne, gives from the American War of Independence a nice example of what prize money could mean even to a victim of the pressgang. 'A Selborne man', he writes, 'was aboard the Porcupine sloop when she took the French India rich ship. I saw a letter from him this morning in which he says his share will come to £300. This will be some recompence to the poor fellow who was kid-napped in an ale-house in Botley by a pressgang.' To Miss White, 19 October 1778; Rashleigh Holt-White, *The Life and Letters of Gilbert White of Selborne* (London, 1901), II, 31.

[7] One may perhaps mention that the novelist Captain Frederick Marryat (1792–1848) had actually served with Cochrane. His novels are therefore worth reading as a story of life in the Royal Navy in the Napoleonic War that is based on the writer's own experience; but, as I have noted elsewhere, Cochrane's own *Autobiography of a Seaman* is not to be trusted as a historical source.

number of guns they carried. They ranged from two-deckers with as few as 60 guns to three-deckers with over 100 guns, and even to four-deckers like the tremendous *Santissima Trinidad* of 130 guns, the greatest ship of her day until she was crippled and sunk as one of Spain's most grievous losses at Trafalgar. The commonest armament of British two-deckers was 74 guns; and these '74's' were far handier in rough weather than the ponderous three-deckers. On the other hand, the three-decker, opening fire with over 50 guns in a single broadside, could deliver a terrific punch. But the speed of a punch was hardly less important than its power; and so the effectiveness of a ship in action depended on the expertness of its gun crews and the quickness with which they could reload and fire. Hence came hours of gundrill, week in and week out. What all this gundrill meant in battle appears in the achievement of Collingwood's gunners on H.M.S. *Excellent*. They could get off three broadsides in 1½ minutes, while their Spanish opponents at St Vincent are said to have managed no more than one broadside in 5 minutes.[8]

After the ships of the line, the frigate was the most important ship of the period; but frigates in general must not be judged by the most famous surviving vessel of this class – the U.S.S. *Constitution*, which so many sight-seers visit annually in Boston harbour. Like Germany's pocket battle ships of this century, the big U.S. frigates, the *United States*, the *Constitution* and the *President* were designed to outshoot any ship that could catch them and outsail any ship that could outshoot them. They were two-deckers, technically rated as 44-gun ships, but they could, and often did, carry over 50. The standard frigates of European navies were single deck ships armed with from 26 to 44 guns. Their jobs in the Royal Navy were to protect convoys, to act as scouts ahead and on the flanks of a battlefleet, to destroy enemy commerce and to maintain the close-in blockade of enemy bases, while the heavier line of battle ships lay further out to sea.

Then there were sloops, brigs and corvettes, all small ships and weak in armament, but essential for scouting, carrying messages, intercepting the enemy's trade and hunting down his privateers.

The number of ships that the Admiralty could allot to its commanders depended on the number it could man, build and keep in repair; and for the last two tasks it needed naval bases. A naval base had, first, to be a harbour in which many ships could lie safely at anchor when storms drove them to seek shelter; and it had also to be capable of defending itself against enemy attacks. But if it was to serve a fleet effectively a base needed much more than this. Its usefulness depended on its supplies of stores – of barrels of salt pork and biscuit and supplies of

[8] Oliver Warner, *Collingwood* (London, 1968), 87.

good water to revictual ships; of powder and shot of all calibres to re-arm them; of masts, spars, cordage, sails and oak plank to repair them.

Serving admirals commonly regarded the dockyards as the Achilles' heel of the Royal Navy. How fair this opinion was is a question that cannot be answered until someone makes a special study of the work of British dockyards in this war,[9] but certain points seem clear.

First, too many of the dockyards the fleet had to use were under-equipped. Thus to the end of the war British ships had to be sent home from the Mediterranean for all repairs which needed dry-docking. Much could, of course, be done at Gibraltar, Malta, Port Mahon (after 1808), and Syracuse (of which some use was made by the force defending Sicily). There new masts, spars, cordage and sails could be supplied. Hulls could be cleaned wherever a ship could be hove down; and Rear Admiral Thomas Fremantle declared himself able to do this even with a line of battle ship at the little base which he most ably improvised at Lissa in the Adriatic in 1812. But major repairs to the frame of a ship or recoppering could only be done in drydock; and that meant a trip to Deptford, Woolwich, Sheerness, Chatham, Portsmouth or Plymouth. Spanish dockyards after 1808 could give little help – understandably when one considers the chaos into which the Peninsular War threw Spain. That Malta would have been vastly more useful if it were provided with a dry dock is obvious, and in due course one was built there. But it was for long doubtful whether Malta would remain in British hands. Pitt's negotiations with Alexander I in 1804–5 nearly foundered over the question of this island on which the Tsar had very definite opinions. Evangelicals in England, with a piety surpassing their information, stoutly affirmed that Britain would forfeit her good faith if she did not give Malta 'its independence'.[10] This attitude was nonsense, because 'independence' meant restoring Malta to that derelict crusading order, the Knights of St John, whose rule the native Maltese detested.

[9] A sensible interim verdict is that of Bernard Pool: 'The fact is that the country could hardly have survived the war if the arrangements for providing ships had not been basically sound and well administered' (*The Navy Board and Contracts, 1660–1832* (London, 1966), 130).

[10] So wrote Lord Teignmouth to Wilberforce (*Life of Wilberforce*, IV, 99). Article 10 of the Treaty of Amiens provided that Malta should be restored to the Knights of St John who would elect among themselves a Grand Master to rule the order; and the British would evacuate the island three months after proper ratifications. But the Knights never held a regular election. One Ruspoli was elected Grand Master at an irregular election held in Russia, but declined the post. The Pope then nominated a Grand Master; but a papal nomination was not the same thing as an election. (W. Porter, *History of the Knights of Malta*, 3rd edition (London, 1884), 392.) The 10th Article of the Treaty of Amiens was thus never fulfilled; and until it was properly fulfilled, Britain was under no obligation to evacuate the island.

The real situation was well described to William Wilberforce by John Bowdler, writing from Valletta in January 1811. Even at that date the Treaty of Amiens' stipulations about the Order of St John still hung like a cloud over the island, and, wrote Bowdler, 'No arrangements, therefore, have ever been made for settling the government permanently, or defining its authority, and the legitimate modes of exercising it'.[11] When such doubts as these prevailed, it is not very surprising that the Admiralty never asked the House of Commons for money to build a dry-dock there until so late that the dock was hardly finished before the war ended. The results of this delay were disturbing indeed to British admirals. They had to keep in the Mediterranean a fleet equal to meeting the rapidly growing French forces there; hence they could not send a ship home for repair until she was replaced; but replacements were constantly slow in coming and there were too many unsound ships in the fleet on which Britain relied for the command of that great inland sea.

Another, and never cured, weakness of the dockyards was their chronic lack of shipbuilding materials. This is a point on which St Vincent has been much criticised. The old admiral had no patience with war profiteers. The leading timber merchants in Britain were united in demanding prices which St Vincent refused to pay and, as his attempts to find other markets were unsuccessful, he left the dockyards very empty. His successor, Melville, soon got more timber but only at the cost of surrendering to the merchants' price ring. Even then it was impossible to get enough oak and though much fir was bought as a substitute in 1804, the dockyards remained short of timber as long as the war lasted.[12]

The Admiralty, however, is hardly to be blamed for this chronic shortage. Rather, the fault lies fair and square on the shoulders of those five hundred and more mainly civilian gentlemen who formed the House of Commons. In England every peace was followed by an outcry for economy at the expense of the armed forces. With each passing year of peace the wisdom of imposing taxes to buy materials needed for the armed forces seemed more like folly, and in one way the very liberties which the English fought so hard to defend were a handicap to them in war. In an autocratic country, like France, ships' timber could be, and was, conscripted; there when the 'marteau national' had imprinted on a tree the mark of its appropriation to the service of the dockyards, it became from that moment sacred; the owner was indemnified by an arbitrary evaluation and was answerable for its safety.[13]

[11] *Correspondence of William Wilberforce*, ed. by his Sons (London, 1840), II, 197–9.
[12] For the full story, *see* R. G. Albion, *Forests and Seapower* (Cambridge, Mass, 1926).
[13] Brenton, *Naval History of Great Britain*, IV, 3.

Not so in England; there the owner of private woodlands was free to sell his timber on the open market, and the government had to pay the market price.

This was precisely the sort of expenditure which members of parliament resented imposing on their constituents in peacetime, and unfortunately their omissions could not be corrected in wartime. Masts, though important, were the least part of the problem, for masts were of pine and excellent white pine was felled and rafted down the Ottawa and St John rivers from the virgin forests of Canada. The crucial difficulty was getting oak – oak plank six inches thick or more to provide the contemporary equivalent for the armour plate of twentieth century battle ships; and 'knees', those bent pieces, (best found in the semi-subterranean timber at a point where the trunk and a great root parted) which were used to bind the cross-beams of a ship's frame to her sides. All this timber had first to be bought in places whence it could be moved to the dockyards. But moving a whole oak tree, even after the lop and top were cut away, was a ponderous task, and oak woods were valuable in proportion to their nearness to waterways. From time to time new canals made new supplies available,[14] but the demands of many years had stripped England of her best forests long before 1803; and as the war progressed, French conquests on land cut Britain off from more and more markets for foreign timber.

Again, hard woods should be well dried and seasoned before they are used; but the seasoning of oak is a slow business for which there was no time in war. So the result of parliamentary stinginess in peacetime was that in one war after another the British were hustled into building and repairing ships with green timber. For this stuff, which would have been so much more cheaply got in peace time and would simply have improved with keeping, the nation had to pay war-time prices; the inflated prices of war time, of course, added to the debt which grew with every war; the growth of the debt scared civilian M.P.s who knew nothing of the sea and naval war, into demanding more misplaced and misnamed 'economies' as soon as peace came; and so the vicious circle went round and round in the eighteenth century and on into the nineteenth century.

But an inflated debt born of panic prices was only part, and perhaps the least part, of the cost of this penny-wise, pound-foolish policy. The worst part of the cost lay in the danger faced by a country whose defence depended on decrepit ships. For in vessels built of unseasoned timber the great fungus growths of dry rot spread fast, and once that

---

[14] E.g. 'In old times *The Holt* [forest] was estimated to be eighteen miles ... from water carriage ... ; but it is now not half that distance since the *Wey* is made navigable up to the town of *Godalming* in the county of *Surrey*.' Gilbert White, *Natural History of Selborne*, Letter IX to Thomas Pennant.

got into a ship's frame, dry-docking, and at least partial rebuilding, might be the only cure. In the Napoleonic war the Admiralty was so short even of unseasoned timber, that it took to the desperate shift of using knees of iron with copper bolts. But here chemistry was against them for no sound union can be made of iron, oak and copper. So in 1808 one finds Collingwood writing that the *Ocean* 'though scarce out of the hands of the builders' was already unfit for the sea owing to the bad wear of iron knees and copper bolts; 'it is the Ships of old construction, into which the late inventions have not been introduced, that can best be depended on for service', he added.[15]

There could be no question of what ships had first claim on such supplies of timber as Britain did secure. Her command of the sea had to be held by her ships of the line, the only ships fit to meet the most powerful ships of the enemy in battle. British ships of the line duly got everything that the Admiralty could give them and first things were put first. But this very rational policy also meant that other things came a very poor second. So the letters which admirals wrote home teem with repeated demands for more frigates, sloops and brigs. But these demands could never be fully met; and when the French did venture out to sea, British commanders often failed to catch and sink them for sheer want of scouting craft to find them. The long roll of Bonaparte's victories on land made this task of hunting down the enemy at sea even harder, for his career of victory turned one hitherto neutral state after another into Britain's enemies; and as neutral ships disappeared, so did a long valued source of information on the high seas.

Smaller craft, particularly frigates and sloops were also wanted to attack French coastal shipping. Ships of the line drew too much water to chase small craft that sailed close in to the coasts; and for want of the smaller vessels for which they repeatedly asked British admirals were never able to put an end to the French coasting trade. And this raises a point which Corbett never tired of stressing, namely, that the real work of exploiting seapower was done by the small ships which hunted down enemy merchantmen. So the Royal Navy was in a most frustrating position. First things were indeed put first; the line of battle squadrons were able to contain the enemy and assure the safety of the homeland; but the command of the sea they held could never be fully exploited for want of small craft to inflict the maximum punishment on the enemy's shipping.

After the problem of providing ships came the problem of finding crews to man them; and of these too there were never enough. In one way the Navy was indeed better off during the Napoleonic War than during the preceding war against the French Republic. In the earlier

[15] Collingwood to the Admiralty, ADM/1/414, in a letter docketed as received in London on 26 January 1809.

ours, the effect on their maritime strength, on which Great Britain depended, might be fatal'; and 'on the most alarming emergency they might be deprived, to an extent impossible to calculate, of their only means of security'.[18]

That puts the matter in a nutshell. Britain's choice lay between ruling the sea and becoming a French vassal state; and, if she was to rule the sea, she could not, to oblige a neutral, excuse from their long established duty of serving in the fleet those British seamen who took jobs on the neutral's ships. So there could be no yielding on that point.

Yet the British government of the day, the All-the-Talents ministry, was by no means uncompromising, and it suggested two concessions. First, they offered to enact a law imposing specific penalties on any British officer who impressed a genuine American; but Jefferson's envoys rejected this out of hand. The proposed act's preamble read 'Whereas it is not lawful for a belligerent to impress or carry off, from on board a neutral, persons who are not subjects of the belligerent';[19] and the Americans would not accept this statement of the British government's right to take its own subjects from U.S. ships. The other proposal was that American seamen should carry documentary protections 'which on all occasions would be implicitly accepted'.[20] The novelty here was not the protections, which were already widely used, but the rash offer that they would be unfailingly respected; and the British were lucky that this offer was not accepted. So many of their own seamen got false American protections that, even when these documents were not always respected, British warships were often seriously undermanned.

Sailors obtained these protections from three types of U.S. officials, namely, notaries, consuls and customs officers; for the last, besides being entitled to a 25¢ fee for putting an official custom house stamp on a notary's protection, sometimes issued the actual protection (Doc. 24a). Under an act of 28 February 1803, U.S. customs officers had also to refuse a clearance from U.S. ports to U.S. ships whose crews were not fully protected. And at this point the British naval historian must make a serious effort to remember that American notaries, consuls and customs officers, like other men, came in the three standard classes of good, bad and indifferent. It is an effort which may demand much of him, for in the British naval archives he will find precious little evidence that any good ones existed. One must not forget, however, that conscientious men of principle would refuse to provide English sailors with palpably false certificates of nationality. Therefore British seamen who

---

[18] A. T. Mahan, *Seapower in its relations to the War of 1812* (London, 1905) 129, citing 'American State Papers, Foreign Relations, III, 133-5'.
[19] Mahan, op. cit. 132.
[20] Ibid. 129.

wanted such certificates went to others – the shysters, the profiteers and the 'good guys' who would cheerfully wink at perjury that hurt no one but John Bull. They duly found them – men like the New Orleans notary who shut his ears to Robert Clark's Edinburgh accent and his eyes to the way the boy evaded swearing on the Bible (Doc. 24a (i)); or the New York customs officer who never asked the Cornishman, Thomas Brown of Falmouth, to utter any oath, but gave him his protection on the say-so of a person intriguingly described as 'Deborah Ann . . . a woman I then lived with' (Doc. 24a (ii)). Observe, too, the advantage of the captive market which U.S. customs officers enjoyed if they could both demand a 25¢ fee for stamping or issuing a protection, and also deny a harbour clearance to American ships whose crews were not fully protected. For that reason one should perhaps not think too badly of English sailors who got false protections in U.S. ports – it might be their one means of getting home. But those who bought them when already at home, in Britain, are another matter; and that brings us to the man who was perhaps the champion shyster of them all, William Lyman, the U.S. consul in London. Whether he did or did not enrich himself with all the half-crowns said to have been paid by the 'many hundreds' of British seamen who got U.S. protections for 2/6d. in the British capital (Doc. 24c) – and it is hard to see who else would have pocketed them – he cannot escape responsibility for the remarkable affidavit reproduced as Doc. 24b below. This printed form bears Lyman's signature in the bottom right hand corner and the official seal of his consular office in the bottom left hand corner. It purports to contain the name, place of birth, residence and description of each member of the crew of the U.S. ship *Wareham*, as sworn by its Captain, Richard Chadwick, who 'Personally appeared before me and made Oath'. But in fact Captain Chadwick had never made oath to anything before Lyman. Instead, the too obliging consul had sent him away with this form ready-signed and blank to fill out as he pleased and at his leisure. Thanks to Chadwick's negligence it was still blank when taken from him by a British captain who forwarded it to Admiral Lord Gambier; and it is hard to quarrel with Gambier's comment that it was 'a convincing proof of the irregularity of these documents and the extensive deceit which they are calculated to shield' (Doc. 24b). Indeed, the racket in phoney protections was so widespread and so notorious that it is scarcely surprising if, as Professors Morrison and Commager put it, British captains frequently pressed off American ships 'any likely looking lad who had the slightest trace of an Irish or British accent'.[21] Too often the lad's accent was far better evidence of

---

[21] S. E. Morison and H. S. Commager, *The Growth of the American Republic* (New York, 1942), I, 401.

biased as Madison's statement, but in the opposite way. The committee, however, at least examined a considerable number of witnesses; the witnesses were men who had reason to know what they were talking about; and they gave evidence on oath. The committee's findings are also made the more credible by the way the British investigated complaints of pressed men claiming American citizenship; and the mere fact that these cases were liable to be investigated gave British officers reason to be careful about what men they took off American ships.

So more Americans than we sometimes suppose may have entered the Royal Navy as volunteers; indeed many chose to continue even when Britain was at war with their own country.[28] Their presence still gave Madison his excuse for war at a moment when it seemed that he had not long to wait for the defeat of Britain which Americans had been very confidently expecting.[29] What a new enemy at this time meant to the government in London cannot be realised by those who think of the War of 1812 merely in terms of the ravaging of Upper Canadian farms, the burning of Toronto,[30] the loss of half a dozen British frigates or damage done by American privateers intercepting Wellington's supplies off Northern Spain. It meant that line of battle ships had to be diverted to protect British trade. That in turn led to Admiral Pellew's squadron in the Mediterranean being cut to 26 ships when the French had 30 ready or nearly ready for the sea and 12 more approaching completion in those waters;[31] and the Admiral's protest that his force was too weak for the duties it had to perform brought him the stark reply that he could have no more because 'the exigencies of the public service

[28] Pellew, writing from Mahon, 12 December 1812, reported that out of 482 Americans in his fleet to whom the question had been put 33 were still undecided, 109 had volunteered to continue serving and 340 had declined; that is, upwards of 22 per cent in this fleet elected to continue serving in the Royal Navy (ADM/ 1/425).

[29] Thus one of Jefferson's reported reasons for never submitting the Anglo-American treaty of 1806 to the Senate for ratification was the belief that 'the measures pursued and pursuing by Bonaparte are of such a nature, that the Government of England cannot much longer exist'. Cited by Channing, *History of the United States*, IV, 362.

[30] Its name was then York and the date was the spring of 1813.

[31] The latest reports of French ships of the line in the Mediterranean at the end of the war from Pellew are as follows (in ADM/1/427 and 428):

	Ready	Building
Toulon	24	4 (8 May 1814)
Genoa		2 (19 April 1814)
Naples	2	1 (10 August 1813)
Venice	4	5 (2 May 1814)
	30	12

Orders reducing Britain's total in the Mediterranean to 26 reached Pellew by 6 October 1812. (Pellew to Croker, 6 October 1812, ADM/1/424).

are at this time so great'.[32] So, to sum up, the disastrous result of Bonaparte's Russian campaign was a godsend for the British, a bitter blow to the Americans, and equally unforeseen by either of them.[33]

From men there is a natural transition to food; and the job of feeding a fleet containing some 100,000 seamen was a vast one. It is also a job that the Victualling Board is commonly supposed to have done very badly. Authors with a nose for topics of the kind popularly termed 'horrific' regale their readers with stories of water so foul that men preferred to drink urine; of salt meat so tough that snuff boxes could be made out of it; and of ships' biscuit riddled by weevils. Such tales may make good reading, but they do not necessarily give a true picture of life in the Navy. Certainly in the conditions of the time it was almost impossible to keep weevils out of old ships' biscuit; and, with scientific detachment, Sir Joseph Banks lists and names five separate species of them which lived, burrowed, mated and multiplied in the hard tack he ate when sailing round the world with Captain Cook in 1768-70.[34] But sailors in the fleet were not necessarily worse off than those on merchant ships. Indeed, I suspect they were commonly better off, and certainly great care was taken to give them healthy rations.

For in this period the Admiralty banished scurvy and gained a new name for Englishmen in American and Scandinavian slang, by issuing lime juice to the fleet,[35] after the value of fruit juice had been strikingly demonstrated at Minorca and Gibraltar in the two great sieges of the American War of Independence.[36] Everything that regulations could do to ensure that only good provisions were issued to the fleet was done. Thus some casks in every shipment of salt beef and pork received by the Victualling Board had to be opened and sampled; purchases of rice, peas, oatmeal, wine, spirits, meal, flour, raisins, vinegar, sugar, butter, tea and cocoa had to be tasted too; and the regulations went the length of specifying that the rice, peas and oatmeal should actually be boiled.[37]

[32] Admiralty to Pellew, 12 February 1813 (ADM/2/926).

[33] Perhaps at this moment,' said Henry Clay in Congress on 4 December 1812, 'the French Emperor may be dictating peace in Moscow', On 5 December the Baltimore *Weekly Register* still more boldly declared that 'Peace before this time has been dictated by Bonaparte'. Neither could know that Bonaparte was already in retreat and that 5 December was the very day on which he abandoned the remnants of his army on the banks of the Beresina to hurry back to Paris.

[34] Banks had, however, already been at sea for twelve months before he wrote this note. *Journal of the Rt Hon. Sir Joseph Banks*, ed. by Sir Joseph D. Hooker (London, 1896), 181.

[35] 'Lime-juicer' to Scandinavians, so a Danish friend assures me; and simply 'Limey' to Americans.

[36] Minorca, with no supplies of orange juice, was hit hard by scurvy and surrendered when only some 600 men of the garrison were still able to march out and lay down their arms. Gibraltar, with good supplies of orange juice, defied both scurvy and the enemy to the end of the war.

[37] *Eleventh Report on the Civil Affairs of the Navy*, 66-7.

elements swept into the fleet by the press, or the criminals imported from the jails. What was resented was the cudgelling and canings by lower ranks of officers . . .'.[44] But that abuse of authority had been one of the grievances of the mutineers of 1797; and, says Hannay, 'when we come . . . to the year 1800, we begin to meet cases in which warrant officers were brought to Court Martial for disobeying the standing order of the ship, which forbade them to strike the men'.[45]

Such was the nature of Britain's first line of defence, the Royal Navy, through these years of danger. Its margin of superiority was never very great after Spain declared war in 1804. 1807, as has been noted, was a critical year when only the strong-arm action against the Danes won safety. It was a crowning mercy that the Spanish revolt against Bonaparte in 1808 followed so soon after Russia's declaration of war against England in 1807. It was also a piece of good fortune that Bonaparte left Turkey to the Russians, instead of helping them partition her and securing thereby Turkish forests and harbours to build ships, Balkan seamen to man them and the closed waters of the Black Sea as a training area for his fleets. Even so the French navy was dangerously close to equality with the Royal Navy by the war's end. Yet, as Winston Churchill has said, 'All great struggles of history have been won by superior will-power wresting victory in the teeth of odds or upon the narrowest of margins'. In this great struggle the will-power of Britons ashore and afloat was equal to the test.

[44] *Naval Courts Martial* (Cambridge, 1914), 67.
[45] Ibid., 65.

4

The Boulogne Flotilla[1]

BONAPARTE'S great Boulogne flotilla was both his most famous threat to Britain and one of his boldest conceptions. He aimed at nothing less than invading and conquering England with no more than a local and temporary command of the sea. This was his purpose for most of the time between 1803 until the date in August 1805, when he realised that war with Austria (and Russia) was inevitable.[2] He did not revive it after the treaty of Tilsit in July 1807, by ensuring peace on the continent, had set him free for new designs against Britain; by that date the coasts of Kent and Sussex were too well fortified for this particular plan to be practical any more. For Britain the critical period of the threat from the flotilla was July and August 1805, in the summer after Spain had declared war on her, and when, as Holland Rose soundly observed long ago, 'the chances of Villeneuve appearing off Boulogne' with up to 51 French and Spanish ships of the line, 'were fairly good';[3] and except on one condition (discussed below) one cannot believe that such an opportunity would be missed by the man who in 1815 dared to invade France itself from Elba, with just 1050 men, and by his boldness

[1] The materials for this chapter are drawn partly from the great mass of documents assembled by Edouard Desbrière in his *Projets et Tentatives de Débarquement aux Isles Britanniques*, supplemented by J. Holland Rose whose important essay 'Did Napoleon intend to invade England?' in his *Pitt and Napoleon; Essays and Letters* amounts to an extended review of Desbrière. Rose's reasons for differing at times from Desbrière are argued with the authority to be expected of Bonaparte's biographer. I have also made some use of Wheeler and Broadley's *Napoleon and the Invasion; the Story of the Great Terror*, but have done so without seeing the reason for the second half of their title. The cartoons from Mr Broadley's collection with which the work is lavishly illustrated reveal abundant hatred and contempt for Bonaparte, but precious little fear; in doing so they give an indication of the temper of England at the time which perhaps makes them the most valuable part of the book. See also, of course, the *Correspondance de Napoleon I*er.

[2] For how he abandoned the scheme from September 1804 (after Admiral Latouche-Tréville's death) until February 1805 when he could count on active help from the Spaniards), see Holland Rose, *Pitt and Napoleon*, 134–5, 145.

[3] Ibid., 145.

So there were the requirements which Bonaparte had to meet. His plan covered all of them. We may consider first the point on which it failed, providing naval protection for his army's crossing; and the weakness of this part of his plan was a personal one – his reliance on that broken reed, Admiral Villeneuve.[6]

We cannot, and need not, retell here the whole story of the naval campaign of 1805. The essential facts which bear on the invasion are that Villeneuve had got away from Toulon with 11 line of battle ships on 30 March, reached Cadiz on 8 April where he picked up one more French and 6 Spanish ships under the Spanish admiral Gravina, and on 13 May arrived at Martinique where he was joined by Admiral Magon with another two French line of battle ships on 4 June. Here he also learned that Nelson had reached the West Indies in pursuit of him. This news meant that he had achieved his first purpose, that of decoying an important British squadron far away from Europe, where the outcome of the war would be decided. Back then toward Europe, with a good head start, Villeneuve sailed on 7 June; and now the details begin to be interesting.

The first detail to note is that, on '20 June', Captain George Bettesworth, of the *Curieux* brig, as he sailed home with Nelson's despatches, caught sight of Villeneuve's fleet, and 'counted 19 sail of the line in lat. 33.12, long. 53 W, steering N. by E., but afterwards N. by W'.[7] On the morning of 9 July Bettesworth was in Lord Barham's office at the Admiralty, reporting to the First Lord the news of Villeneuve's return which nobody else in Europe had had the means of learning;

---

to do that Bonaparte too commonly took liberties with the truth. He was in any case very inconsistent in stating the time he would need for the crossing, as A. Fournier noticed (*Napoleon I: a Biography* (London, 1911), I, 341 n). The man whose estimate I accept on the time the flotilla needed to get to sea is the British admiral, Lord Keith, and he reckoned 6 tides, or 3 days, necessary (Sir John Laughton, ed., *Letters and Papers of Charles, Lord Barham*, III, 181); moreover, Bonaparte himself supports Keith on at least three occasions – twice to Villeneuve (*Corresp.* Nos. 8700, 9022) and once to Ganteaume (*Corresp.* No. 8998). Of the other figures listed in Fournier's note, one, of 12 hours, may be accepted as a correct statement of the time required for an actual Channel crossing by boats once they had already got out of harbour; another, of 6 hours, would seem to be the mere wishful thinking of a man whose great fault was his impatience; a third, of 14 days, agrees with the estimates of Decrès and Ganteaume and is no doubt the time needed to transport all the paraphernalia which caution might dictate; but Bonaparte was too bold a gambler to be bound by the dictates of caution.

[6] One hates to criticise so unfortunate a creature as Villeneuve; it is too like kicking a man who is down; but the poor devil does seem to have been one of nature's born losers.

[7] *The Times*, 10 July 1805; but the newspaper made the error of transposing the figures. It was in fact on 19 June that Villeneuve was sighted and he had 20 ships.

and promptly Barham took steps to meet the situation. But then came what, to use the kindest possible language, can only be described as a deplorable piece of stupidity. The *Times* newspaper somehow learnt Bettesworth's story and instead of intelligently keeping silent, published it, in the very words just quoted, for all the world to read on Wednesday, 10 July. Of course it was known in Paris within the week. So Bonaparte, informed of his own fleet's progress by his enemy's journalists, was able to draft his definitive orders in a letter to Villeneuve, dated 16 July.[8]

It is a most interesting document. It required Villeneuve to pick up the French and Spanish squadrons sheltering in Ferrol; he was then to proceed to the Straits of Dover; he was permitted to increase his fleet by taking over the French forces in either or both of Rochefort or Brest; his course to the Straits was not to be up the Channel, but round Ireland and Scotland and thence to the Texel, where he was to pick up the Dutch fleet as his final reinforcement. Then came the loophole clause, which enabled Villeneuve to wreck his master's concept – permission to anchor in Cadiz 'if owing to engagements you have fought, or considerable gaps in your fleet or other accidents we have not foreseen, your situation should be considerably modified'. (Doc. 14b).

The fact that Bonaparte's naval plan broke, through the weakness of the human instrument who was to carry it out, does not mean that the plan itself was bad. For observe, first, the route – round Ireland and Scotland. That took note of the standing British practice, duly followed on this occasion, for their squadrons to rendezvous in a crisis at the western end of the Channel; and it enabled Villeneuve, if he chose, to sidestep this move on the part of his opponents. Second, Villeneuve was not required to pick up more than one of France's western squadrons in Brest or Rochefort. If either remained, the British would have to divert some ships to watch it. Corbett indeed argued that, had Villeneuve attempted to pick up Ganteaume's fleet in Brest, he could not have sidestepped the British; instead the result of Trafalgar would have been anticipated by some weeks, for he was sure that Cornwallis would have beaten Villeneuve outside Brest, as Nelson later beat him outside Cadiz, in a battle which would have been finished before Ganteaume could get to sea.[9] Perhaps; but Cornwallis was not a Nelson – no one was; also, as Corbett acknowledged, Villeneuve would have had the stronger fleet;[10] and there is besides a grim question which Corbett did not discuss – assuming Cornwallis did defeat Villeneuve's combined Franco-Spanish squadron, would he, immediately after taking the punishment that even the victor must take in a hard fought fight, have

---

[8] *Corresp.* No. 8985.
[9] *The Campaign of Trafalgar* (London, 1910) 240.
[10] Ibid., 253, n.l.

been in any state to stop Ganteaume's fresh and undamaged fleet of 21 ships of the line?

But Villeneuve did not have to pick up Ganteaume from Brest. Instead, he was permitted, and actually tried, to join Allemand who was already at sea with 5 line of battle ships. Villeneuve could then have sailed round Scotland with the 29 ships with which he did in fact set out from Ferrol on 13 August, plus Allemand's five; at the Texel he would have found another ten Dutch ships ready to join him; and he would then have entered the Channel with over 40 ships to oppose to Admiral Keith's eleven. In this crisis the British would, of course, have reinforced Keith by summoning aid from their forces at the western end of the Channel; but how long would that take? The news would first have to reach the Admiralty in London; then an order would have to be sent to the fleet. The telegraph could pass the order to Plymouth in, probably, well under an hour. But then a dispatch boat would have to carry the order out to the fleet at sea; the ships ordered east would have to sail the full length of the Channel; and the British would be lucky if they regained control of the Straits in less than the three days which Bonaparte needed to get his flotilla to sea and deposit between 150,000 and 170,000 men in England in relays. Then the French fleet, with its mission accomplished, would have found in Antwerp a safe haven in which to shelter from the reinforced British.

But all hope of Bonaparte's achieving any such success as this evaporated on 15 August, when Villeneuve picked up from a Danish merchantman a cock-and-bull story, carefully planted by a British officer, of an English fleet of 25 ships of the line advancing upon him.[11] That night, without checking this story, Villeneuve turned south to run to Cadiz, as Bonaparte's order of 16 July instructed him to do 'if owing to engagements you have fought ... or other accidents we have not foreseen, your situation should be considerably modified'; and that was that.

Before leaving the naval side of Bonaparte's planning on this occasion it is but fair to note how little his order of 16 July to Villeneuve supports the criticisms commonly made of him by British authors. They accuse him of giving his admirals impossibly rigid orders. But his order to Villeneuve of 16 July 1805 failed for want of rigidity; it left too many options to a weak man's discretion.

Bonaparte's plans for the crossing itself were also shrewdly laid. His 'real point of landing', as he told George Bingham years later, 'would have been somewhere between Deal and Margate', i.e. in or near Pegwell Bay.[12] This choice assured him of his other three requirements –

[11] Ibid.
[12] Bingham had sailed to St Helena with Bonaparte. His notes on his conversations with him are in 'More Light on St Helena', *Cornhill Magazine* (1901) 28–9.

a short voyage; supplies for his army, which should be abundant in East Kent at harvest time; and, best prize of all, not one, but three harbours, Ramsgate, Broadstairs and Margate. None of these ports could be very readily assaulted from the sea, but neither could they be defended on the landside, and therefore, as the Duke of York warned the British government, they would fall into 'the enemy's power whenever he possessed that district of the country'. [13] So securing these places would involve little more than a matter of marching once the French were ashore in force; and the march would be short. Next, as Bonaparte told Berthier, 'I shall have to besiege Chatham and Dover and perhaps Portsmouth'.[14] The inclusion of Portsmouth is interesting; it reveals his very natural intention to destroy Britain's sea power by striking at her naval bases, if necessary, but he certainly hoped that this siege would be unnecessary. For his grand objective was London; and 'had I arrived there', he said to Bingham, 'I should have offered very moderate terms of peace, taking care, however, so far to cripple you that you could have done us no further mischief'.[15]

This was one of the plans which the Duke of York had been preparing to meet since the war began. How far it could have succeeded in 1805 depends on a number of factors. The French had the advantage of surprise that should always belong to the attacker. They could choose where to land, while the British had no means of knowing which of the possible alternatives they would pick. So the Duke of York, though well aware of the danger of dispersing his forces, had no choice but be ready to meet attacks coming from a variety of landing places. However poorly the different types of craft in the flotilla sailed, the actual crossing should have been no problem in good weather and while the French controlled the sea, although considerable confusion might occur in both the voyage and the landing. In the face of the English coast defence batteries the landing – or landings if more than one beach were assaulted – might well have been costly for the first flight of troops to go ashore. But, with the Martello towers unfinished, those batteries should still have been overrun and the landing should have succeeded. How heavy a toll of the invaders would be taken by Britain's gunboats would depend on how much close support Villeneuve's heavy ships could give the landing craft as they approached the shore.

Greater difficulties for the French were likely to begin after the landing. The objective, as noted, was London where Bonaparte hoped to be able to dictate peace. The approaches to London from East Kent were flanked by Dover and blocked by the Lines of Chatham. Dover would have to be taken, or masked, and the Lines stormed, or

[13] York to Lord Hobart, 25 August 1803. WO/30/76.
[14] *Correspondance de Napoleon Ier*, No. 8957.
[15] Bingham, op. cit.

outflanked by way of Maidstone, before the capital could be attacked.
A flank march round Chatham by Maidstone, however, would give the
British opportunities for counter-attack which the Duke of York would
have welcomed; and mere field artillery (with no bigger gun than the
12-pounder) could hardly master the defences of Chatham. That was a
job for a regular siege train of 24-pounders. We have seen that Bonaparte would land these guns and their ammunition at Margate, Broadstairs and Ramsgate, and that to gain these ports would be merely a
matter of marching once he was ashore. Still, the landing and the march
would both take time, the unloading of the guns and ammunition
more time, and no boats could come in until the ports had been seized.
Next, his advance to Chatham, some forty miles away, would again
take time, and could hardly begin until teams for the guns and ammunition waggons had somehow been found. Once arrived in front of the
Lines the French would have to devote still more time to the indispensable preliminaries of any siege – reconnaissance, bringing up their
siege equipment, sapping and digging in their batteries – before they
could start the serious jobs of mastering the powerful artillery in the
Lines and breaching its defences. Yet that artillery had to be silenced,
practicable breaches made, saps dug up to them and counter-scarps
blown in before the assaulting columns of infantry swept forward
through the sap to charge up the breaches and overwhelm the last
defenders of the Lines.[16]

How long all these operations would take is a question to which it
would be most unwise to attempt a precise answer. But it is hard to
believe that an enemy who invaded Kent could accomplish them all in
time to arrive before London within the four days of landing that
Bonaparte expected;[17] and even if he did cover the distance in that time,
he would no longer find London a defenceless city. For London, north
and south of the river, 'field fortifications', of entrenchments and

[16] A 'sap', in sieges, was a trench, or sunken road, wide enough to permit
two waggons to pass, by which ammunition could be safely brought up to the
attackers' guns and infantry advance to the assault when a practicable breach
was made. The 'counterscarp' was the outer side of the moat, or ditch, encircling
a fort; it should be 'revetted', that is, supported by a solid wall of masonry,
which had to be blown in with a petard before the assailants could enter the
moat from a sap as they advanced to storm the breach. I should note here that the
French attack on Chatham would hardly be a regular siege. The English works
there consisted of a fortified bridge-head designed both to defend Chatham docks
and to hold a crossing of the River Medway, on whose right bank they stood.
The French could therefore attack one front only, and their task would be the
harder, because the English would be able to reinforce and resupply Chatham
from the west. But the methods used to attack the defences covering the east
bank of the Medway would have to be those used in the attack on any fortified
place.

[17] O'Meara, A Voice from St Helena, I, 349.

palisades, had been planned in detail, but not constructed. Three days was the time reckoned necessary for their construction on the south side;[18a] and even after passing Chatham, the enemy could not start attacking them until he had overcome the advanced works prepared on Shooter's Hill. Meanwhile Dover would be undergoing a separate siege, and it was certainly much the handiest supply port for the enemy, if only he could seize it. It was important to the British, too, as a harbour through which the Duke of York intended to throw reinforcements into Kent to act against the rear of an enemy threatening Chatham or London. It had its own garrison, with provisions for 40 days, and by 1805 it was also well fortified. So the French could hardly have taken it before they lost the command of the sea.

Such were the tasks facing a French force that succeeded in landing; now for 'the other side of the hill'.

News of the arrival of Villeneuve and Ganteaume in the Channel would reach London as fast as the telegraph could carry it; and probably even before the French landed a number of moves would be started. First among them we may note that the Court and the treasure from the Bank of England were to be moved to Worcester; the artillery and stores of ammunition at Woolwich, and the other arsenals on the Thames, were to be shipped to the Midlands by canal.

These plans make two things clear. One is that the British did not count on being able to hold either their capital or their riverside arsenals. There they were wise. The arsenals had no fortifications to protect them, once the defences of Chatham and Shooter's Hill had fallen. As for London, the earthen entrenchments planned for her defence would certainly buy time through compelling the enemy to mount a formal attack; and time was most valuable. But mere earthworks could hardly be expected to resist long under the bombardment of properly handled siege guns,[18b] and so London might well fall. The second point that appears from these plans, however, is that the English did not propose to let the loss of their capital end their resistance. With their arms and treasure safe they would have the means to continue the struggle; and the French would be in for a nasty disillusionment when they found that the capture of London marked only the beginning, not the end, of their attempted conquest of Britain.

The next plan the English had ready was to remove all horses and

[18a] In July 1804, the Duke of York wrote to Pitt that the defences on the south side of London 'possibly might be accomplished by 500 men and 300 horses in three days' (cited by Holland Rose, *Dumouriez and the Defence of England*, 236). Note the equation between days and men; and the number of men and horses listed is small for a city of London's size.

[18b] Because, of course, of the relative weakness of mere earthen entrenchments as compared with the solid masonry of a regular fortress; on which, see Chapter V below.

draught cattle from areas likely to fall into the hands of an invader. This would perhaps not have been too easy a job. It might have well been hard to round up all the animals; and herds of loose horses being driven away from the coasts would for a while have cluttered roads also needed by the troops. Yet the British had planned it carefully,[19] and it would have been an important measure; for, the French were prepared to carry no more than 9,632 horses in their flotilla (Doc. 14e). This petty number is scarcely a fifth of what an army of some 150,000, or more, men would need; and it has an obvious bearing on the ability of the French to besiege Dover, Chatham, Shooter's Hill and London.

For sieges required an enormous amount of material. First, there were picks, shovels, gabions and fascines[20] for use in excavating the saps and making the gun emplacements. Every French engineer battalion was normally equipped with '1,700 pickaxes, 170 miners' picks, 1,700 shovels, 1,700 long handled shovels, total 5,270 intrenching tools; 680 felling axes, 1,020 bill hooks, total 1,700 cutting tools; 1,802 artificers' tools; 253 miners' tools; and 8,318 kil. weight of machinery and stores'. Thirty-five waggons and 230 horses were needed to move all this equipment,[21] with which to dig the saps and gun-pits, fell and split trees to make plank for gun platforms and cut brush for fascines and gabions.

Then, when the gun emplacements were made, and saps dug from points safe from the defenders' artillery provided the sunken roads along which ammunition waggons would come up to the guns, there was the business of supplying the ammunition itself. A clue to the amount of ammunition that might be wanted for a siege is provided by the amount which Wellington actually used in capturing Badajoz. This totalled 2,523 whole barrels of powder, each weighing 90 lb., 18,832 rounds of 24-pounder shot and 13,029 rounds of 18-pounder shot.[22] And how, one asks, were the French to move such a tonnage of ammunition and stores up from the ports of East Kent to Chatham, Dover, Shooter's Hill and London if the country had been swept clear of horses and draught cattle? Even assuming that they did bring 9,632 horses with them, they would not get all these ashore until the sixth tide

[19] On this matter of 'driving the Country', see the End Note to Chapter II; and the map opposite p. 338 of Rose's *Dumouriez and the Defence of England* which shows the organisation prepared for carrying it out in the county of Dorset in 1801.

[20] 'Gabions' were baskets able to hold enough earth to stop a musket ball and big enough to cover a man while he was digging in a sap. 'Fascines' were bundles of brushwood used for the same purpose.

[21] Major General Sir John Thomas Jones, Bart., *Journal of the Sieges carried on by the Army under the Duke of Wellington in Spain between the Years 1811 and 1814*, 3rd. ed. (London, 1846), II, 386.

[22] Ibid., I, 209–10.

had released the last portion of their flotilla from Boulogne and its neighbouring ports; and no arm was more essential to a general campaigning in a hostile country than the cavalry on which he must rely for reconnoitering his enemy. So there was a limit to the number of teams the French could improvise by putting cavalry chargers between the shafts of ammunition waggons; and they would need teams for their field artillery as well as for their siege train. One must, then, be careful not to underrate the length of time that the Lines of Chatham would hold the French up. Every day gained there was an asset to the British, as reinforcements of Regulars, Militia and the now well-trained Volunteers converged on the capital.

The reason why time was so important was that in the earlier phases of the invasion the French would enjoy certain very clear advantages. We have already noticed the advantage of surprise which belongs to the attacker; the French were right in supposing that they would start with a big superiority in numbers; and in my opinion a good deal too much has been made of the fact that Bonaparte would have needed six tides to get his whole force away from France. That he accepted this delay seems clear from his repeated demands for 'the mastery of the Straits for three days only'; and even in the age of sail troops could be moved faster by sea than they could march by land. Hence the build-up of French troops should have handsomely out paced the arrival of British reinforcements.

The figures would be somewhat as follows.[23] In 1803 the Duke had alloted Kent 2,000 cavalry and 18,000 regular infantry and Militia, not counting the garrison of Dover. To these in 1804 the Southern District (containing Kent and Sussex) could add 1,521 Yeomanry and 10,257 Volunteers (Doc. 27), and if General Sir David Dundas, the district commander, alloted half of them to Kent, the county's garrison would total 2,760 horse and 23,128 foot. In addition the Duke had planned a general reserve of 20,000 regular troops for the Southern District and in 1804 prepared to move a total of 15,000 Volunteers, drawn from London and either the Eastern or Southern District, to whichever district was invaded.[24] But he could not take more troops from Sussex, which was equally in danger from Boulogne; nor could he draw more from the Eastern District which had to be ready for invasion from the

[23] Note that I say 'somewhat'. I am dealing with 1805 but the British figures I have found come from 1803 and 1804. The various recruiting measures adopted in 1803–5 should have enabled the Regulars in Kent to receive some reinforcement. But additional troops would be wanted elsewhere too, and an expeditionary force of 6,000 had been sent to the Mediterranean; hence I believe the figures I give should be near enough for the rough balance I strike here, in which, it will be noted, I also attempt no estimate of the casualties likely to be inflicted on the French in the landing.

[24] Duke of York to the Earl of Harrington, 29 March 1804 (WO/30/76).

ports of Holland as long as the French commanded the sea.[25] Reinforcements from more distant parts of Britain would take longer to arrive. So, even if it took six tides for all the 167,000 French troops to get to sea, we have this result; the first lift would carry to the chosen Kentish beach nearly 28,000 men, a total greater than the whole force in the county. Twelve hours later the next tide should bring another 28,000 to give the French a 2-1 superiority. By the end of the third day all 167,000 French troops should have sailed. But the British would have marched well if all the 35,000 first reinforcements had arrived in the county by then; and, had they done so, the invaders would still outnumber the defenders by approximately 167,000 to 60,000, or nearly three to one. These figures underline the importance of whatever toll the English coast defence batteries might take of the first flight of the invaders before their guns were overrun; also of the amount of confusion into which the squadrons of the French flotilla fell during the voyage and the landing, of delays in getting the siege train ashore and in finding horses, and of the resistance, first, of the Lines of Chatham and then of Shooter's Hill and London. For by 1805 much had been done to increase the British artillery and most of the 300,000 and more Yeomanry and Volunteers had been pronounced fit to serve with the Regulars. So the ultimate superiority of force should lie with the defenders.

In assessing the prospects of the campaign too much should not be made of the difference in ability between Bonaparte and the Duke of York. Bonaparte was indeed a supreme strategist. But the confines of East Kent offered him limited room to manœuvre; and he by no means always shone as a tactician. Indeed, on occasion, as at Eylau, Borodino and Waterloo, one might call his tactics clumsy; and he had sheer luck, rather than his own skill, to thank for the victory of Marengo. On the other hand Lieutenant Colonel Burne's professional study of his leadership in Belgium and Holland stamps the Duke of York as decidedly abler than the Beaulieus, Macks, Weyrothers and Hohenlohes who presented Bonaparte with his more resounding triumphs. The Duke had also the advantage of having made an intensive study of the ground on which he expected to fight. Superficially, his plan to reinforce East Kent through Dover may look like a dangerous division of his forces against an opponent who knew supremely well how to use the advantage of concentration. But the value of this move would depend upon its timing; and it would have an excellent chance of disrupting a French siege of Chatham if it could be launched while the Lines still

[25] The seriousness of this threat of course depends on the number of troops and vessels the French had in those ports; but it would not be easy for the British to secure up-to-date and reliable information on either point once their blockading squadrons were driven off by a superior French fleet.

held. Even its defeat should not have been fatal to the force attempting it since they had the fortress of Dover on which to fall back. It is most improbable that Bonaparte was unaware of the potential threat to his rear; and this was no doubt one of his reasons for planning to besiege both Dover and Chatham. Hence the Duke's plans for defending England had the merit of creating a situation in which Bonaparte himself would have to divide his forces. As for the conduct of the troops it seems unlikely that the fighting between Frenchmen, who were used to victory, and Englishmen, who were not accustomed to submitting to invasion, would have been anything but desperately stubborn; and every day's delay in achieving his expected victory would have made the invader's situation more serious.

Time meant more to the defenders than simply moving additional troops against the enemy. It meant regaining the command of the sea, to cut the invaders off from France and set the stage for a possible disaster to the enemy akin to Hitler's loss of over 200,000 troops in Tunisia in 1943. For no really significant number of troops could be smuggled either way across the water once a blockade over the French Channel ports was re-established.[26] Supplies would be still harder get past the blockade; and the ability of the French to fight on would depend on the amount of ammunition they got over before the British regained the command of the sea.[27] Really, then, the prospects of a French success seem very largely to boil down to a matter of will-power; would the British fold up if the capital fell or would they not? It was certainly not in George III's character to do so; and Pitt had another reason for continuing the struggle than obstinacy or his expectation of the fleet's return.

That reason leads to the important condition, mentioned above, which might have prevented Bonaparte from launching his invasion even if Villeneuve had appeared off Boulogne with upwards of 50 line of battle ships. By August Pitt's diplomacy was bearing fruit and the Third Coalition of Britain, Russia, Austria and Naples was already forming against France. In the event this was to cause Bonaparte to cancel his invasion plans for 1805 (not that he then dropped his flotilla plans for ever; on 28 August he is found saying that he expects to return to the coast after a few battles in Germany).[28] It also recalls another factor which has a direct bearing on the invasion of England,

[26] At Elba Count Bertand told Major Vivian that even after the British regained control of the sea the French 'could have kept possession of some small ports and could have smuggled men over' ('An Interview with Napoleon', Rose, *Pitt and Napoleon*, 175). True; some men might have got over, but not enough to make a difference.

[27] Captured British ammunition, being of different calibre, could not be used in French weapons.

[28] *Correspondance de Napoléon Ier* No. 9150.

because it imposed an obvious limit on the number of troops which Bonaparte could allot to the Channel crossing. It is that a nation engaged in war against one foe must be ready to guard itself against other potential enemies. Among the continental powers Bonaparte despised Russia whom he knew to be negotiating with England but who was too remote to hurt him. He did not fear Frederick William III of Prussia, a diffident and vacillating man who could always be cheaply appeased with George III's electorate of Hanover. He was more concerned about Spain. To keep an eye on her he established at Bayonne a camp for a corps of observation under Augereau, in 1803, even though Spain was an ally who financed his war against Britain before actually becoming a belligerent. The power he had most cause to fear was Austria, who was both nearer than Russia and stronger than either Prussia or Spain.

Now it is true, as has often been pointed out, that early in the summer of 1805 Bonaparte took certain steps which in fact provoked Austria to join the Third Coalition. One was crowning himself King of Italy on 28 May and another annexing Genoa on 4 June. It has been suggested that he did both with the deliberate intention of causing a continental war which would enable him to abandon the dangerous business of invasion without loss of face. But this suggestion hardly survives close examination. It gives Bonaparte so much more credit than he deserves for understanding and considering other people's feelings. Even so he was careful to explain the coronation to the Austrian emperor, Francis II, in terms that are, for him, almost apologetic; and he annexed Genoa expressly to strengthen his hands against England. It had many seamen; its dockyards were to add a number of 74-gun ships of the line to his Toulon fleet; and he did not expect its annexation to lead to war. In fact, nearly two months were to pass before he began to realise how much his annexation of Genoa had offended Austria. As late as 27 July, he was writing to his stepson and Viceroy in Italy, Eugene Beauharnais, to reassure him that he need have no fear of Austria. Two days later, on 29 July, he received more serious news, and instructed Talleyrand to take steps to calm the Austrians. At last, on 3 August, he was convinced that they were arming. Again, he directed Talleyrand to reassure them; but from that point on he realised that he must be ready to fight them. As late as 22 August, however, Bonaparte was still writing Admiral Decrès, his Minister of Marine, and his fleet commanders, Ganteaume and Villeneuve, pressing for action. 'Sail', he urged Villeneuve, 'lose not a moment; enter the Channel with my assembled squadrons. England is ours. We are all ready, everything is embarked. Show yourself for twenty-four hours and all is over'.[29]

[29] *Correspondance de Napoléon Ier* No. 9115. On those '24 hours' see note 5, above p. 79.

The very next day, however, he received news which made him realise that the game was up. The little Kingdom of Naples demanded that France withdraw her Army of Occupation from its territories; and Bonaparte learnt of the arrival in Malta of a British force of 6,000 men which had left England as long ago as 19 April and whose destination had been a mystery to him ever since. Both portended war in Italy. But 6,000 British and the whole of the petty Neapolitan army, even with the support of the 10,000 Russians in Corfu (then held by the Tsar), could not make much of a dent on French power in that country. War in Italy must mean war with Austria. Promptly then, and in quick succession, Bonaparte first despatched a virtual ultimatum to Austria on 24 August requiring her to keep no more than eight battalions in her Venetian province and one in Tyrol; and then on 25 August he sent Murat into Germany to reconnoitre the roads leading to the upper Danube. From that moment on the threat of the Boulogne flotilla was a thing of the past; first, it was to be put in cold storage for the duration of the war in Europe; and, second, before that war was finished, it was made obsolete by the completion of the new fortifications on the south coast of England.

So ended Bonaparte's hopes of a swift conquest of England with the Boulogne flotilla. It is perhaps a pity that he was unable to attempt it – a pity because his chances of victory, once he had landed, would seem far less promising than he supposed; and certainly the absence of over 150,000 French troops across the water, locked in battle with the English on the outskirts of London, would have given the continental powers such a chance to overthrow the supremacy of France as had not come their way since Bonaparte returned from Egypt in 1799 and would not come again until after the misery and tragedies of 1812.

Even if it was a failure, the Boulogne invasion scheme is still worth examining as one of the more remarkable achievements of the great Corsican's genius. We today may be better equipped to evaluate it than were men of Rose's and Corbett's generation. For some of the older readers of this book are likely to have taken part in landing operations. Others may know that in the Hitler war Britain's Combined Operations Command was set up in 1940; that early experience was gained in Commando raids on France and Norway and large scale rehearsals followed, in North Africa, the Pacific and Italy. But still four years passed before British, Canadian and American armies were ready to invade a German-held France from England at a time when the main enemy forces were engaged against the Russians from the Baltic to the Black Sea, when yet more were tied down in Italy and when the Allies possessed overwhelming seapower. In two years Bonaparte prepared for an invasion in the reverse direction, without an assured command of the sea and when the main British armies had no other enemy to fight. Our verdict that the organisation of the threat from Boulogne was a supreme achievement of Bonaparte's genius may, then, surely stand, even when it is admitted that he made a number of mistakes; and also when we admit that some of his mistakes were big ones, as the mistakes of great men are apt to be. For he started with next to nothing – a fleet of only 13 ships of the line ready for the sea, a negligible flotilla and no harbours capable of sheltering an adequate one.

We have already seen something of what Bonaparte managed to do for the French navy. By 1805 he had 11 line of battle ships ready for the sea at Toulon which, with one more at Cadiz, made 12 in the Mediterranean. From the fleet he had sent to the West Indies during the peace of Amiens he managed to get Gourdon's squadron of 5 back past the British and safely into Ferrol. Another 5 were made ready at Rochefort and also Ganteaume's 21 at Brest; and beside these he had the Dutch fleet of ten at the Texel. So in two years he raised France's strength at sea from a mere 13 ships to about 50; and once Spain had entered the war as his ally, he was near to equality in mere numbers. The job, of course, meant finding materials to repair his vessels, shipwrights to work on them and crews to man them; this all had to be done at a time when he had also to find ways and means to build and man the flotilla; and he achieved both tasks simultaneously – a fact of significance for anyone who wishes to assess the potential seapower of Napoleonic France.

In preparing the flotilla Bonaparte had two problems. The first was to produce the boats, a job for French-controlled shipyards all the way from Holland down to ports on the Bay of Biscay. The other was somehow to get his newly constructed invasion craft away from the ports where they were built and up the Channel to Boulogne and its neighbouring harbours, a task involving a voyage round the peninsula of Brittany for many of them. In the face of Britain's cruisers the job of assembling them was to prove both dangerous and slow.

Bonaparte's plans for the flotilla harked back to those he had concerted with Admiral Latouche-Treville in 1801. Of the invasion craft then built disappointingly few survived, but at least decisions had been made about the types of vessels to be used. First, there were *Prames*, three-masted vessels, 110 feet long, 25 feet wide and drawing 8 feet of water. Next were *Chaloupes cannonieres*, or gun-brigs, 76 to 80 feet long, 17 wide, with two masts, and drawing 5 to 6 feet of water. Then came *Bateaux cannoniers*, or gun-boats, of three different models, measuring some 60 feet long, 14 wide and drawing $4\frac{1}{2}$ feet; and *Péniches*, or pinnaces, 60 feet in length, 10 in width and drawing $3\frac{1}{2}$ feet of water. These pinnaces were undecked open boats. In addition to their crews, the *Prames* were intended to carry 120 soldiers, the *Chaloupes cannonières* 130, the gun-boats 100 and the pinnaces 60 soldiers.[30] Besides these there were also specially fitted horse transports, converted fishing boats, packet boats and other assorted craft.

The qualities of any boat depend on the purposes for which it is designed. Since the purpose of Bonaparte's flotilla was to enable men to land on enemy beaches, before a harbour was captured, he needed above all else craft which could be run well inshore and grounded in shallow water. As landing craft, the best were the smallest, the pinnaces and the gun-boats whose shallow draft would enable the soldiers they carried to leap overboard into no more than $3\frac{1}{2}$ feet and $4\frac{1}{2}$ feet of water respectively before advancing up the beach. The gun-brigs and *prames* drew an amount of water which would seem to require them both, and certainly the *prames*, to be beached on a falling tide; and there they would have to wait until the water had receded enough to enable the men to go over the side and up the shore. But Bonaparte did not produce many *prames*, and this seems wise. The situation of men cooped up in *prames* stranded off shore, and waiting for the tide to fall, while British coast defence batteries played on them, would not be enviable. They could only hope that their fellows in the pinnaces and gun-boats would be swiftly able to charge up the beach and capture the batteries; but, as we shall see, this was likely to pose some problems too.

Then there is that bugbear of all combined operations, the problem of 'runnels', or low and often long strips of a beach where the water deepens at places closer to the shore than the spot where the landing craft run aground; and there, of course, one is liable to find oneself suddenly out of one's depth after disembarking in much shallower water. Runnels were not too serious an obstacle in 1942–4 when every man went ashore in a Mae West life jacket and his ammunition consisted of copper bullets that should be waterproof. But the cartridges of 1803 were mere paper envelopes containing a musket ball and a charge of powder.[31] Once a soldier had soaked these by plunging into deep water, he would be disarmed of everything but his bayonet until

[30] These details are taken from Desbrière, *Projets et Tentatives*, III, 90 and the notes on the diagrams on the folding page opposite.

[31] Hence the name 'cartridge paper'. To load his musket the soldier first bit off a corner of the envelope and poured a little powder into the 'pan' as 'priming'; then after closing the pan, he poured the rest of the powder down the muzzle of his flintlock and rammed the ball home after it. This procedure explains a passage in Private Wheeler's letters on the capture of Cambrai during the advance from Waterloo toward Paris. There was some resistance before the walls were carried by escalade. Then, writes Wheeler, 'We were, as usual, received by the people with vivas, many *of whom had forgot to wash the powder off their lips caused by biting off the cartridges when they were firing on us from the wall.*' (B. H. Liddell Hart, ed. *The Letters of Private Wheeler, 1809–1828* (London, 1951), 175; italics mine).

he could be issued with a fresh supply; and Bonaparte's only answer to runnels was to require that all invasion troops be practised in swimming. Clearly, then, the French might have encountered a number of difficulties in the mere disembarkation even after they had reached the shores of England.

But first they had to reach England in flat-bottomed craft designed to be run ashore in shallow water; and these boats would certainly have been useless for an invasion if they had not been so designed. Yet this essential requirement naturally raised another difficulty. It meant that no boat could have a proper keel, and that is why they sailed so poorly in any but a following wind. The *prames* each had three very shallow keels; but, as Desbrière notes, this combined with the method of their construction, was disastrous for the solidity of their hulls.[32] The *chaloupes canonnières* also sailed badly. The gun-boats were well rigged, but for want of keels they too could not sail close to the wind and were ill designed to weather a heavy sea. The pinnaces were also well rigged, and well designed for rowing in calm, too, but incapable of resisting a serious squall.

To these defects must be added another; from a nautical point of view all these craft were loaded down with too many guns. In part, perhaps, this was the result of Bonaparte's early hopes that his flotilla might fight its own way across the Channel. Yet, even when he had dropped that idea, he still needed fire-power to cover the troops' landing in the face of the English coast defence batteries. A less headstrong and impatient man might have preferred to find this fire-power some other way and designed special support craft to give covering fire to troops disembarking from landing craft unencumbered with artillery. But designing military novelties was not Bonaparte's forte;[33] and in any case once his plans were adopted and his great programme of building the flotilla started, he could hardly have changed his designs too drastically without creating intolerable confusion. The weight of the guns still had the effect of straining the hulls of his craft whenever they were grounded. Even worse, the *bateaux canonniers* had no means of traversing their guns and could only aim them by pointing the boat itself at the

---

[32] '*Le système de trois quilles, avec le procédé d'assemblage employé, était désastreux pour la solidité des coques.*' *Projets et Tentatives* III, notes to folding chart opposite p. 90.

[33] In fact, he sometimes seemed obtuse about them. For example, he had no use for observation balloons, which earlier French revolutionary generals had employed; and in 1807 he 'ordered the withdrawal of all rifles from his army' thus leaving his light troops with smooth bores only and putting 'the French in Spain at a permanent disadvantage in skirmishing' (Michael Glover, *Wellington's Peninsular Victories*, 174). Yet the rifle was not a new weapon. He left it to the English to produce the real military inventions of the war, Congreve's rockets and the Shrapnel shell.

intended target.[34] Finally, their unseaworthiness made it unsafe to anchor them outside the harbour in any but calm summer weather.

I have suggested above that Bonaparte's chances of success in England, even if peace continued on the continent, were much poorer than his self-confidence led him to suppose; and among the assets of the British I listed the likelihood of confusion developing in the flotilla during its voyage and the landing. The reader is now in a position to assess the likelihood of confusion for himself. Not counting horse transports and other assorted vessels, the French proposed to come over in landing craft of four principal types with very different qualities. The job of getting away from the French ports would take six tides, that is, three days. Among the invasion craft there were to be over 300 pinnaces, which could not survive a strong squall. Hence a change of weather in those two or three days could badly disrupt the departure timetable (quite apart from the dangerous surf it might raise on the beaches); and a change of weather during the crossing might lead to a wholesale disaster among the pinnaces. Even in favourable weather there is no saying how far the ill-designed *prames* and *chaloupes can-onnières* would drift off course while the oared pinnaces could go directly to their beaches. Hence it is impossible to say in what time or what sort of order each flight, starting from four different French ports, would arrive at its appointed beach. In fighting terms that raises the question of how soon the commander of each flight of landing craft could call on properly organised units to obey his orders; or for how long after landing the French army would find itself no more than a jumbled medley of petty detachments, some from one unit and some from another. Nor can one guess how many soldiers could still fire a musket after the landing or how many would have nothing left of their ammunition but sodden paper envelopes spilling wet powder and loose musket balls into water-filled pouches. In the case of the first flight these confusions would have to be sorted out under fire; for nothing should have stopped the British coast defence gunners from showering the newly arrived French with grape- and case-shot until someone could lead a successful assault on their batteries in their earthen entrenchments. One can think of easier tasks than organising such an attack in these circumstances; and mounting the entrenchments themselves would also be difficult.

Another thing that would seem extremely difficult is bringing such a massed and mixed armada to its chosen beach by night – the

---

[34] This is one of a number of defects noted in Admiral Montagu's description of a captured gunboat, cited by Holland Rose, *The Life of Napoleon I*, I, 485–6. (I identify this boat by its measurements given by Rose as 58½ feet long, 14½ feet wide, and drawing 3 feet of water at the bow and 4 at the stern. These conform fairly closely to those given above from Desbrière).

commando's ideal time for landing. Nor should it be supposed that the coast gunners would have been unable to punish the invaders even if they did succeed in making their landfall by night. The English would naturally follow the ordinary military precaution of having sentries patrol the beach through the hours of darkness; and one may presume that their batteries would be ready to fire 'light balls'. These contrivances, wrote Jones, were 'of excellent use for discovering working parties' during sieges;[35] and to them one may attribute the 'sudden blaze of light' which greeted the British on that night of 'frightful carnage' when they stormed Badajoz.[36] The far likelier event of a daylight landing would have given the British gunners a still better chance to hammer their assailants; and their means of doing so therefore require a little attention here.

The commonest weapon in the coast defence batteries was the 24-pounder gun, which threw much heavier metal than the field pieces with which General Menou had tried and failed to defeat Sir Ralph Abercromby's landing at Aboukir Bay on 8 March 1801. The ammunition was of three types. First, there was round-shot, or cannon balls, which might be described as a marksman's weapon, capable of respectable accuracy at a considerable range, and hence useful for smashing the boats while they were still well out to sea. Then there were case- and grape-shot, not weapons of precise accuracy, but projectiles designed to shower an area with musket-balls, much as a sportsman's shot-gun scatters its pellets in a particular pattern. These were effective up to 300 yards,[37] but little, if any, further, and would come into play when the actual landing began. Third, there was something new, which, at least as far as its manufacture went, long remained a secret British weapon. This was the projectile which we still call (but, alas, mis-spell) after the name of its inventor, Major Henry Shrapnell.[38] It was a type of case-shot whose case was burst, not by the propellant charge which threw it from the gun but, by any one of four fuses, each designed to burn for a different length of time before it exploded the case and scattered its lethal shower of bullets. This type of case-shot could 'be fired with an effect equally close and connected to any distance within the range of the piece'; and so, continues our authority, artillery supplied with shrapnel 'need not advance within musket shot of the enemy to make use of this kind of fire with its full effect, and are not so subject to have their guns charged either by cavalry or infantry'.[39]

[35] Jones, *Journal of the Sieges*, I, 368.

[36] Napier, *History of the War in the Peninsula*, IV, 14.

[37] Major Charles James, *A New and Enlarged Military Dictionary* (London, 1810) *sub* 'Shot'.

[38] This is the spelling I have found on one or two documents where it appeared to be his signature.

[39] James, *Military Dictionary*, *sub* 'Shot'.

So these were the weapons of the defending gunners, round-shot to sink boats of the invading flotilla or shrapnel to kill and wound the occupants of the open-decked pinnaces well before they could land; then case- and grape-shot would blast the French as they came ashore. Good gunners were expected to fight their pieces, literally, to the muzzle. 'Never abandon your guns till the last extremity', reads the standard manual. 'Your last discharges are the most destructive; they may perhaps be your salvation and crown you with glory.'[40] The sort of price the French were likely to pay for assaulting beaches defended in this manner is perhaps best suggested by the casualties the British suffered in capturing Badajoz. 'Three thousand five hundred men [were] striken in the assault, sixty officers and more than seven hundred men being slain,' records Napier, adding 'this frightful carnage took place in a space of less than a hundred yards square'.[41]

Yet it should not be concluded that the Bonaparte who planned the invasion of Britain was a mere butcher, preparing to send his men to pointless slaughter. Great objects are never cheaply bought. Determination and bold leadership can overcome forbidding handicaps. Though his craft were poor sailors, they were still navigable, or those built in Holland, Le Havre, Brittany and the Bay of Biscay ports would never have reached Boulogne. In reasonable summer weather, and with the French fleet in command of the sea, they should have made the crossing somehow. Though the casualties in the first landing might be heavy indeed, the numbers of the French in the first flight should be great enough to afford them, while the English gunners were but few – just the gun crews of about a dozen men to each gun. As long as the enemy held the initiative, and his objective was unknown, it was pointless to disperse more along all the beaches, from Selsey Bill to the North Foreland and westwards past Reculver to Whitstable where the French might land. To spread troops so thinly would only ensure universal weakness and leave the defenders without concentrated bodies of men for counter-attack. Obviously, too, the French could count on the fire of the flotilla and supporting fleet doing something toward neutralising or softening up the British defences; even if this did not dismount a gun, any damage done to the *chevaux de frise* on the entrenchments would make it easier to storm the batteries with fixed bayonets. So the first invaders to reach the English coast ought to have succeeded in over-running the shore batteries and capturing or bayoneting their gun-crews. The second flight of landing craft to leave Boulogne should therefore have found a peaceful, if corpse-littered, beach controlled by the now reorganised units of the survivors of the first flight.

[40] Ralph Willet Adye, *The Bombardier and Pocket Gunner*, 4th ed. (London, 1804), 27
[41] Napier, *War in the Peninsula*, IV, 122.

The second flight would still, of course, be liable to the same confusion on the voyage as the first flight and would require time to get organised – another gain to the defenders; yet it does seem that the landing should have been possible, given decent weather and command of the Straits.[42]

On the voyage, then, it only remains to notice the extraordinary energy shown in producing the invasion flotilla which on 8 August 1805, mustered in the French Channel ports 18 *prames*, 320 *chaloupes cannonières*, 572 *bateaux cannoniers*, 349 *péniches*, 405 horse transport supplemented by 10 packet-boats, 81 fishing boats adapted to carrying men and horses (in Calais) and other assorted craft (Doc. 14e). All these had been assembled by a man who in March 1803 had possessed no more than 28 *chaloupes cannonières* and 193 *bateaux cannoniers*, left of the armament of 1801, and of these few only 27 were fit for service, and a number had decayed beyond repair.[43] The energy by which Bonaparte transformed such weakness into the impressive strength of 1805 seems beyond praise.

But this was only part of the achievement his energy produced. The threat of 1805 was based on capacious harbours which had scarcely existed in 1801; and Bonaparte developed them also in the short space of two years. In 1801 France's much smaller flotilla was dispersed along the coast from Flushing in Holland to St Malo and Morbihan in Brittany. This was enough to arouse the English and set them to work on plans for defending their island which they were to improve and develop in 1803–5. But there was little immediate danger until the French could concentrate their forces somewhere; and, as the weakness of their fleet gave them little hope of an assured command of the sea, the place of concentration had to be near the narrowest part of the Channel. Calais, Gravelines, Dunkirk and Ostend, to the north and east of Cape Gris Nez, were the existing ports in that area, but none of them was to play

[42] I say this after duly noting Holland Rose's comment on the invasion 'nearly all naval authorities pronounced [Bonaparte's] naval schemes impractical and highly dangerous' (*Pitt and Napoleon*, 145–6); also his quotation from Admiral Russell's comment on a captured gun-boat, 'these vessels in my mind are completely contemptible and ridiculous' and hence the Boulogne flotilla must be a blind to cover a real attempt made elsewhere; and the Dutch Admiral Verhuell's plain warning to Bonaparte that the expedition was not feasible and 'nothing but disgrace could be expected' (*Life of Napoleon*, I, 486). These comments are sound enough of an invasion attempted by the flotilla *without* the command of the sea; and Russell's comment is dated 23 November 1803, when the French had no immediate prospect of commanding the Straits. But if, as hoped, Villeneuve and Ganteaume had appeared in the Channel with 50 line of battle ships in 1805, they would have produced a major change in Bonaparte's prospects; and as from 1804 on his plans were based on a local command of the sea, these comments hardly seem applicable to the later period. Certainly Bonaparte did not let them deter him.

[43] Desbrière, *Projets et Tentatives*, III, 29–30.

more than a secondary role in 1805. Squadrons of a flotilla putting to sea from all of them, even Calais and particularly Ostend, were too liable to be intercepted by the British fleet in the Downs; but it was hoped that with winds from the west, and still more from the south-west, the fleet from the Downs would have difficulty in getting round Cape Gris Nez.[44] Therefore bases south-west of the Cape were chosen. It is true that this point would matter little if ever the French could win and hold the mastery of the Straits. But in the beginning Bona-parte had supposed that he might get across, by surprise, in fog or on a long winter night; and at the worst he then hoped the flotilla could fight its own way through the opposition of the lighter English ships. The work of making four new harbours to the west of Cape Gris Nez was begun when he still imagined that to attack England he need merely evade her superior fleet; and it continued after he had realised that this was a false hope. Nor was he necessarily wrong to continue it after. He had not only invested much work and money in the job by that date; it was at any time mere good sense to start his invasion from the points where the enemy would find it hardest to thwart him.

The first of these new bases was, of course, Boulogne. A harbour of a sort already existed there, formed by the estuary of the Liane river, and, such as it was, it had played a part in the plans of 1801. Three small harbours nearby were also to be used. These were Etaples, on the estuary of the Canche south of Boulogne; to the north of Boulogne were first Wimereux, on a river of the same name; and beyond Wimereux and only a little south of Cape Gris Nez, Ambleteuse on the estuary of the Slack.

The four things that Bonaparte wanted from his harbours were, first, space enough to shelter all the boats in his flotilla; second, exits that would permit the whole flotilla to get out to sea in one tide;[45] third, protection from attempts at mischief by the British; and, fourth, water enough at all stages of the tide to float craft whose heavy arma-ment strained their hulls when they were aground.

The first two of these things were quite incompatible. As we have seen, the strength of the British army at home in 1803–5 was such that Bonaparte was compelled to prepare to invade Britain with far larger forces than any previous ruler of France had had to consider for the purpose. It proved possible, with great exertions, to make harbours large enough to shelter such a fleet; it was not possible to provide those harbours with exits that would let the whole flotilla out in one tide.

---

[44] Ibid., III, 304.

[45] '*Il serait inutile*,' he had written on 21 February 1798, '*de faire des travaux longs et couteux au port de Boulogne pour le rendre susceptible de contenir un plus grand nombre de bateux qu'il n'en peut sortir en une marée.*' Cited by Desbrière, *Projets et Tentatives*, III, 150.

The alternative to keeping his boats in harbour was to anchor them outside in a position that would enable them to defend themselves against
the English with their own broadsides. Latouche-Tréville himself had
suggested doing this outside Boulogne in the summer of 1801; and there
it could be done in summer. The road of St Jean had sufficient depth
and a good bottom, though anchors were quite often lost there; but it
was too open and exposed to winter winds to be safe except in summer.
In the event the attempt to keep boats there at other seasons was to lead
to serious losses. The bay at Etaples was also not a good enough
anchorage. It was early suggested that the anchorage off the beach at
Wissant might be made a safe shelter for about a hundred boats;[46] and
the Bay of Authie south of Etaples was also considered. But Wissant is
north-east, instead out of south-west, of Cape Gris Nez and the Bay of
Authie was also found unsatisfactory. So, from north to south, Ambleteuse, Wimereux, Boulogne and Etaples remained the invasion ports;
the fact that six tides would be required for all their shipping to get to
sea had to be accepted; and Bonaparte had to content himself with
requiring of Admiral Bruix (who commanded the flotilla till he died in
the spring of 1805) and from his harbour engineers basins to float enough
craft and the best harbour exists that could be devised; from the army
he required protection against the English with forts and coast defence
batteries.

The amount of sheer hard labour involved in making these harbours
is scarcely to be imagined by those accustomed to watching modern
dredging operations, with a mechanical scoop shovel heaving mud into
waiting barges which then tow it away and dump it. The job fell into
two parts, excavating basins and making new channels to the sea. The
method of improving the channels was to force the streams to run
straight out to sea, and the tide to ebb and flow straight in and out, by
laying dikes of fascines to direct the current, and so making the water
scour its own new channel between them. Deepening the basins was a
job for working parties of thousands of soldiers from local regiments
toiling with shovels and thousands of wheel barrows; a long, weary,
messy job of moving mud and sand. The great advantage of the barrow
for this work is that, with its single wheel and light load, it can be run
along a plank laid over mud where a cart would sink. There were delays
caused by Bonaparte's own impatience; for he began by rejecting the
proposals of Admiral Bruix, for Boulogne, and his chief harbour engineer, Sganzin, for Ambleteuse, only to be compelled to return to these
plans later. In each case Bonaparte wanted something quicker and
simpler to achieve. Yet these early errors were corrected, and the
workers laboured on, driven by the keenest mind and most restless
and tenacious will in Europe. How far sheer overwork contributed to

[46] Ibid., 162.

Bruix's death in the spring of 1805 it would be rash to say, for he had long been a consumptive; but he was certainly given no rest.

The results were impressive. Boulogne had been described in 1776 as *'un des plus mauvais ports de la Manche'*;[47] even if the earliest, and later rejected, plans for enlarging it had been completed, it would have then held only 100 *chaloupes cannonières*.[48] But in August 1805, with a new semi-circular basin and anchorages on either side of its channel it held 14 *prames*, 187 *chaloupes cannonières*, 221 *bateaux cannoniers*, and 239 *péniches*, besides 3 *bombardes*, 9 packet-boats, 2 corvettes, 44 horse transports and nearly 300 boats of other types. In place of its old and narrow S-shaped channel it had a new exit running straight out to sea between two long dikes. Ambleteuse also had a basin, separated from the channel of the river Slack by a dike of basket work and opening to the sea through two long dikes; it held 3 *prames*, 25 *chaloupes cannonières*, 107 *bateaux cannoniers*, 4 *péniches*, 17 horse transports and several Newfoundland fishing boats. Etaples held 36 *chaloupes cannonières*, 108 *bateaux cannoniers* and 72 horse transports and a number more assorted craft; and at the obscure fishing village of Wimereux the labours inspired by Bonaparte had produced a harbour capable of holding 4 *corvettes*, 32 *chaloupes cannonières*, 36 *bateaux cannoniers*, 56 horse transports and 35 other craft with an exit that permitted them all to get to sea in two tides. Forts and batteries enough to keep the English off had been built too.

So that was the situation in early August 1805. A flotilla capable of lifting 167,000 men was lying in Bonaparte's invasion bases. 93,000 men were standing by to embark on the first two flights of landing craft, to storm the beaches and seize the harbours of Margate, Broadstairs and Ramsgate. From the Texel to Paris semaphore telegraph crews stood ready to pass the message of the French fleet's arrival and start the rest of the invading army on its march to Boulogne. Across the water the garrisons of the new fortifications of Chatham and Dover were waiting to receive the invaders; already – as we shall see – the Duke of York had issued provisional orders to set upon the road a vast army to join them in their fight for the defence of their homeland (Doc. 27). All that was wanting was the fleet needed to cover the Frenchmen's crossing; and if only Bonaparte could have found a Suffren, instead of merely a Villeneuve, to command his navy, what a battle might have been fought in East Kent!

Of course, as everyone knows, it did not happen; yet the margin by which Bonaparte failed to invade Britain would seem more uncomfortably close than some Englishmen have cared to admit; and the energy he flung into his novel task, and the results he achieved, were

[47] Ibid., 141, citing the report of the engineer de Briche.
[48] Ibid., 151.

surely magnificent. Since, in the very period this book treats, Captain Barclay took Tom Cribb in hand to prepare him for his return bout with Molineaux,[49] sportsmen have known that a fight may be won or lost in the training camp, before ever the bell rings for the opening round to start; and as love of wine and women, or sheer idleness, has led too many promising young pugilists to kiss their hopes for championships goodbye, so nations too can court disaster by neglecting their means of defence while they still have time – a weakness of which France herself was to provide such dismal examples between 1866 and 1870 and again between 1934 and 1940. But there was nothing slack or negligent about Bonaparte's preparation for his contest with Britain in 1803–5, and yet all his labour was to be lost. His moment of opportunity passed when Villeneuve failed to appear in the Channel and the Austrians led him into a continental war that lasted nearly two full years. That war gave the English time to complete the task of making the coasts of Kent and Sussex secure against any invasion that could be launched from Boulogne. How their soldiers went to work with almost equal energy and prepared for their contest with the flotilla so thoroughly as to prevent it from ever happening, is the subject of the next section.

[49] Fought at Thiselton Gap near Wymondham in Leicestershire on 28 September 1811. Barclay, a veteran of the Walcheren campaign and a physical fitness enthusiast who had walked 110 miles in 19 hours and 27 minutes, had some very modern ideas. He not only put Cribb through many miles of roadwork to improve his stamina, in addition to the usual sparring. He also fed him on straight beef steak – the modern doctor's 'high protein reducing diet'. By these means he punished the champion's weight down from a ponderous 16 stone to a trim and nifty 13 stone, at which Cribb needed barely 20 minutes fighting to thrash the great American negro who had so nearly defeated him in their first encounter.

5

Fortifications: Britain's Counter to the Boulogne Flotilla

> 'In yon strait path a thousand
> May well be stopped by three;
> Now who will stand on either hand
> And keep the bridge with me?'

said Horatius Cocles in Macaulay's poem; and the purpose of fortifications is to enable small bodies of men to hold key places against greatly superior numbers. The places that need to be fortified are those a nation cannot afford to lose, such as its great cities, its arsenals or its naval bases; places where an enemy's advance can be delayed, such as passes through mountains, river crossings, like the Pons Sublicius for which Horatius fought so well, or, in Britain's case, landing beaches; and places from which a force may threaten the rear of an enemy who ignores them.

The Duke of York could hardly have chosen a better example of the value of fortifications to an embattled nation than the one he gave in his report on defence – the example of Belgium in two eighteenth-century wars.[1] The wars were those of the Austrian Succession and the French Revolution. Belgium had of old been strongly fortified, but by a curious arrangement the ruling power there (which was Austria in both 1744 and 1792) had no right to provide garrisons. Instead the Dutch Barrier treaties gave Holland the right to hold the Belgian fortresses which lay between her borders and France. During the War of the Austrian Succession these Dutch garrisons were often under strength and ill officered. Yet it still took Marshal Saxe, in an unbroken career of victory, four years to conquer the country, as the job of capturing its cities individually led him on from one laborious siege to another. In the decades that followed this war, however, Austria, with Belgium restored to her, became France's ally, and in the 1780s the Emperor

---

[1] Duke of York to Lord Hobart, 25 August 1803 (WO/30/76).

Joseph II saw no reason why he should pay a foreign power to garrison his territory against his own brother-in-law, Louis XVI. So, as the one means of getting rid of the Dutch, he pulled down all the barrier fortresses.

But Joseph II had hardly been dead for two years before events took the turn which he had regarded as impossible. Louis XVI, helpless in the hands of a revolutionary government, declared war on his nephew, the new Austrian emperor, Francis II. At Jemappes, on 6 November 1792, the French under Dumouriez decisively defeated a far smaller Austrian army; and this one stroke delivered all Belgium to the victors. The next spring saw a total reversal of fortune. The Austrians, returning with a strongly reinforced army, routed Dumouriez at Neerwinden on 18 March and regained the entire country. But their success too was temporary, and 1794 saw yet another turn-around. Then Jourdan's victory over the Austrians at Fleurus on 26 June led to Belgium falling once more into French hands, there to remain until Bonaparte's defeat in 1814. So in each of these three campaigns victory in a single day's fighting settled the fate of a country which Saxe, and Marlborough before him, had taken years to conquer.

The fortunes of France in the same period show the other side of the coin. As soon as the Austrians and their allies had swept across Belgium to the French border in 1793 they were stopped in their tracks by a properly fortified frontier; and the siege and capture of Valenciennes alone cost them the best part of that summer. It has been well said that 'Vauban's fortresses probably saved Paris' during the early campaigns of the French Revolution;[2] and certainly Joseph II's dismantling of Belgium's fortresses made it impossible to save that country once either side had gained a decisive victory in the field. It was therefore unfortunate that Britain in 1803 was almost as naked of permanent fortifications as Belgium had been in 1792–4.

The defences of the two south-coast naval bases at Plymouth and Portsmouth had indeed been usefully, though insufficiently, improved since the French and Spaniards had threatened them so gravely in 1779. But between Portsmouth and the Thames the coast had few defences – a small fort, in poor repair, at Sandgate, Dover's ancient and inadequate castle, and refurbished Tudor forts at Walmer, Deal and Sandown.[3] Two reasonably effective forts gave some protection to the Thames – at Tilbury and Sheerness;[4] and the latter also protected the entrance to the Medway. But London was an open city with one antiquated fortress, the Tower, at its centre. Chatham dockyard had

[2] Theodore Ropp, *War in the Modern World* (New York, 1962), 43.
[3] This is not the Sandown in the Isle of Wight. The Sandown Castle here intended is in Kent, between Deal and Walmer.
[4] But Sheerness needed considerable repair.

no defences on the right bank of the Medway. The naval base at Deptford and the great arsenal at Woolwich were quite unprotected. The only fortress in East Anglia, at Landguard Point between the mouths of the Orwell and the Stour, was so decrepit that the officer commanding the Eastern District reported nothing could make it any good except pulling it down and rebuilding it (Doc. 23).[5]

It may seem extraordinary that the country should still have been so defenceless after facing threats of invasion in nearly every war of the eighteenth century.[6] But it is always hard to change a nation's inherited prejudices; and Cromwell's dictatorship had left the English with a prejudice against 'militarism' that was too strong for even the alarm of 1779 to overcome. In that year the combined Bourbon fleets of France and Spain had ruled the Channel for some six weeks in August and September; the defences of Plymouth, according to its harried governor, had been so feeble that the French had only to land there in order to be masters of the dockyard 'in less than six hours'.[7] The situation at Portsmouth was better only because the garrison commander there kept his head instead of losing it; and Lord North's government was roundly abused for its unpreparedness.[8] But when Pitt, urged on by the Duke of Richmond, his Master General of the Ordnance, attempted to get these bases better fortified in 1785, his estimates for the purpose were defeated in one of the House of Commons' more remarkable debates. Vigorous speeches were made on both sides. MPs heard Richmond's proposals defended by no less competent a professional than Admiral Lord Hood and denounced by a windbag who declared that fortifications were mere 'seminaries for soldiers and universities for Praetorian bands'.[9] Then the house divided – exactly evenly on either side; and the government's proposals were defeated on the casting vote of the speaker. In spite of this defeat Pitt and Richmond did manage to do something for Portsmouth and Plymouth by raising a special corps of soldiers to fortify them.[10] The rest of the coastline, and the interior of the country, remained as naked of defences as ever. The invasion scares

[5] North of East Anglia Hull had been fortified as far back as the reign of Henry VIII, and Tynemouth and Berwick in the reign of Elizabeth I; but I have found no report of the condition of these places in 1803. The sea approaches to Edinburgh were defended by a small new fort at Leith, which mounted five 24-pounder guns and four 15-pounders and had been completed in 1793 (K. W. Maurice Jones,) *History of the Coast Artillery in the British Army*, 79).

[6] The one exception is the War of the Spanish Succession.

[7] Cited by H. Butterfield, *George III, Lord North and the People* (London, 1949), 61–2.

[8] For the events of the critical summer of 1779, see A. Temple Patterson, *The Other Armada*.

[9] *Parliamentary Debates*, XXV, 1117 and 1114.

[10] The Corps of Royal Military Artificers raised in 1787 and modelled on a similar body raised to repair the fortifications of Gibraltar. Their origin is

of 1797–8 and 1800–1 also failed to produce any permanent fortifications; yet they had two results of some importance. They caused the Commander-in-Chief and his staff to make a very thorough study of all the problems of defending Britain; and they also secured for the Army authority to build the temporary defences of entrenchments and palisades called 'Field Fortifications'.

In 1803 the Commander-in-Chief found himself once again facing an enemy who controlled all the coasts opposite England from Brest to the Dutch ports, whence William of Orange had set sail on his successful invasion of Britain in 1688; and this time the enemy also possessed the German ports on the Ems and Weser. Britain's assets in 1803 were her navy's superiority over the French and Dutch fleets, the strength of her army at home and Bonaparte's shortage of landing craft. It was certain, however, that Bonaparte would use all the resources of France and Holland to overcome his weaknesses; and while he did so, Britain could afford to lose no time in increasing her own strength. That meant, first, enlarging her army still further and, second, adding to the natural strength which her topography gave her.

How Addington, and his successors, went about increasing the British army will be told in another chapter. As for topography, the south coast offered the enemy both the shortest crossing and at some points the shortest line of advance on London once he had landed. But southern England also offered the defenders excellent defensive positions in which to stop a French advance. It was crossed by three roughly parallel ranges of hills, all running north-westwards from the coast. From East to West these ranges were the North Downs which blocked the advance of an enemy landing west of Hythe; to this the Weald added a second barrier if he landed west of St Leonards, and the South Downs a third if he landed west of Beachy Head. Likewise the river Medway offered a defence against an enemy advancing on London from East Kent.

North of the Thames Admiral Lord Keith advised the Commander-in-Chief that most of the Essex coast was made reasonably safe by the difficulties of navigation among a host of sandbanks (Doc. 2). From Clacton northward there were several good landing beaches. But north of the Thames the voyage was too long to be done with rowboats; an enemy who came by sail could hardly get to sea except in the sort of

---

described in T. M. Connolly, *The History of the Royal Corps of Sappers and Miners* (London, 1855), I, 55 and their defects are castigated by C. W. Pasley, *Course of Military Instruction*, (London, 1817), II, iv. The Duke of Richmond, their founder, wished to make them an effective field force which would make good the Royal Engineers' lack of other ranks and in 1792 was training them in bridging and mining. But Richmond's successors, Cornwallis and Chatham, let them stagnate as mere maintenance crews for fortresses. See also Glover, *Peninsular Preparation*, 38, 104, 186.

weather that made it impossible for the Royal Navy to keep its stations off the ports of Holland; and in such weather the surf breaking on east coast beaches would make landing there a very hazardous and uncertain business. If, however, an enemy did get ashore at or north of Clacton, but few strong defensive positions lay between him and London.

Taken all together these points may make the tasks of the defenders reasonably clear. Moving from the centre outwards, London had to be fortified on the north, east, south and west. The line of the Medway had to be strengthened with a bridgehead both to protect the naval base and arsenal at Chatham and to provide a sally port from which an enemy in East Kent could be counter-attacked. Plymouth and Dover each needed strengthening; and landing beaches on both the south and east coasts had to be protected.

There were two methods by which these tasks could be done – by either permanent or 'Field' fortifications. That, of course, meant two government departments were involved, the Ordnance for permanent fortresses and the Commander-in-Chief for 'Field Fortifications'; and it is clear, even through the discreet medium of official documents, that progress was hampered by friction between these two departments. The Duke of York, who would have to meet the French in the field, was in a hurry to get things done; so were his subordinates, the General Officers commanding Districts, of whom the chief were those two able and experienced men, Sir James Craig in the Eastern District and Sir David Dundas in the Southern District. There is no question that the Duke's very considerable patience was much tried by the lethargy of Lord Chatham at the Ordnance. One senses, too, some jealousy among Ordnance officers of the way the army hurried to defend with field works places where the Ordnance would have preferred permanent fortifications.

The army's field works had certain real advantages. They were cheaply and quickly built. The troops themselves usually provided the labour and few materials were needed. The speed with which these defences could be thrown up accounted for much of their cheapness, for in many cases they were not built at all. Instead, their sites were surveyed; palisades, guns and planks for gun platforms were assembled at their sites; but actual construction was left to be done after the enemy had landed. Meanwhile the ground continued to be cultivated by its owner and no rent was paid for it. The most important place where fortification was thus left to the last minute, and hence never done, was London itself. The soldiers were hardly satisfied with an arrangement that left the capital an open city until enemy forces were already ashore on English soil. But, with a sound psychology, recalling the poster which bade Londoners to 'Keep calm and dig' in the Munich crisis of 1938, the Duke of York recognised that the job would provide 'useful and animating labour to an overgrown population that might otherwise become dangerous and desponding';[11] and in July 1804 he informed Pitt that the defences on the north side of London should be finished in four days by 5,000 men with 800 horses, and on the south the job should be done in three days by 500 men with 300 horses.[12]

So far so good; and it was unlikely that the enemy would be able to break through from either the east or the south coast to London in a mere three days. Yet this solution was not a satisfactory one. It is obvious that entrenched camps, of palisaded earthen embankments, were far weaker and less able to withstand siege artillery than regular fortifications of solid brickwork a dozen or more feet thick. There is also the less obvious point that no earthen embankment was weaker than a new one. The soil thrown up to make it needed much time to pack down and acquire its full potential strength. That lesson had been cruelly rubbed in at Yorktown. There Cornwallis had reckoned on finding sanctuary from the very superior forces of Washington and Rochambeau. But as soon as de Grasse's success over Admiral Graves in the battle of Chesapeake Bay[13] enabled the French to land their siege guns, Cornwallis discovered that 'our *fresh* earthern works do not resist their powerful artillery';[14] and four days after writing these lines Cornwallis was Washington's prisoner. Just one more week's resistance might have brought a very different result. By 24 October Admiral Graves was back in Chesapeake Bay with a reinforced fleet and 6,000 troops under Sir Henry Clinton. But all to no purpose; while Graves and Clinton were at sea, the weakness of Cornwallis's redoubts had lost a war.[15]

In 1803 the British hoped that earthworks would serve their purpose on the ground and that at least in the early days of his invasion an enemy would be weak in artillery. They based this hope on the difficulty of bringing such heavy things as guns ashore across open beaches, and bringing too all the tonnage of ammunition without which guns are useless. Indeed, even if the enemy succeeded in capturing a port, his troops in the field might still remain weak in artillery if he could be prevented from landing or collecting horses or draught cattle to provide

[11] York to Hobart, 25 August 1803. WO/30/76.

[12] *Pitt Papers* No. 245, cited by Rose and Broadley, *Dumouriez and the Defence of England against Napoleon*, 236.

[13] In what William B. Willcox nicely describes as 'one of the least inspired and most decisive naval battles of the century' (*Portrait of a General; Sir Henry Clinton in the War of Independence* (New York, 1964), 424).

[14] Cornwallis to Clinton, 15 October 1781: B. F. Stevens, *The Clinton-Cornwallis Controversy, growing out of the Campaign in Virginia, 1781* (London, 1888), II, p. 188 (my italics).

[15] But, it does not necessarily follow that Clinton's earlier arrival would have turned the campaign into a British success. The 'different result' could also have been a still greater disaster for Britain, and Clinton never gambled so boldly as on this occasion. For the risks he ran, see Willcox, p. 435.

gun teams. So far, then, British hopes were reasonable, although the opponent whose assault they were expecting was the greatest artillery-man of all time; and in any case, 'beggars cannot be choosers'. A nation which in her years of peace and prosperity had failed to prepare for a defensive war had no option but accept a second-best solution when the crisis came.

It was still unfortunate that work on her defences was checkered by so much friction between the Ordnance and the Army. This section, on the fortifications with which Britain first countered the special threat of 1803–5 and went on to make the Boulogne flotilla virtually useless, may begin with certain places where serious friction between the two depart-ments occurred. From them we may proceed to the defence of London and end with the fortification of the beaches (which also brought difficulties between the Army and the Ordnance).

In the first group we may start with the great naval base of Plymouth, on whose docks, workshops and stores of oak planks, masts and rigging the efficiency of the fleet depended. Here Lt General John G. Simcoe, commanding the Western District, wanted redoubts to prevent an enemy landing in the river Yealm and advancing on the base 'by the great Plymouth road'. The officer commanding the garrison engineers objected on the grounds that detached works would be too easily taken. A quick decision was necessary to enable the base to be strengthened, one way or another, as fast as possible; and the Duke gave it. Simcoe, as the man responsible for defending the place, was to carry out the plan he preferred.

Dover was an even more serious problem. It was certain that an enemy must attempt to seize a port as soon as possible after landing; and no port was handier to his bases at Calais and Boulogne. Alter-natively, if the enemy landed in East Kent and won his opening battle on the beaches, the Duke did not intend to retreat north-westwards on London. Instead he planned to fall back on Dover itself. There he would face his opponent with a choice either of advancing toward the capital, and so laying his rear open to a counter-stroke, or of eliminating Dover first, and so giving time for reinforcements from the north and west to assemble in front of London. But it was doubtful if Dover castle could be held against an enemy who had seized the Western Heights which overlooked the town; and even supposing the castle were held, it was doubtful if its garrison could prevent the enemy from using the port at night once the Western Heights were lost. It was therefore essential to crown the heights with defences in which troops could stand a seige if they were attacked or from which they could assail the enemy's rear if they were not.

For a post of such importance a regular fortress was obviously the ideal. The question was one of time. The Duke's advisers were General

Sir David Dundas, commanding the Southern District and his chief
engineer, Colonel Twiss. When they reported that with the resources
then available field works could not be completed before the end of the
summer of 1803, the Duke, on 20 July, requested Lord Chatham to
consider 'the expediency of immediate measures being taken for
occupying Dover heights by respectable and permanent works,
according to the suggestion contained in the concluding paragraph of
Colonel Twiss's Report'.[16] How or why nothing had yet been done by
the following March are questions to which I have found no answer;
but evidently nothing was; and on 30 March 1804 the Duke was writing
to Lord Hobart, Secretary of State for War, on the subject. He enclosed a letter 'of yesterday's date' from General Dundas, giving 'the
united opinion of that officer and my Lord Keith (the Admiral Commanding in those Seas)'.[17] Dundas warned that Dover was 'in its present
state open to be carried by a sudden descent of the enemy', but it could
be made secure by three to four weeks work at a cost of less than £1,000
if a plan which he enclosed were promptly adopted.[18] The Duke therefore requested that he might be empowered to order Dundas to get to
work fast. But the authority the Duke wanted did not come swiftly;
and on 12 April he is found writing again, this time to Lord Chatham,
to explain his opinions on Dover once more; and he concluded, 'The
mode of Fortifying in the first instance I should wish to be such as to
secure the Heights against a Coup de Main, by working on a Plan (if
possible) which would afterwards be converted into a Permanent
Work'.[19]

On this one may comment that after the Duke had passed the problem of the Western Heights to another department on 20 July 1803 he
needed cabinet authority to take it back. But Lord Chatham, the
Master General of the Ordnance, was both the head of that department
and a member of the cabinet. It looks as if he had used his position in
the cabinet to speak against the Duke's proposal and in favour of the
'respectable and permanent works' for whose erection he had been
requested to consider 'immediate measures' nine months earlier. The
Duke's letter shows that he could not get on with the job until he had
made a direct application to the minister who was blocking him; and
meanwhile he had lost two of the 'three or four weeks' required to get
the work done. After this it was done, and in 1805 the veteran,
Dumouriez (now an exile in England), could write simply 'Dover is
unassailable';[20] but the delay and the friction had both been unfortunate.

[16] York to Chatham, 20 July 1803 (WO/30/76).

[17] York to Hobart, 30 March 1804 (WO/1/627).

[18] So wrote Sir David Dundas on 29 March 1804 (WO/1/627).

[19] York to Chatham, 12 April 1804 (WO/30/76).

[20] Rose and Broadley, *Dumouriez and the Defence of England against Napoleon*,
375. These temporary fortifications, set on a steep slope which invited erosion,

Chatham was another point which the Ordnance department wished, with good reason, to defend with permanent fortifications and where the soldiers, with equal reason, felt they could not afford to wait. Like Plymouth and Portsmouth, Chatham had one of the dockyards on which the maintenance of the fleet depended. As we have seen, the town lay on the right bank of the river Medway, that is, the bank exposed to an enemy landing in east Kent. The river itself was a barrier of some value against an enemy advancing westwards and if its right bank once fell into the hands of the French, it would be an equal hindrance to a British force counter-attacking toward the east. On 2 July 1803, therefore, the Duke instructed General Dundas to 'proceed with all possible expedition to take such preparatory measures as will determine the position and nature of the field works which you point out as essential for protecting the dockyard and affording security to a body of troops on the right bank of the Medway'.[21] The reaction of the Ordnance Board was swift and hostile; and on 12 July the Duke was writing to Lord Chatham to counter objections raised by Lt General Robert Morse, the Inspector General of Fortifications. A week later he sent Lord Chatham plans for a Tête de Pont to cover a bridge that was to be thrown across the Medway for the defence of Chatham; he added that 'if undertaken with vigour' the work 'may be speedily completed', and that he hoped to see it done 'with the least possible delay'.[22] But again he was to be disappointed of swift action; and not till 4 June 1804 could he report that the lines of Chatham were nearly finished.[23]

The defences of London were of two kinds, those designed to block the approaches to the city, and the defences on the perimeter itself. We have seen that the perimeter defences were surveyed, but never built; also that, if a time came when they were needed, the Duke intended to have the work done by the Londoners themselves. He described his plans for the perimeter defences as follows: 'On the Right bank of the Thames the Line rests upon the River above Deptford and passes along the ridge of the Norwood hills, then turning by Streatham and Tooting to the River behind Wandsworth Crick. The continuation of the Line upon the Left bank of the Thames in front of London passes behind the River Lea by Stratford and Lea Bridge to Stamford Hill; from thence it takes the ridge of Ground by Hornsey Wood, Highgate and Wilsden Green; and again turns by Holland House and Little Chelsea to the Thames.'[24] These lines, he continued, gave the defenders

in due course deteriorated badly. But Dumouriez's verdict on their condition in the critical year of 1805 is still interesting, as coming from a man involved in the abortive French plans for invading England in 1779.

[21] York to Dundas, 2 July 1803 (WO/30/76).
[22] York to Chatham, 19 July 1803 (WO/30/76).
[23] York to Lord Camden, 4 June 1804 (WO/30/76).
[24] York to Lt Gen. Lord Cathcart, 15 July 1803 (WO/30/76).

'angular points of great command behind which the Troops intended for support have in all directions comparatively short lines of communication'[25] and, all told, 'the features of the country' were 'singularly adapted for defensive positions'.[26]

So far, so good; but two weaknesses must be noted. The first was the river Thames itself. If they were to make use of their 'comparatively short lines of communication' the defending troops must be able to cross it; and it was then spanned by only three bridges, London Bridge, Blackfriars Bridge and Westminster Bridge.[27] This lack of bridges was a handicap to more than the defence of London. Whether the enemy landed on the south or the east coast, reinforcements would have to hasten to meet him; and the route of many of them would pass through London. They too would have to cross the river; and both to speed them on their way and improve the city's own defences the Duke called for a ferry. He picked the 'stairs at Blackwall' to serve the ferry at one end; and to enable troops to embark (or disembark) at the other side at any time of the tide, he requested a raft between rows of piles to be prepared on the opposite bank.[28]

The other weakness was the need of a garrison. If London were formally beseiged, no fewer than 180,00 men would be required to defend it.[29] This was more by some 50,000 than the grand total of all the Regulars and Militia in Britain in 1803. Much of London's garrison would therefore have to be provided by the Volunteers. These, as we have seen, were all cavalry or infantry; and who, in that case, would serve the guns that were to be mounted in London's fortifications? The best answer one can give to this question is that a complete investment of so large an area as London was hardly to be attempted by any force the French had a chance of landing. Therefore, as the Duke observed, they were most likely to attack one front only; and there the defenders could concentrate all their professional gunners.

Yet the Duke was obviously still worried about giving London enough artillery for its defence. In July 1803 he required from Gen. Harrington 'a return of all Master Carpenters and Smiths who would undertake with their workmen to prepare the platforms for the Artillery' and a return of all inhabitants of the city who knew how to work the guns once they were in place.[30] To Lord Hobart in August he expressed the hope that 'a few batteries' might 'be constructed on Ground of the least value on either side of the Thames where the Volunteer companies might be

[25] York to Lord Hobart, 28 August 1803 (WO/30/76).   [26] Ibid.

[27] See William Faden's *New Pocket Plan of the Cities of London and Westminster with the Borough of Southwark* (London, 1797).

[28] York to Lord Hobart, 26 March 1804 (WO/30/76).

[29] York to Hobart, 25 August 1803 (WO/30/76).

[30] York to Lord Harrington, G.O.C. the London District, 26 July 1803 (WO/30/76).

trained in the use of the Great Guns'.[31] So, as far as he was able, he spared no pains to develop every resource that could be used to defend the capital.[32]

The 'bold and commanding feature' of Shooter's Hill was the point chosen for defences to cover the approaches to London from the South. It had the merit of giving some protection to Deptford and Woolwich also. Here it was decided to build a permanent fortress, a task in due course completed by the Ordnance; and, to give the position some security in the meantime, the Duke reserved to himself, 'under the Head of Field Works, to order Defences round the Hill to be thrown up'.

The northern approaches to London offered a less easily settled problem. The Duke was quick to start building an entrenched camp at Brentwood; and he wasted little time in having the possibilities of flooding the Lea valley studied by John Rennie, the famous engineer and future builder of Waterloo bridge. Rennie produced his report suggesting ways in which it might be done on 8 August, and on the 12th the Duke wrote ordering Lord Cathcart to engage contractors to carry out his chosen alternative. His aim was to deepen and widen the main stream by building sluices to cut 'off the four branches of the Lea ... on the Left bank so as to prevent the drain they occasion from ... the principal branch of the river'. The 'two sections of the river formed by *Budding Mill Stream* and *Distillers River*' were also to 'be prepared for inundation' in order to hinder the enemy's approach to the main stream. [33]

Both the camp and the sluices added to London's security. But both were unpleasantly close to the city; and what the East coast needed was some position, like Dover on the South coast, which the enemy could not capture without being delayed or ignore without danger to his rear. Positions near Colchester and Grinstead were both being considered in August 1803. Neither was satisfactory; and the difficulty of making any decision induced York 'to delay a final determination until I shall have an opportunity of examining the ground in person'.[34] After apparently considering Sudbury and Braintree as well

[31] York to Hobart, 25 August 1803 (WO/30/76).

[32] But this is, of course, one area where the Duke's authority was very limited. He could invite carpenters and smiths to volunteer to bring their workmen to make gun platforms; he could not require them to do it. He could order money spent on Field Works for actual use against the enemy, but not to provide mere training facilities for Volunteers. He could suggest that particular companies of Volunteers should be trained for special duties; he could give them no orders until they were called out on 'permanent' duty. In short, he had to depend on the goodwill of others to carry out all his very practical suggestions described in this paragraph. I have found no record of what results these suggestions actually produced.

[33] York to Cathcart, 12 August 1803 (WO/30/76).

[34] York to Sir James Craig, 19 August 1803 (WO/30/76).

as Colchester and Grinstead he finally proposed 'an Entrenched Camp in Front of Dunmow'. It was 'a more retired situation, but one calculated to meet the same cases of an operation on the part of the Enemy'.[35]

There remains the matter of defending the coast itself. It was, of course, in the moment of landing that an enemy could best be defeated; and the point was well recognised. The problem was how to do it. There were so many beaches on which the enemy might land that an attempt to guard them all would spread the defending troops too thin and make the defence weak everywhere. The standard, and as far as it went correct, method of defending the coasts of England's recent wars had been to hold the main bodies of her troops at inland points whence they could launch a counter-attack once the place of the enemy's landing was known. The defence of the beaches themselves was left to small bodies of artillery, whose guns might open fire on the ships of the enemy's flotilla at sea as soon as he came in range of round shot and attack his landing craft and his troops with grape and canister, as they approached and crossed the beaches. The sites where these coast defence batteries were needed were the same in one war as in another; and when war broke out again in 1803 they were quickly re-established. So something was done, and done early, to prepare to take toll of the enemy in his moment of greatest weakness.

But this was not a good enough solution. Mere coast defence batteries could not stop a determined and powerful enemy who ignored his punishment and swept ashore regardless of his losses. So much had been proved by the British themselves in Egypt on 8 March 1801, when Sir Ralph Abercromby's troops had made good their landing at Aboukir Bay in the face of the 15 guns and 1,600 French infantry. It was, indeed, only too likely that the coast batteries would not merely fail to prevent a determined enemy from landing but would be captured by him; and then he might find them a very useful substitute for his own guns, which he was expected to have difficulty in getting ashore. So a perceptive staff officer had written of the coast defence batteries in April 1798 that 'in whatever way I regard them they appear to me as more calculated to promote the views of an Enemy then to resist [his] descent'. Accordingly this officer, one Major Thomas Reynolds, had recommended that the guns and their crews be placed 'in a Simple Tower of Brickwork' (Doc. 21a).

At that time Major Reynolds' suggestion had not been adopted. The danger passed too soon as the French chose to invade Egypt, not England, that year. In 1799 they had been thrown on the defensive by the early victories of the Austrians and Russians in the War of the

Second Coalition. Finally, in 1801–2 they had made peace after their victory at Hohenlinden. But in 1803 the idea of building towers was energetically revived.

This time it was Col. Twiss, Dundas's chief engineer in the Southern District, who proposed them; and on 11 August 1803 the Duke of York is found pressing the idea upon Lord Chatham. In view, he wrote, of 'the peculiar description of Armament with which this coast is threatened – composed of a multiplicity of small vessels . . . it is highly probable the disembarkation of an enemy will be undertaken for a considerable series of time after the arrival of the leading vessels upon the coast'. Hence 'the possession of the Sea Batteries [was] an object of the greatest moment'; towers would be 'perhaps the least expensive of all permanent works' and would do away with 'the necessity of those temporary defences resorted to at the commencement of Every new war'.[36]

Once again the Duke's patience was to be sorely tried. The towers were permanent fortifications which the Ordnance department must design and build; and Lord Chatham was bleakly uncooperative. In February 1804, he wrote to the Secretary of State for War that as towers were 'entirely novel in principle and connected with an infinite variety of details, I should be unwilling to occupy the time of the [Engineer] Committee on this point unless your Lordship continued to feel a desire to receive a report on the subject, and . . . the idea was generally approved by His Majesty's Confidential Servants'.[37]

Again the Duke of York refused to be beaten by obstructionism at the Ordnance; and he turned that department's jealousy of the army to his own advantage by offering to build the towers himself. Since the Ordnance was 'already charged with the erection of great and extensive works', he suggested to Lord Hobart on 31 March 1804 that the towers 'might possibly be erected under the Head of Field Works'.[38] This threat apparently stung the Ordnance into action, and on 10 April it produced, from the office of the Inspector General of Fortifications, what can only be described as a report of quite astonishing fatuity. It declared that batteries in towers had 'little or no advantage over any other battery' because the enemy might destroy the gun carriages 'with a few shells thrown from small Mortars'. Placing batteries in towers would also be much more expensive than leaving them on the ground; and towers took much longer to erect; so on the ground the guns should remain. On the other hand towers loopholed for musketry could be useful for defending guns on the ground 'and might be applied to some

[36] York to Chatham, 11 August 1803 (WO/30/76).
[37] Chatham to Hobart, WO/1/783, cited by Maurice-Jones, *The History of the Coast Artillery* 99.
[38] York to Hobart, 31 March 1804 (WO/30/76).

of the batteries upon the Coast of the South District' which were
deemed to be not 'sufficiently protected against an Assault'.[39]

On this report one can only comment that silencing your enemy's
guns by smashing their carriages or killing their crews with the high-
arcked fire of mortars was one of the standard ploys of siege warfare and
would have been just as effective against guns in field works as against
guns in towers; but unlike the guns in field works, which might be
captured by assault, the guns in towers could not be silenced unless
their mountings were smashed by mortars. Then, second, there was an
obvious answer to the threat of mortars, which was in due course to be
adopted; it was simply to equip some towers with 5½-inch howitzers,
which could return with interest the fire of any mortars the enemy might
place where the flat trajectory fire of guns or carronades could not reach
them. Third, for all its penny-pinching thrift, this report still did not
evade the task of building some towers; but, fourth, alike in range and
rate of fire the musketry, for which the report's towers were to be designed, was a far feebler defence than the case- or grape-shot of well-
served artillery.[40] Fifth, and finally, the towers might have been half-
built in the nine months already wasted by 10 April 1804.

Very properly then this report impressed nobody; and the idea of
building towers was referred to a committee. Meanwhile the Duke
had explained very clearly what he wanted and where he wanted it.
He wanted to strengthen the defences of southern England because the
enemy's concentration of men and shipping at Boulogne 'evidently
marks a determination to land upon the Coast of Kent or the nearest
part of the Coast of Sussex'. The Addington government had apparently
told him he could have no more than ten towers for this purpose. Of
these he wished to place one at each of the following places – Reculver,
the entrance to the Sandwich river, Eastware Bay, Dungeness, Dym-
church, the Greedy Gut near Rye Harbour and the end of the Pett Level;

---

[39] 'Observations and Opinions upon the Matters mentioned to Lt Gen.
Morse and Brigadier-Gen. Twiss when they had the honor of attending H.M's
Cabinet on the 18th Instant.' Inspector General's Office, 26 April 1804 (WO/
30/75).

[40] 'Grape-shot' consisted of a number of iron balls 'put into a thick canvas bag
and corded strongly together, so as to form a kind of cylinder whose diameter
is equal to that of the ball which is adapted to the cannon'. In 'Case-shot' the
balls were put in a 'tin case . . . in diameter a little less than the calibre of the
gun or howitzer'. (James, *Military Dictionary*, sub 'Shot'.) When these projectiles were fired, they burst so as to spray a whole area with the iron balls, in the
manner of a shot gun. They were effective up to a range of 300 yards (ibid.). The
rate of fire depended on the efficiency of the gun teams; and in a crisis a first-
class gun team might get off as many as ten or twelve rounds a minute (ibid.).
The muzzle-loading smoothbore musket of the day was very inaccurate at
ranges over 100 yards, and it took a very well-trained man to get off as many
as three rounds a minute.

and three 'in Pevensey Bay betwixt Hastings and Eastbourne'. He added, 'I should further consider it of great moment if the Government would approve of Two being placed betwixt Beachy Head and Brighton'.[41]

Another six months passed, in the course of which Addington's government fell and Pitt returned to power, bringing Lord Camden to replace Lord Hobart as Minister for War, but unfortunately leaving his brother, Lord Chatham, at the Ordnance. Meanwhile the Ordnance committee had got down to serious work, and as its members came up with a solution that was to transform the defence of England their names deserve mention; they were N. D'Aubant, William Twiss and Thomas Nepean. After considering two types, one square with 4 guns and one round with one gun, they finally recommended a round tower carrying on its top 'one 24-pounder gun and two Carronades, all mounted on traversing platforms to fire over a high parapet, the crest of which is about 33 feet from the foundation'. These towers had a diameter of 26 feet. Their walls were of brickwork 5 feet thick. Up the centre rose a solid brick pillar, also 5 feet thick, which supported a bomb-proof dome. They were divided into three stories – the roofless gun platform at the top; the men's sleeping quarters in the middle; and the bottom, which had neither door nor windows, was the magazine for storing provisions, water and ammunition. The entrance was by a ladder to a door in the second story; and from the second story a stone stairway, contrived in a specially thickened part of the wall, led up to the gun platform (Doc. 21b).

The Committee's conclusions were passed to Lord Chatham through the same General Morse whose foolish comments of the previous April were cited above. He now explained that the square towers with 4 guns cost five times as much as the round towers with one gun and two carronades and had only one third more fire-power. On this ground he ruled that the round tower was good enough for all situations, and his ruling was adopted.[42] This was unfortunate because the ingenious traversing gear (an invention of Lt Col. Nepean) proved disappointing.[43] In fact, none of the towers seem to have been actually equipped with the one 24-pounder and two carronades, and a report of 1810 shows that the strongest armament any tower carried was one long 24-pounder and one $5\frac{1}{2}$-inch howitzer, and some two-thirds of the towers had only the 24-pounder gun.[44] So the ultimate strength the towers added to England's south-coast defences was sadly less than had been intended.

But there is one striking novelty in recommendations submitted by

[41] York to Lord Hobart, 10 April 1804 (WO/30/76).
[42] Morse to Lord Chatham, 6 October 1804 (WO/30/78).
[43] Lord Charles Somerset: Report of the State of the Sussex District, 30 August 1807 (WO/30/71).
[44] Report of Lt Col. A. Christie, 7 and 8 April 1810 (WO/30/81).

William Twiss on 12 September 1804[45] – that is, before Lt General
Morse had ruled against the square tower. Twiss proposed a total of no
fewer than 74 towers. Credit for this tremendous improvement on the
mere ten for which the Duke of York had named particular sites in
April should certainly go to William Pitt. The defects of this statesman
as a war minister have been drawn by Fortescue with a vigour that is
sometimes mistaken for prejudice by those who have difficulty in
grasping the military arguments on which Fortescue based his verdict;
but Pitt was a far bolder spender than Addington and on this occasion
he made the right decision.

In the end only 73 towers were built in the Southern District – 27 in
Kent and 46 in Sussex; but this was enough to defend the threatened
beaches with chains of towers spaced at intervals of 500–600 yards.
That distance left no point which could not be swept with grape- or
case-shot by one tower or another. The towers themselves were impregnable to troops without proper battering guns. Food and water,
stored with ammunition in its magazine, enabled each tower to stand a
siege; and throughout the whole 'series of time' required for the
enemy's disembarkation, as landing craft arrived one after another, the
gun crews could keep up their fire with grape- and case-shot from
24-pounder guns, supplemented by some $5\frac{1}{2}$-inch howitzers. By
October 1806 the towers were so nearly completed that the Duke of
York could recommend that the field works made in 1803 be given up.[46]
And here a little arithmetic may help civilian readers appreciate the
value of what had been done by covering the endangered beaches of
southern England with towers so spaced that their fields of fire inter-
locked and so strong as to defy any assault that mere infantry might
attempt.

Understand, then, that case-shot came into two forms, 'heavy' and
'light'; and it appears that one 24-pounder round of 'heavy case' would
contain 84 balls, each weighing six ounces, one 24-pounder of 'light
case' contained 232 balls of two ounces' weight and one round of
$5\frac{1}{2}$-inch howitzer contained 100 two-ounce balls. This means that a
single round of 'heavy' 24-pounder case-shot had nearly the same

[45] Twiss: Report on the South Coast of England, 12 September 1804 (WO/
1/629).

[46] He made this recommendation on 8 October in a letter to William Windham
which he quotes on 8 December when he wrote again to Windham to request a
reply to his earlier letter. (York to Windham, 4 December 1806, WO/1/633.)
The reader will note how Windham had left an important letter unanswered for
nearly two months – one example of why he was such an unsatisfactory minister.
As the sites of field works had to be rented, every month's delay in dispensing
with them meant so much more money lost. For a fuller account of these towers,
see R. Glover, 'Martello Towers', The Queen's Quarterly (Kingston, Ontario,
Spring 1938), 66–77.

killing power as a volley of musketry from a company of 100 infantry-men; a single round of 'light' 24-pounder case had more than double the killing power of a volley of 100 infantrymen. Further since, as we have seen, well-served guns could, over short periods, be fired ten or twelve times in a minute, one Martello tower mounting a 24-pounder gun and a $5\frac{1}{2}$-inch howitzer should be able to spray the area of beach it covered with up to 3,300 lethal projectiles per minute. Take these facts all together and it seems fair to say that to attempt an assault landing in the face of England's new towers would be courting disaster.

Pitt may take credit for financing another defensive work of first rate value – the Royal Military Canal which encircles the rear of Romney Marsh. As its name implies the marsh was an area of reclaimed swamp, protected from the Channel by a sea-wall and drained through five sluices which let water out at low tide. To the west of it, across Rye harbour, lay a similar stretch of land, the Pett Level. On the seaward side of the marsh Dungeness Point stretched far out into the Channel. Its beaches offered an easy landing in almost any state of wind or tide, for one or other side of the point was nearly always sheltered from whatever quarter the wind blew. Excellent, however, as these landing beaches were, no one appears to have worried very much about them in the early months of the war. There seemed to be such a simple and obvious way to seal off an invader who landed on Dungeness. Between such an invader and the rest of England lay the full expanse of Romney Marsh; the marsh had been reclaimed from the sea; and it was supposed that in a crisis, it could be returned to the sea. Plans for doing this had been made in the previous war (Doc. 22a); and, in writing to Lord Hobart on 25 August 1803, the Duke of York said quite simply, 'To give further security to this line of coast I have directed measures to be prepared to ensure the inundating of Romney Marsh'.[47]

If the inundation of the marsh could be ensured in time, that line of coast would indeed seem safe; but the question was – what measures would do this? As winter turned into the spring of 1804 this question began to worry General Dundas. He reported that it would take three or four tides to complete the inundation. This meant that an enter-prising enemy should be across the marsh and up the hills beyond before enough water could be let in to hinder anybody, if flooding were delayed until he landed. Therefore the inundation would be useless unless it was completed before the enemy sailed. But to flood the land before it was necessary would be a very serious matter. The marsh's 28,000 acres of excellent pasture would be lost for the duration of the war and, in view of the damage salt water does to vegetation, the job of restoring the land after the peace would be a slow one. So Dundas

[47] York to Hobart, 25 August 1803 (WO/30/76).

asked for explicit instructions; and on 14 March his enquiry was passed on to Lord Hobart's office.[48]

There were three reasons why this question should go to the minister. First, liaison with the local people through the lord, lieutenant of the counties was his job. Second, if the marsh with all its wide acreage of grazing land was to be destroyed by salt water, very considerable compensation would have to be paid to the farmers; and only the ministry could find the money. Third, if anyone in England was able to get forty-eight hours' advanced warning of when the French were coming, it was the minister, for he was the man who controlled the secret service money. Clearly, then, this was not a question which the Duke of York could answer; and unfortunately the ministry had no help to give him. Instead, after leaving the letter unanswered for two weeks, they recommended that General Dundas should follow the suggestions of his chief engineer, Brigadier General Twiss. From this fatuous evasion Dundas could glean one thing only – the Cabinet was not going to promise compensation to farmers.

No responsible soldier could be satisfied with such an answer, so Dundas and his staff sought some other way to make this stretch of coast secure. The canal was their solution. Their recommendation, dated 18 September, is a curious document, written in two columns, one by Lt Col. John Brown, of the Royal Staff Corps, and one by Dundas himself, and it was accompanied by a map (which seems now to be lost) (Doc. 22b). It is unlikely that Dundas and Brown had read each other's contributions before giving them to a clerk to copy, for on one point they contradict each other. Dundas regarded the canal as a mere supplement a 'partial inundation'; Brown correctly said the canal would render 'unnecessary the doubtful [sic] and destructive measure of laying so large a Portion of the Country waste by Inundation'. But Dundas, with a Scot's shrewdness in money matters, added that such a waterway 'would not be totally unproductive and (would) be of use for commercial and Husbandry purposes'. And there he was dead right; until about 1850 income from the canal's tolls largely exceeded the cost of its maintenance.

Brown, who must be credited with the planning, wished the canal to be '60 ft wide at the Top, 40 at the Bottom and Nine Feet deep, which would always ensure from 7 to 8 feet (of) Water'. The earth dug up should all be thrown on the inside of the canal to make a rampart. On the far side of this rampart, and sheltered by it, there should be 'a great Military Road'. The route of the canal would be right at the foot of the high ground which overlooked the marsh and rose immediately in its rear. A fortification so designed and placed, wrote Brown, might be deemed impregnable; and Dundas added, 'Did such an obstacle

[48] Brownrigg to Sullivan, 14 March 1804 (WO/1/629).

present itself, the attempt on Romney Marsh would probably not enter into an Enemy's contemplation'.

This was the first proposal of the Royal Military Canal; and it has been seen that, while Dundas was still thinking of a 'partial inundation', Brown regarded any inundation as a 'doubtful' measure. Brown must already have looked closely into water levels, or he could not have been so positive that a cut nine feet deep would ensure seven to eight feet of water; and he continued his studies after the proposal for the canal was mailed. When he had finished them, no room for doubt remained. 'The highest spring Tides in the mouth of Rye old harbour rise 17 or 18 Feet,' he discovered, 'the Neap Tides not more than 11 or 12 feet'. On the west, but not the east, side of Romney Marsh the sluices could admit enough water to 'form on this side (at Spring Tides only) a sufficient Barrier'. The Neap Tides on the other hand 'would produce no other effect than that of filling a few Ditches'. As for the Pett Level, it had no sluice capable of admitting enough water, so it had been intended to cut the dykes; but, commented Brown, 'The Tide once admitted in this manner will infallibly enlarge and deepen these Cuts' and 'as much or more Water will run off during the Ebb as went on in the Flood'.[49] In short, his investigations showed that it was useless to flood Romney Marsh and that the canal was needed behind the Pett Level too. Brown described these findings in a letter he sent directly to the Duke of York on 3 October.

That letter should have settled the question if it still needed settling; but in fact, when Brown wrote it, the main decision was already taken. On 26 September the Duke had written to Dundas, 'The great work proposed of cutting a canal betwixt the Rother and the Beach in Hythe Bay . . . is approved by His Majesty's Government'. In short, within the space of eight days the Duke had both made up his own mind and persuaded Pitt to sanction a proposal for whose cost Dundas had been able to give only the roughest of estimates. 'I am now,' continued the Duke, 'to sanction its being immediately undertaken under your authority' – so the Ordnance department would have no chance to delay this job. The measurements were to be those Brown proposed. The military road would, 'of course, only commence from beyond Hythe, where the present Great Road along the Coast goes in Front of its Line'. Then the Duke added a new note: 'the General Direction of this Work should be given (under your Authority) to Mr Rennie, the Civil Engineer'[50] – the same who had planned the inundation of the Lea valley.

These decisions being made, work was promptly begun and, at Pitt's insistence, under contract. The contractor, however, went bankrupt within a year, and then the work was carried on under John Brown's

[49] Brown to the Duke of York, 3 October 1804 (WO/30/78).
[50] York to Dundas, 26 September 1804 (WO/1/629).

direction. In August 1806, the stretch between Hythe and Rye was formally opened by the Duke of York. The new waterway, nineteen miles long and backed by the rampart sheltering the military road, turned Romney Marsh into an island detached from the rest of England, and so made some thirty miles of excellent landing beaches useless to the enemy. By August 1807 the last stretch, running from the river Brede to the coast at Cliffend, was nearly finished too as a second line of defence behind the towers which then covered the beach.[51]

Here we may leave the subject of fortifications. Some more work was still to be done. Thus the east coast beaches from Aldeburgh southwards to St Osyth were to be defended by 29 Martello towers of a later and improved model.[52] Some ports were further strengthened, like Plymouth where by June 1804, the Ordnance were nearly ready with a plan for permanent fortifications to replace the field works Simcoe had raised the previous summer.[53] On the Isle of Wight more regular works did much for the safety of this island which in 1779 the French hoped to seize as an advanced base; new fortifications at Milford Haven were to help secure England's communications with Ireland. Such works as these were to increase the nation's strength in the later stages of the war. The importance of the particular works described above (excepting Simcoe's redoubts at Plymouth, which illustrate the conflict between the Ordnance and the army) is that they were designed to meet the special threat of the famous Boulogne flotilla. The field works at Dover, Chatham, Shooter's Hill and about London, and the early coast batteries, were the only defences the enemy would have had to master if he had landed in 1804-5; and we have seen that he might have

[51] For a fuller account of this subject, see R. Glover, 'The Royal Military Canal', *The Army Quarterly*, October 1953, 97-107, with a map.

[52] The circular platforms on the top of those South coast towers which I have seen have one heavy iron post at the centre and within the parapet a step on which is placed a rail. It appears, then, that the traversing gear on which the guns in these towers were mounted was a bar, or spoke, which rested at the centre on the post and at the circumference on a wheel designed to run on the rail; and that the guns were traversed all together by rotating the whole bar which supported them. In the rather larger towers of the East coast the gun platform is divided into three circular bays, like a clover leaf. Each bay has its own centre post, and its own step and rail at the circumference. Thus the eastern towers could carry the full three guns intended for the round towers in the South; moreover, each of these guns could be traversed and aimed independently. The greater size of the East coast towers also enabled them to accommodate their garrisons better.

[53] This was, of course, work for the Ordnance Department; on which the Duke wrote, with relief, to Lord Camden on 4 June 1804, 'I am happy to learn from your Lordship that a Plan is nearly decided for finishing the Works at Plymouth'. One notes here that York had not heard about this plan from the Ordnance Department, which was responsible for it – more evidence of inter-departmental friction; also that even at this date the Ordnance was not ready to start work, a strong justification of the Duke's action in getting Simcoe's Field Works built the previous summer.

overcome them. But by 1807, when the treaty of Tilsit had ended the fighting on the continent, and England was once again France's only enemy, her new fortifications, the Royal Military Canal and the chains of Martello towers, had transformed the nature of the war. Between them they made it pointless to attempt an invasion across any beach within the range of the Boulogne flotilla – a fact which perhaps needs the more emphasis because of today's widely held belief that Trafalgar had made 'any revival of [Bonaparte's invasion] threat impossible'. But that greatest of contemporary naval strategists, Lord Barham, has left us his clear verdict that Trafalgar did nothing of the kind. Instead within four month's of Nelson's splendid victory there he was expressing his fear that Bonaparte's recent defeat of Austria would bring 'an immediate renewal of his design to invade this country'.[54] At the date when he wrote these words, on 11 January 1806, the new towers and canal were probably doing more to increase than to reduce England's danger. For they were still unfinished, and therefore could add nothing as yet to the strength of her coast defences; but they were started, and so served notice on Bonaparte that the time in which he could hope to use his flotilla was limited. That time ran out in the autumn of 1806, when the Duke of York opened the principal part of the Royal Military Canal in August and in October reported the towers ready for service.

This month of October 1806, is famous for the campaign of Jena and the great advantages Bonaparte gained from his overthrow of Prussia. But it also deserves to be remembered as the month in which he lost the advantages for which he had worked so long and hard in making new Channel ports and building the flotilla to threaten Britain. From now on he could no longer expect to crush the English with any such temporary command of the Channel as he had hoped Villeneuve and Ganteaume would gain in 1805. Henceforth the only strategy left him, apart from harassing British trade, was that long-drawn, and never completed, drive to create a fleet capable of thrashing the Royal Navy on the high seas. Simultaneously her new coast defences, which made her so much safer at home, made it all the easier for Britain to spare troops to give Bonaparte trouble elsewhere, in Sicily where they doubled the garrison which denied him this island; in the Ionian islands, most of which they reconquered from him; and above all in Spain, which a British expeditionary force under Wellington's command was to make the graveyard of so many of Bonaparte's hopes. Take these points all together and, despite the glamour of Jena and the capture of Berlin, October 1806 was perhaps a month in which Bonaparte's losses outweighed his gains.

One of the most interesting, and by some perhaps least expected, features of the story is the ability and energy displayed by the Duke of

[54] *Barham Papers*, III, 108.

York. He knew how to delegate responsibility. His method was first to appoint able subordinates, like Craig and Dundas, then to call on them for recommendations and to support them to the hilt. His principle, as declared in his decision on the Field Works at Plymouth, was sound; the officer 'with whom responsibility rests ought not to be denied the resources which in his judgment are most applicable to the defence'.[55] But he was far from being the puppet of his own subordinates. When confronted with alternatives he was quick to come to his own decisions – for example, in the case of the river Lea. Where problems were hard to resolve, he stepped in to take the responsibility himself, as in the Eastern District, where he would make no final decision between Colchester and Grinstead without 'an opportunity of examining the ground in person';[56] and then he came up with a solution, the entrenched camp at Dunmow, which was not one of the original alternatives. Yet he still was careful to consider the feelings of the man on the spot, writing to Craig that he expected 'to be aided by your presence and advice'.[57] His energy and drive are as conspicuous as his ability both to respect his subordinates and to make his own decisions. We have seen how soon after receiving Rennie's report on the Lea he made his decision on the alternatives it proposed; and before that he had already won Addington's approval of whatever cost might be involved. Likewise within a week of receiving Dundas's and Brown's proposal of the Royal Military Canal, he had both made up his own mind and gained Pitt's approval for that job too. The work, as he wrote Dundas, was to be '*immediately*' undertaken under your authority'[58] and the word 'immediate' is one of the commonest in the Duke's vocabulary at this period. His language is consistently that of a man who knows the value of time – a very important soldierly quality.

All through one must remember both the sluggish obstructionism of the Ordnance department and the prejudice of the English people against spending money on fortifications. It is clear from what he wrote to Hobart on 25 August 1803, that the Duke was embarrassed by reports that he was recommending 'a *System of Permanent Works for the Defence of Great Britain*'.[59] Yet thanks to his drive and persuasiveness a very useful number of permanent works were built. So, to sum up, no small part of the reason why the Duke and Bonaparte never met in battle on English soil lies in the energy which the Duke devoted to making the much vaunted assault from Boulogne too risky to be attempted. It seems fair to say that a man who could do this should rank among the great Corsican's more effective opponents.

[55] York to Hobart, 25 August 1803 (WO/30/76).
[56] York to Craig, 19 August 1803 (WO/30/76).
[57] Ibid.
[58] York to Dundas, 26 September 1804 (WO/1/629). My italics.
[59] WO/30/76.

6

Raising Men for Defence and Counter-Attack, 1803-1814

Sir John Fisher, the famous First Sea Lord of the Admiralty in the early years of the century, liked to describe the army as 'a projectile fired by the Navy'. If he meant that the best contribution the Navy could make to winning a war, as distinct from merely not losing it, was to land the army where it could defeat the enemy, he was right. For the Regular Army was the nation's sole offensive striking force; and that remark is not in the least derogatory toward the Navy. The importance of the Royal Navy in our period is beyond challenge. One decisive defeat at sea would have been the end of an independent Britain. But still the Navy was essentially a defensive force. It could, and did, prevent French armies from landing in England. It could, and did, cut off French foreign trade, and force French women to do without silks and set French chemists to work discovering how to make sugar out of beets instead of West Indian sugar cane; but it could not overthrow Bonaparte's empire. It also could, and did, convoy British troops to various theatres of war; but the task of counter-attack – in the colonies, in Italy, the Baltic, Spain and the Netherlands – required soldiers. The British army was, of course, never large enough to master the French singlehanded. But when used on sound strategical principles and well led in the field it contributed much to the eventual success of the allies on land. Its reputation also contributed much to the success or failure of British diplomacy.

This chapter, then, must deal with the raising of men for foreign service as well as for home defence. About 50,000 men of Addington's peace-time army of 130,000 were already overseas, serving as garrisons in India and the colonies, when the new war began on 18 May 1803. Then some of them were very soon in action in the West Indies where General Grinfield (who was forewarned to be ready) quickly captured the enemy colonies of St Lucia, Tobago, Demerara and Essequibo, as the first steps in conquering France's Caribbean empire. In the same year, and on the other side of the world, more British regulars were to march with Arthur Wellesley and Colonel Stevenson against the Mahrattas and share with the East India Company's army the victories of Assaye and Argaum. In 1805 Pitt sent the first small British expeditionary force to the Mediterranean, under the same General Sir James Craig whom we met above as the district commander in East Anglia in the earlier months of the war. These were some of the men with whom Sir John Stuart was to rout the French at Maida on 3 July 1806. They were the advanced guard of the considerable forces employed in succeeding years to garrison Sicily, to seize Alexandria in 1806, to capture most of the Ionian islands, to launch a diversion in eastern Spain in 1812 and liberate much of Italy in 1813 and 1814. More troops had to be found to reconquer the Cape of Good Hope in 1806, the islands of Bourbon (or Réunion) and Mauritius in 1810 and Java in 1811. Others were to take part in the abortive attacks on Buenos Aires in 1806 and 1807, and to help defend Canada in 1812–14. In Europe itself 26,000 troops took part in the attack on Copenhagen in 1807 and nearly 40,000 in the Scheldt expedition of 1809. In short, the great effort of the Peninsular War from 1808 on was by no means the only, although it was the biggest, land operation carried out by Britain in the years 1803–14.

All these operations must be mentioned here, for the great difficulty with so vast a world-wide struggle as the Napoleonic war is always to see the thing as a whole. Yet that is the way contemporaries had to see it. Responsible ministers in London had constantly to be balancing the merits of one theatre of war against another; and if some operations they undertook look in retrospect like petty sideshows, many of them still contributed to the security Britain finally won at the great peace treaty of Vienna. For, after the reborn reputation of the British army and the personal prestige of Wellington as the one allied commander whom the French had never beaten, Castlereagh's chief bargaining strength at that conference lay in Britain's possession of the former colonies of her enemies, Dutch as well as French.

Of what we have called Britain's 'four separate and ill-coordinated armies' only two, the Ordnance Corps and the Regular Army, could be used for foreign service. But that does not mean that the Militia and the Volunteers were useless. Not the least of the great principles of war is 'Security', in this case the security of the home islands of the British people. If Bonaparte had ever successfully invaded England, all the oversea efforts of the British army in 1803–14 would have been as futile as Wolfe's death at Quebec would have been if, at the hour when he engaged Montcalm, French troops were occupying London as a result of Louis XV's success in the attack which he, too, had planned to launch against Britain. In each case the Navy was the essential first line of defence – indeed, in 1759 it was virtually the only line of defence. In the later war the Militia and the Volunteers had this value, that by supplementing the garrison for home defence they released Regulars for foreign service. The recruiting of all Britain's land forces must therefore be discussed in this chapter. The Militia may be dealt with first, for on them there is least to be said. Next may come the Regulars, both Army and Ordnance Corps; and, third, the Volunteers.

When the war began, Addington was far more ready to meet than was Bonaparte to launch an invasion. 81,000 regulars were at home to garrison Britain; and 50,000 men of the Old Militia had been called out and their battalions were forming under officers of whom the majority cannot have been novices at soldiering.[1] But it was certain that Bonaparte would spare no pains to increase his means to attack England. Therefore Britain had to increase her own strength and the first step was to call out the 25,000 of the Supplementary Militia.

In Ireland, which had its own laws, the Militia was a force of men who voluntarily enlisted for home defence. England and Scotland in 1803 used conscription to fill their Militia. Its members were selected by ballot out of lists of all men of military age in every shire and the officials responsible for the balloting were the Lords Lieutenant of the counties. No man who was ballotted was compelled to serve in person if he could induce a 'substitute' to serve for him. The most persuasive inducements with substitutes was money, and the safest way of securing that money would be on hand in time was to insure oneself against being ballotted. So war brought insurance clubs and great, if briefly enjoyed, wealth was often the reward of the substitute who was willing to take somebody else's place in the Militia.[2]

As was well known at the time, the men who voluntarily joined the Militia in this way were the very ones who would have been readiest to enlist in the Army. For that reason the raising of this conscript force always checked the recruiting of the Regulars; and Sir John Fortescue has accordingly denounced the system of allowing substitutes to serve in the Militia as one of the outstanding abuses of the period. That it hindered efforts to develop the nation's full offensive strength must be acknowledged, but whether it was really avoidable is another question. Politics is the art of the possible; and the fact that no government attempted to raise the Militia without allowing substitutes sheds an interesting light on the real freedom of the English people under even the old and unreformed Parliament. Though no figures are available, it is very likely that in 1803 the system had the merit of bringing back many old hands into the Militia, men who had been disbanded in 1802 and for

[1] See above, pp. 43-4.
[2] E.g., in 1803, Sergeant Butler got 'no less than £20 for entering the Militia as a substitute for a Mr G.'. (T. H. McGuffie, 'Bounty Payments in the Napoleonic Period', *Army Quarterly* (1946), 276).

a price were ready to serve again. Further, the man who joined the Militia as a substitute was not necessarily lost to the Regulars. In 1799, when Pitt needed troops for the Alkmaar campaign, a special act was passed to permit militiamen to volunteer for the regulars. This particular act (unlike an ill-fated predecessor) was such a great success that it was to be imitated on other occasions. It would, of course, never have been necessary if normal recruiting methods had produced enough men; and similar acts in later years were also passed to supplement the regular recruiting service as carried on under the Commander-in-Chief's direction. This must be examined before we pass to other methods.

The Duke of York took over the command of the army in 1795 determined, as he often said, 'that no officer, upon whom the duty of leading troops to the field may devolve, should ever be subject to the same disadvantages under which he had laboured';[3] for during the Netherlands campaigns of 1793-4 he had suffered much from the way his army was recruited in Britain. This service, too, had decayed during Pitt's ten years of peace, and it had provided the Duke with wretchedly inadequate reinforcements in the Netherlands campaigns. As early as April 1793, one of his brigades was found to be encumbered with 'recruits ... totally unfit for service, being mostly either old men or quite boys, extremely weak and short'.[4] Even some of his better regiments 'had been completed by independent companies, hastily raised for rank, and were wretchedly deficient in appearance, efficiency, discipline and equipment'.[5] Again in the spring of 1794, a witness writes, 'the recruits for General Abercromby's brigade arrived a few days ago; they much resembled Falstaff's men and were as lightly clad as any Carmagnole battalion'.[6] When the Duke returned to Britain he found himself compelled to break up whole new battalions which had been 'raised for rank'. Though, as will be seen, this system of recruiting could be useful when well handled, in 1793-4 it produced 'crude and hasty levies' in which 'very few ... officers have served before and none of the men have ever had a Firelock on their shoulders'; in some cases the men carried their contempt for their officers to 'an open, bare-faced state of mutiny'.[7] Such battalions could only be reduced, their men being dispersed to units capable of training and disciplining them, while their officers, one fears, were legally entitled to go on half-pay at the taxpayers' expense for the rest of their lives.

[3] Anon., 'Review of the Military Establishments of Great Britain and the Services of the late Duke of York', *United Service Journal* (1834), 436.
[4] Harry Verney, *Journals and Correspondence of Sir Harry Calvert* (London, 1853), 53.
[5] Anon. 'Review of the Military Establishments ...; *United Service Journal* (1834), 435.
[6] Verney, *Journals of Sir Harry Calvert*, 187.
[7] Fawcett to Hewett, April 1795 (WO/30/13).

After this, 'recruiting for rank' fell into abeyance for several years and the Duke took steps to bring regularity and order into the army's more usual method of raising men. He revived the post of Inspector General of Recruiting and appointed to it General Henry Fox, the brother of the famous politician. Fox was soon succeeded by General Hewett who held the post until 1804 when he was succeeded by General John Whitelocke. In 1807 the post was again abolished, but its duties continued to be performed under the Adjutant General.[8]

The Duke also divided England into fifteen recruiting districts, Scotland into four, and at about the same date Ireland was divided into five. Each was given a staff consisting of 'an Inspecting Field Officer, an adjutant, a sergeant major and requisite number of depot sergeants'.[9] This organisation provided two things, a headquarters in each district to supervise the recruiting parties detached from regiments to raise men, and a body of instructors to start the men's training. In 1796 a third was added, a hospital mate to inspect the men;[10] and from then on there was some assurance that recruits with the physique of Falstaff's men would be accepted no longer. In 1802 District Surgeons, in place of mere hospital mates, were appointed to carry out the physical examinations.[11] After passing his physical examination one step more was required before the recruit became a soldier; he had to be attested before a magistrate who was expected to make sure that the recruit knew what he was doing and was sober enough to understand the meaning of the soldier's oath.

Within this organisation regiments of the Army did their own recruiting, detaching for the purpose small parties of an officer, a sergeant, a few reliable men and a drummer; and the Ordnance Corps used the same method. These parties had no easy job to get good men, for service in the army was emphatically unpopular, and with reason. Up to 1806 enlistments were for life, with garrison duty in an Invalid Battalion to occupy a man's declining years, if he lived so long. But too many soldiers did not live long and the enemy's bullets were far from being the worst danger they faced. The great dread of the day was service in the West Indies where yellow fever and malaria exacted an appalling toll. The soldier's pay was miserable – 1s. a day. 'On the Continent', wrote the Duke of York to William Windham on 18 March 1806, 'where there is comparatively speaking little or no trade or manufactures and consequently little means for the Employment of the Population otherwise than in agriculture, the Pay and advantages of a soldier are equal if not superior to that of the Handicraftsman and

[8] General Order, 1 June 1807 (War Office Library).
[9] H. Marshall, *Military Miscellany* (London, 1846), 72.
[10] Ibid., 61.
[11] Ibid., 63.

therefore is a sufficient inducement for a man to enlist. . . . But in this Country where all Labor is so exceedingly high and where such inducements are held out to the lower Class of the People either to engage in manufactures or to be employed at Sea' (Doc. 30) the soldier's wage of 7s. a week meant a lifetime of abject poverty. By comparison civilian artisans were earning 18s. a week in 1800 and 28s. a week in 1806;[12] and the soldier's daily shilling was by no means all his own. Out of it he was required to buy his food and replace any article of equipment or clothing that he lost before it was due to be replaced. He was also expected to forego any family life. 'Marriage', runs one of the standard manuals, 'must be discouraged as much as possible. Officers must explain to the men the many miseries that women are exposed to and by every sort of persuasion they must prevent their marrying if possible';[13] and 'miseries' was the right word. No decent married quarters were provided; and the rule was that when regiments went overseas 'Women only in the proportion of Six to every Hundred Men will be permitted to embark. They should be carefully selected, as being of good Character and having the inclination and ability to render themselves useful; it is very desirable that those who have children should be left at home'.[14] And, one asks, left at home to live – how? Parliament granted no marriage allowance to the soldier's wife, though one was paid to the wives of conscripts in the Militia.

Parents in decent working class families understandably deplored their sons entering such a calling as this. 'Alas', said the mother of one recruit, 'now you have finished it. Now you are lost to us and to yourself'.[15] Another, who claims to have 'spent a dissolute youth' even before he enlisted as a seventeen-year-old, believed that 'no parents ever felt more deeply the combined emotions of tender regret at my leaving them so young . . . and at the disgrace which my wayward conduct had, as they imagined, brought upon myself'.[16] When Rifleman Harris was ballotted as a soldier in the Army of Reserve, his father, though only a shepherd on a Dorset farm, 'tried hard to buy me off',[17] but, only too naturally, could not manage it; it would have cost him £20; and one doubts if a shepherd could have earned much more than that in half a year.

[12] These figures are from Marshall, *Military Miscellany*, 68.
[13] *Rules and Regulations for the Cavalry* (1795), 74.
[14] General Order for Troops destined for Continental Service, 15 April 1807 (War Office Library).
[15] *Recollections of an Eventful Life chiefly passed in the Army*, by a Soldier (Glasgow, 1825), 66.
[16] William Surtees, *Twenty Five Years in the Rifle Brigade* (Edinburgh, 1833), 2.
[17] *Recollections of Rifleman Harris*, ed. by Henry Curling (London, 1928), 00. The Army of Reserve, like the Militia, was a conscript force. It was raised in 1804 and is discussed below.

Clearly, then, decent young men of the lower classes had very good reasons for staying out of the army; and the point should be borne in mind by those self-appointed judges who are more eager to condemn the Duke of Wellington for his blunt remarks on soldiers than to check their facts. When the Duke roundly declared that British soldiers were 'the scum of the earth, the mere scum of the earth . . . fellows who have all enlisted for drink' or 'from having got bastard children [and] some for minor offences',[18] he was describing men who had chosen a profession that decent working class people of the day abhorred as a 'disgrace'; and other witnesses support him with very similar language. Thus 'A Practical Recruiter', writing in 1837 when the Duke's verdict had still to be published, warns that those most ready to take the sergeant's shilling were often 'the very worst characters, deserters from other corps, or men who have deemed it prudent to leave home [after committing] . . . some serious offence. A third class is composed of the sturdiest of our yeomen who, having increased the population of their parish without permission of the clergy, are glad to escape the consequences by sheltering themselves under the licence of the camp' (Doc. 29a). And on occasion, when 'proof . . . of Guilt' was 'not sufficiently evident' to guarantee a conviction, one even finds cases of criminals who had already been arrested being excused trial on the condition that they volunteered to enlist 'in His Majesty's Regiment abroad'.[19]

This last quoted case concerns Ireland where juries had a reputation for looking at certain offences with a lenient eye. But Ireland probably provided the British army with its best men. There, as on the Continent, there was 'comparatively speaking little means for the Employment of the Population otherwise than in agriculture'; and Ireland's tragic poverty made the soldier's shilling look an attractive wage even for a decent man. In this period, too, the government ceased to require 'recruits . . . to swear that they were Protestants'.[20] With their ranks thus opened to Roman Catholics, English regiments, even before the Union, began to find Ireland their best recruiting ground, with results that were embarrassing during the troubles of 1797-8. On 22 April 1797 the Duke of York is found writing that 'as almost the whole of the Recruits of the Infantry of the Line are Irish, it would be by no Means a politick measure to send any of the regular Battalions to Ireland';[21] and that is why the rising was suppressed by Fencible regiments and by English Militia battalions which had to be asked to volunteer for service outside the country before they could be sent across St George's Channel.

But even when it had gathered in all the drunkards, all the fugitives

[18] Stanhope, *Conversations with the Duke of Wellington*, 13-14, 18.
[19] Duke of York to Charles Yorke, 14 March 1804 (HO/50/397).
[20] Marshall, *Military Miscellany*, 61.
[21] Duke of York to George III, 22 April 1797. (Windsor Archives 8409.)

from justice, all the unwed fathers, and all the Irishmen whom it could collect, the army still did not get enough men. In a passage that is most revealing, especially for the light it sheds on the price the nation paid for its West Indian colonies, the Duke informed Windham on 18 March 1806 that 'the continual drain which is occasioned by the common casualties of the Army, particularly in our Colonial Possessions, causes such an Annual Deficiency as has, as yet at least, never been supplied by ordinary recruiting' (Doc. 30). And here the phrase 'common casualties' excludes losses in battle (for which indeed there had been little opportunity since the end of the Egyptian campaign in 1801).

When ordinary recruiting failed so badly, it was necessary to try extraordinary methods; and 'The only Plan . . .,' wrote the Duke, 'which has certainly to a degree succeeded has been to permit Officers, under certain restrictions, to raise Men for Rank, allowing them to receive the usual Bounty'. On the continent, he explained, 'Armies are formed by giving a Property to the Captains in their respective Troops or Companies and obliging them under pecuniary Risk to keep them constantly complete'; and that system made it 'both an Object and Credit to them to use every exertion upon the Recruiting Service'. But in Britain 'where no temptation whatsoever is offered to the Officer to exert himself on the recruiting service, but on the contrary he finds himself exposed to great pecuniary risk and responsibility, that branch of the Service must be materially impeded' (Doc. 30). In days when commissions were purchased, however, a step in rank was the equivalent of a lot of money; so in 1801 the Duke had returned to what he called raising men for rank 'under certain restrictions'. The restrictions were, first, that this time, unlike 1793–4, no complete new battalions should be raised; instead 'two Companies of one Hundred Rank and File' were to be added to existing infantry regiments; and, second, the persons who sought rank by recruiting would not be the uninstructed civilians thanks to whom so 'very few officers' in the new levies of 1793–4 had 'served before'. They were to be officers who were already qualified for promotion by purchase, namely 'the Captain-Lieutenant, the two Senior Lieutenants and four Senior Ensigns'. If any one of these declined the opportunity or failed to 'acquit himself to the utmost of his ability' he was to be replaced by 'some Officer of more Zeal for the Service, either . . . the next in Seniority from his own Regiment or . . . an Officer from another Corps as His Royal Highness may think proper'; no 'Subaltern who has not been an Officer Two Years' would be allowed to get his captaincy in this way; and, finally, a time limit was clamped down by which each officer seeking new rank had to get his men within three months.[22]

[22] 'Circular to Regiments of Infantry at Home, Colonels commanding Regiments, Army Agents and the Inspector General of Recruiting, 13 February, 1801.' (General Orders and Circular Letters, 1801–1806; War Office Library.)

This experiment was enough of a success for the Duke to attempt to repeat it in the summer of 1803 when officers in similar positions in 41 regiments of horse and foot were offered promotion for raising men, ten each for a cornet or ensign to become a lieutenant or thirty for a lieutenant to become a captain. This scheme was not a success. At about the same time balloting began for Addington's new conscript Army of Reserve; like the raising of the Militia this caused a rush for substitutes and in the face of that competition it was feared that the officers would be unable to get their men. In the circumstances, however, it was judged fair to award them their promotions; and the Duke still thought well enough of the plan to let four Irishmen, each aided by officers ready for promotion, to try to raise whole new battalions in 1804. Three of these battalions were accepted, and their officers confirmed in their new rank by February 1805; but one was not. Its aspiring colonel, the Honourable Mr Browne, was found to have made 'Stipulations . . . with several of his officers for pecuniary considerations . . . in direct violation of his Instructions in the 5th Article of his Letter of Service',[23] and all the men raised by the not-so-honourable Mr Browne were drafted to other battalions. After these one more battalion was raised in Ireland by 'recruiting for rank'; and that was the end of the system which had 'to a degree succeeded'.

There was one other idea which the Duke suggested to William Windham as early as 1806, namely 'engaging the permanent Non-Commissioned Officers in the Volunteers' for the recruiting service (Doc. 30). Windham did not adopt it; but this suggestion may well have influenced Castlereagh's remodelling in 1809 of the Local Militia he had created in the previous year. As such, it makes a natural transition to special government measures for increasing the Regular Army.

The first of these was Henry Addington's Army of Reserve Act, which has already been mentioned. If, in preparing this measure, Addington relied much on Lord Hobart, his Secretary of State for War, he was wise; for Hobart was a professional soldier who had seen active service in the American War of Independence and had also been Inspector General of Recruiting in Ireland in 1788–9. Between them they produced a plan which in 1807 Henry Dundas (then Lord Melville) urged Castlereagh to revive.

Addington had observed that Pitt's act of 1799 permitting Militiamen to volunteer for the Regular Army had been, up to a point, a great success. Large numbers of men had come forward and there had been much enthusiasm. The enthusiasm, however, was not unconnected with the 'bounty'. This was a lump sum of money expended in various ways when a recruit was attested. Some of it was used to buy the new equipment the man needed; some was used to reward the party that

[23] Gordon to King, 28 February 1805 (HO/50/400).

recruited him; and some went to the recruit himself, though recruiting sergeants showed great ingenuity in diverting as much as possible of this to their own pockets. The militiamen of 1799, who were already equipped and were not gathered straight from civilian life by recruiting parties, will have received an unusually large proportion of the bounty; and in that debauched old Georgian England too many men knew exactly what they wanted money for – drink. Then, and on subsequent occasions when this method of reinforcing the regulars was used, the Militia regiments involved lapsed into a state of Bacchanalian disorder which, in Castlereagh's words, 'revolted the feelings of Militia officers'.[24] Yet in 1799 the plan had produced the men the nation needed for foreign service, and the ballot had refilled the depleted Militia regiments. So Addington went about conscripting a new force which, like the Militia, would be required for home defence only and, also like the Militia, would be raised by ballot from the lists of men of military age in every county, with substitutes permitted. From this home defence force men would be allowed at any time to volunteer for 'general service', but no Militia officers would have their feelings revolted, because the new force would be part of the Regular Army from the start. It was to be called the Army of Reserve, and the act creating it required 50,000 men to be raised.

The results achieved were no doubt somewhat disappointing and were summarised by Fortescue as follows: 'By May, 1804, when the Act was acknowledged to be dead', he writes, it 'had produced a nominal total of 45,492 men, of whom 2,116 had been discharged as unfit or for other causes, 589 had died and 5,561, nearly one ninth, had deserted or been claimed as deserters by other corps, leaving 37,136 as nominally effective. Of these, however, 7,000 were young and undersized and had to be drafted to garrison battalions until they could grow up. Thus while paying for 45,000 men the country gained the immediate services of little more than 30,000';[25] and Forescue regarded this result as an 'utter failure'.[26]

That is hardly a fair judgement. First, the large number of 5,561 conscripts or substitutes who deserted was unfortunately not abnormal. Some recruits were quick to regret their bargain with the state; and on his very next page Fortescue records that of 3,481 men raised by

[24] Londonderry, *Castlereagh's Correspondence*, VIII, 56. On the other side Rifleman Harris reports his service with a party recruiting Militia volunteers: 'We worked hard . . . I may say that for three days and nights we kept up the dance and drunken riot. Every volunteer got ten guineas bounty, which, except the two kept back for necessaries, they spent in every sort of excess, till all was gone' (*Recollections of Rifleman Harris*, edited by C. Hibbert (London, 1970), 110).

[25] *County Lieutenancies and the Army*, 73.

[26] So his table of contents refers to the above quoted passage.

ordinary recruiting in the last half of 1803 no fewer than 291 deserted, a very similar proportion. Yet none of those 3,481 men were conscripts, dragged into the army against their will; all had been attested before civil magistrates as genuine volunteers. Then, too, this age knew that unattractive character, the professional 'bounty-jumper', who enlisted only to receive his bounty and then steal off (Doc. 29b). Moreover, May 1804, the month in which Fortescue says 'the Act was acknowledged to be dead', was also the month in which the government that passed the act fell and was succeeded by a government which had no intention of enforcing it. For Addington resigned on 9 May, to be succeeded by Pitt; and the Lords Lieutenants of the counties were never called upon to make good the deficiencies in the Army of Reserve by enforcing the ballot again, to secure the 4,500 men who had never been raised or replace the deserters, the dead and the 9,000 and more undersized children or unfit men whom they had accepted the first time. Yet upwards of 30,000 men were gained for national defence, and one of Pitt's own colleagues, Henry Dundas, was later to write; 'I never could figure a reason why the Army of Reserve was laid aside, unless because it was necessary to run down the administration which introduced it'.[27] Within not too long at time, no fewer than 19,533 of the 30,000 effective men the act produced had volunteered for general service; and, though fear of competition caused by the act had led the Duke of York to cancel his plan to have officers raise men for rank, it in fact did far less damage to normal recruiting than had been expected. As Henry Addington's brother Hiley was later to show, the raising of the Army of Reserve did not diminish the number of men gained by regular recruiting by 'more than one fourteenth, as was demonstrated by documents laid on the table' in the House of Commons;[28] and, though the act assigned all the men of the reserve to the Army, the Duke evidently allowed a number to join the Ordnance Corps (Doc. 25).

The Army of Reserve also enabled the Duke of York to make another reform. This was providing a number of regiments with second battalions, in a manner that can best be described as instituting the famous 'Cardwell System' of the future a number of years before ever Edward Cardwell (1813–86) was born. These second battalions had four purposes; to provide recruiting parties to raise men for both battalions; to receive and train all recruits; to provide drafts of fit and properly trained men to keep their first battalions at full strength for service at all times; and to be themselves as ready for service and 'as efficient as Circumstances will permit'.[29] In short, as the Duke informed

[27] Londonderry, *Castlereagh's Correspondence*, VIII, 55.
[28] *Parliamentary Debates*, 27 July 1807, 952.
[29] General Order, 18 November 1807; and Circular to General Officers commanding Districts, 3 December 1807 (War Office Library).

Windham, each regiment's second battalion was 'a nursery for the first, a system which has been so far crowned with success, as may be seen not only by the actual strength of the first Battalions of those Corps, but by the number of men in the second Battalions who are already enlisted for General Service and who from the complete state of their first Battalions are not yet able to join them' (Doc. 30). All told, then, Addington's Army of Reserve seems the best recruiting measure that any British government had yet devised.

But Pitt could not carry on his predecessor's system for he had come to power with a promise to surpass Addington's best efforts to strengthen the country. In some ways he fulfilled his promise. We have seen how much more boldly than Addington he supported the Duke of York's plans for fortifying the coasts; likewise how his government improved the dockyards' supplies of ships timber (though at the cost of surrendering to the timber merchants' price ring); and he was greatly to increase the number of gunboats for inshore defence. But in strengthening the Regular Army he fell far behind Addington.

The new recruiting measure he adopted was called the Permanent Additional Force Act. It was passed on 25 June 1804, and repealed on 26 May 1806. Oddly, the best comment on its failure perhaps comes from William Windham, who was to replace it in 1806 with a vastly worse plan. In a conversation recorded by Francis Horner, in August 1805, Windham said that 'in preparing his measures [Pitt] thinks more of the House of Commons than of their operation; [he is] satisfied if they will look well in statement – like those improvers of ground, who will build a house that shall look most picturesque to spectators on the outside, though within it be incommodious. Mr Windham instanced the Parish Recruit Bill [i.e. the previous summer's Permanent Additional Force Act] and said this was the most satisfactory solution he had been able to give of Pitt's failure in this and many other plans, when Mr Fox had observed to him that surely these were occasions on which it was Pitt's interest to summon all his talents. Speaking of his going through military details – military cars, rockets, catamarans, etc. – Windham observed that Pitt's judgement on such matters was generally bad, though he had a great talent in stating them'.[30]

Here Windham put his finger on a pitfall into which parliamentary legislators constantly tumble. They know their measures will be defeated unless they can get votes to pass them; hence they think too much of getting the votes and too little of how their plans will work after the votes have been cast; and no one is a more dangerously persuasive advocate of bad measures than such a supreme orator as Pitt.

Features of the Army of Reserve Act which, with some reason, were

[30] *Memoirs and Correspondence of Francis Horner, M.P.* Edited by his brother, Leonard Horner (Boston, 1853), I, 340.

thought bad were two borrowed from the Militia, namely, first, using the ballot to compel a man to serve and then excusing him from that duty if he could induce somebody else to serve for him. Together, as we have seen, these led to insurance clubs being formed to provide money for bribing substitutes to relieve the unwilling conscript of his duties; the money from insurance policies and other sources skimmed off for home defence the men most willing to enlist; and the two-fold result was both to hinder regular recruiting and compel the army to offer larger and larger bounties in an attempt to keep pace with the competition. To sidestep these admitted evils Pitt's new measure required each parish – somehow – to contribute a number of men to make up a quota required of the whole county. The men need not come from the particular parish concerned; the parish officers could accept men who came from places as far as twenty miles off in same county or ten miles off in a neighbouring county, but no further. They were to be paid one guinea for each man of their quota whom they produced and fined £20 for each man by whom they fell short of their appointed quotas. The men when raised – or if raised – were to go to the Army of Reserve, with which the act also amalgamated Addington's Supplementary Militia. Like the men of the Army of Reserve they were required for home service either for five years or until six months after the end of the war; they were to join the new second battalions the Duke of York had created and to be encouraged to volunteer for general service.

The act had two good features. It simplified the nation's military organisation by uniting the Supplementary Militia with the Regular Army; and it supported the Duke of York's system of giving regiments second battalions as 'nurseries' for their first battalions. But its great object was to raise men and here it miserably failed. It gave the wretched parish officers no means of compulsion and they had no idea of how to raise men without it. In May 1806, when the act was on the point of being repealed, one M.P. stated that 'In England there were no less than 14 counties in which not a man had been raised by the parish officers'; and he added that 'he thought it a great objection to the bill that, in the course of 18 months, it could not be understood by those whose duty it was to execute it'.[31]

That would indeed seem a pretty damning objection to any bill; and for the parish officers the Permanent Additional Force Act had just one happy loophole. It permitted them to accept men only 5 ft 2 in. tall where the army's recruiting regulations required men to be 5 ft 4 in. tall. For the shrewder and less principled parish officers that margin of two inches between the requirements of different regulations made possible an unhallowed traffic with the recruiting sergeants raising men

[31] *Parliamentary Debates*, 6 May 1806, 17.

for the army; and from places as far apart as Waterford county in
Ireland and Leicestershire in England M.P.s reported of their own
knowledge that the men their counties were credited with raising
through the parishes were in fact undersized recruits gathered by
regular recruiting parties who then handed over to the parish officers.[32]
For each one of these men the parish officers escaped a £20 fine and
got one guinea to share with the recruiting sergeant; and it was in the
interest of both parties to ignore the ten and twenty mile limits imposed
by the Act. It is only necessary to add one more point to demonstrate
the full measure of Pitt's failure: when his act was repealed the fines
due under its provisions from all the parishes of the United Kingdom
amounted to no less than £1,800,000, for a total of 90,000 men required
but not delivered.[33] It was, then, fortunate for the nation that in the
spring of 1805 he repeated his successful measure of 1799 with another
act to permit volunteering from the Militia. This time, however, he got
only 9,000 men, though he wanted 17,000.

The reader may find it hard to believe that anyone would defend
such an act as the Permanent Additional Force Act after its author, Pitt,
had died and his government fallen in January 1806; yet it was defended,
most vigorously. From the opposition benches the former members of
Pitt's cabinet fought hard for it on the grounds that though it had got
off to a very poor start recruiting had recently improved and the bill
was apparently beginning to produce results. Spencer Perceval put it
this way: 'In the last 15 weeks (the act) had produced an average of
258 per week, which would give 13,200 in the year; in the last 10 weeks
an average of 277, or 14,600 in the year; and in the last five weeks an
average of 356 per week, being at the rate of above 18,000 in the year'.[34]
How far this recent spurt was due merely to more and more parish
officers realising that bargains could be made with recruiting sergeants
for runts under 5 ft 4 in. high, who could be palmed off as parish
recruits, no one can say; but Perceval was good at figures and he made a
persuasive case out of them. The other friend of Pitt's act was the Duke
of York himself. He valued it as a means of building up his second
battalions, for whose future he feared; and fear of what was to come is
perhaps the real explanation of all the support Pitt's act received, for,
incredible as it may seem, the new secretary of state for war and colonies,
William Windham, really did produce a far worse one.

Windham is a minister of whom it is impossbile to write without
sympathy or to regard as anything but a national disaster. The sheer
charm of his character commands the sympathy; he was a Whig who
had won and held the friendship of that staunch Tory, Dr Johnson;

[32] *Parliamentary Debates*, 6 May 1806, 16, 17.
[33] Fortescue, *County Lieutenancies and the Army*, 164.
[34] *Parliamentary Debates*, 17 April 1806, 792.

he was one of the finest speakers in the House of Commons in its greatest age of oratorical brilliance; and already in 1806 a man of much political experience. Yet he was never a success. His nickname of 'Weathercock' Windham suggests part of the reason. He could be trusted to see all sides of a question – but never to see them all at once; and hence he repeatedly changed his mind while protesting his consistency. At the war department, however, he had no chance to change his mind. He went there already the prisoner of his own past utterances. He had denounced the Volunteers as a useless extravagance – and had done so, as Perceval pointed out, with all the authority of the 'colonel' of one of the most utterly inefficient Volunteer companies in the country. He had denounced the ballot too, as the cause of the hot market for substitutes for the Militia which drew off possible recruits for the regulars and so kept bounties high; but it never occurred to him to cut out the market in substitutes by firmly requiring all balloted men to serve in person. He accepted a cabinet post that made him responsible for the strategy of a nation fighting a war and felt no responsibility for aiding the country's continental allies. Instead, after inheriting from Castlereagh, his predecessor, an expeditionary force prepared for action and a fleet of transports to carry it overseas, he permitted every one of the transports to be scrapped except the few needed to maintain communications with the Channel Islands.[35]

Once in office he was sufficiently impressed by the Duke of York's warning that the Volunteers were important for the country's defence to refrain from actually abolishing them; but, as will be seen, in the name of economy he abolished everything that made them efficient for the purpose. His method of dealing with the competition for men which arose over allowing substitutes to volunteer for the Militia in place of balloted conscripts was to abolish the ballot and so ensure that none but freely enlisted volunteers – the very men the army wanted – would ever enter the Militia. He imagined he could solve the Army's recruiting problem by making service in that force popular; but the most conspicuous part of his method of making military service popular was to limit the time a man served to seven years. This was a measure well designed to rid the army in due course of all who disliked soldiering, but at the cost of emptying the very ranks it was Windham's duty to fill. He did indeed introduce a new scale of pay, which would give 1s. 6d., in place of 1s., to the man who re-enlisted after his seven years were up and 2s. to men who re-enlisted after fourteen years. But these rates were still far below what artisans could earn; and his pensions for old soldiers, though an undoubted humanitarian reform, were too distant an inducement to be very persuasive in getting young men to enlist. All the while that Windham in the name of reform was thus crippling

[35] Londonderry, *Castlereagh's Correspondence*, VIII, 47–8.

the military power of England, and declining to lift a finger to aid the
nation's allies, Bonaparte was going from strength to strength on the
continent. He had struck down the Prussians at Jena and Auerstädt in
the autumn of 1806; he led his armies into Poland that winter; and
while the All-the-Talents ministry, with Windham as Secretary of
State for War, stood by and watched, with nothing to offer their allies
but money, Bonaparte was preparing for the final campaign that was to
bring him the peace of Tilsit.

Windham however, placed great hopes in a measure to be called the
Training Act; and this was duly passed on 6 July 1806. It empowered
the government to conscript 200,000 Englishmen a year – and it
applied to England only – for twenty four-days' training; and a century
later Sir John Fortescue remarked that this act had never been
repealed. In fact, it hardly needed to be for it was never enforced, nor
worth enforcing. If it had been used, 24 days' training was too little to
make soldiers of raw civilians. No means of disciplining the 200,000 men
was provided, except that a 'constable would stand by', as Windham
put it, while a sergeant was supposed to drill them; no officers to
command them were provided at all; and Windham could not even
give a straight answer to a questioner who asked 'whether the men,
when at drill, were to be under the command of the sergeant or of the
constable'.[36] All told, the one really effective thing that Windham did
to strengthen the army was to pass another act to permit volunteering
from the Militia. But this applied only to Ireland and produced no
more than 4,000 men.

Mercifully the All-the-Talents ministry fell in March 1807, and the
Duke of Portland formed a cabinet of Pitt's followers with Castlereagh
at the war ministry.

There Castlereagh found himself confronted by a most unsatisfactory
situation. Nobody knew the state of the Volunteers. In spite of the Duke
of York's warning of the value of the Regulars' second battalions, 54
such battalions had been threatened with disbandment by Windham
unless they raised 400 men each in six months. As a result, no fewer
than 1,113 separate recruiting parties were out after men in 1806–7,
where the total had been only 405 in 1805–6. The numbers of men
enlisted in the past year had indeed risen as a result, but not in proportion to the cost of recruiting them; every recruiting party detached from
a weak regiment reduced its strength and efficiency still further; in
spite of all this activity the army was still 35,000 men short; and of these
35,000 men 23,000 were needed to bring the threatened 54 battalions
up to an average strength of 700. As for the Militia, it too was under
strength by nearly one fifth, being 18,000 men short of its establishment
of 95,823 for England, Scotland and Ireland. In short, Portland's

[36] *Parliamentary Debates*, 27 June 1806, 863–4.

government took over a country which no longer possessed the means to aid its allies; and vigorous measures were clearly necessary to enable Britain to play an effective part in world affairs.

It was now that Lord Melville (formerly Henry Dundas) urged Castlereagh's to copy Addington's precedent of the Army of Reserve; but Castlereagh felt he could not do it. That law had been enforced by a £20 fine imposed on balloted men who refused to serve; the same fine had been imposed by Pitt's act on parishes which failed to produce their men; and £1,800,000 had been due in those fines when Pitt's government fell. But Windham had not collected them. Instead, he had remitted the whole by act of Parliament. After that, a new Army of Reserve Act, enforced by a fine, was unlikely to command any respect.

Therefore, Castlereagh, ignoring Lord Melville's warning that he would 'disgust your most respectable Militia officers',[37] decided to invite men of that force to volunteer for the Regulars again; and of the 28,000 for whom he hoped, he got 27,505.[38] It was an excellent reinforcement, both in the matter of numbers and because every man of them was already a trained soldier. Of course, it left the Militia reduced to little more than half its official strength. But, as the men had been enrolled in 1803 and the term of Militia service was five years, they would all have to be replaced in 1808 anyway. By reviving the ballot, in defiance of Windham's objections, Castlereagh was able to repair the loss to the Militia and to do so in time to give its new men some months of useful training before the men enlisted in 1803 had to be discharged and replaced. This was not the last time the Militia were to be called upon either. In 1809 Castlereagh was to turn to them for 28,492 and in 1811 Palmerston got another 11,453 from this source.[39] Still more calls than these might have been made on the Militia, if it had not been for another measure of Castlereagh's, which will be discussed shortly.

This measure was connected with the Volunteers who must now be examined.

During the earlier war against the French Republic a number of Volunteer units had enrolled for home defence; and Addington had wisely retained some of them after the peace. When war broke out again, he encouraged volunteering, not in the most clear-sighted manner possible, to be sure, but still effectively. First, in June 1803, he laid down one set of requirements, under what were known as the 'June Allowances'. These allowed pay for eighty-five days' training a year to the Volunteer units which qualified for them and in return required them to serve anywhere within their military district.[40] But this was not

[37] Londonderry, *Castlereagh's Correspondence*, VII, 78.
[38] Fortescue, *County Lieutenancies and the Army*, 186.
[39] Ibid., 223, 257.
[40] Ibid., 75.

enough; and in July Addington passed a Levy en Masse Act, which, in
Fortescue's words, empowered the government 'to drill every able-
bodied man whether he liked it or not';[41] but the act was accompanied
by a pledge that it would not be enforced provided enough men came
forward to join the Volunteers. To cope with these additional Volunteers, Addington provided the 'August Allowances' which granted these
late comers to the movement pay for only twenty days' training a year,
but required them to serve anywhere in the kingdom.

So there were two different sets of Volunteers. The first, on the June
Allowances, being paid for eighty-five days' training, should be far the
better trained and more useful; but could only be employed in their own
military district. The second, on the August Allowances, could be
employed anywhere, but because they could only be required to do
twenty days' training, could not be expected to be as efficient and hence
as worth employing, as the men on the June Allowances. Next Addington made perhaps his most damaging political blunder. After en-
couraging thousands to volunteer by his Levy en Masse Act he was
caught off balance by the success of his own policy; and so, not knowing
what to do with the thousands who came forward, he issued a ruling on
18 August that limited the number of Volunteers in any county to a
total that must not exceed six times the number of the Old Militia in
that county. This limitation produced an uproar that was too strong
to be withstood; and he laid it down by a new ruling of 31 August that
all offers of Volunteers would be accepted but those over and above the
total allowed by the rule of 18 August were to be supernumeraries
'without any allowance of pay, arms or clothing and without claim to
exemption from any ballot'.[42] And the key words there were the last;
one thing that did much to make volunteering popular was that it
excused men from being balloted for either the Militia or the Army
of Reserve.

The difficulties that the Ordnance department had in finding
weapons for all the 300,000 and more Volunteers have been described
in Chapter II; and so have the Duke of York's excellent arrangements
for providing Inspecting Field Officers to make regular reports on the
progress of the Volunteers, to assist them in their training and serve as
their staff officers on operations. These arrangements were preserved
by Pitt, who also made some improvements, especially in the discipline
of the force, by passing the Volunteer Consolidation Act of June 1805.
But this act still left untouched the different obligations of Volunteers
on the 'June Allowances', who were required to serve only in their own
military districts, and those on the 'August Allowances' who were
required to serve anywhere in the kingdom. The distinction quite

[41] Ibid., 66.
[42] Ibid., 78.

understandably embarrassed the Commander-in-Chief, who, on the very day before the bill finally passed, wrote to Lord Camden, the Minister for War, that though he was 'sanguine that all such limitations would be abandoned on the appearance of an Enemy ... as an Officer in Chief Command I am not at liberty to rest the Safety of the Country upon any speculative opinion'; and, he added, of Volunteers totalling 'nearly 25,000 Rank and File in the Metropolis, only 13,400 can be *ordered* upon extended service'.[43] But in this matter Pitt and Lord Camden left the Volunteers as they had found them.

January 1806 brought Pitt's death and the advent of the All-the-Talents ministry which sent Windham, with all his genius for confusion, to rule the war department. As I have said, Windham was urged by the Duke of York to retain the Volunteers on the ground that they added materially to the strength of the country; but in his own mind he believed them to be a useless extravagance – 'painted cherries which none but simple birds would take for real fruit' was one of his un-flattering descriptions of them.[44] Torn between his own publicly stated views and the Duke's professional advice, Windham compro-mised, and so secured the worst possible solution. He did retain the Volunteers; but he also abolished their Inspecting Field Officers, cut their training allowances, cut the number of days' training required of them and refused to promise them any future clothing allowances. He also, as we have seen, suspended the use of the ballot for conscripting militiamen; and yet the government's power to disband unsatisfactory Volunteer units and so render them liable to be balloted had been the strongest inducement to those units to be efficient. So the results of Windham's impact on the Volunteers may be summed up as follows. He did not save the country the whole expense of maintaining these 'painted cherries'; but he did abolish everything calculated to preserve the real usefulness for which the Commander-in-Chief valued them. And he did these things at a time when it could be stated in the House of Commons that most of the Volunteers 'had been reported fit to act with troops of the line'.[45] This alone is surely enough to justify our calling Windham 'a national disaster', quite apart from the effect of his policies on the Regular Army, the fatuity of his Training Act and his failure to aid his allies.

When Castlereagh in the spring of 1807 took up the job of restoring Britain's military powers, he had naturally to consider how to make the Volunteers efficient again; and he lost little time in restoring their

[43] Duke of York to Lord Camden, 4 June 1804 (WO/30/76).
[44] It was a most unfortunate phrase which his opponents never let him forget and constantly quoted against him.
[45] By Sir Henry Mildinay on 26 June 1806. See *Parliamentary Debates* for that date, p. 21.

Inspecting Field Officers. Without their 'superintendence', he wrote, 'Government could have no security of the faithful application of the allowances granted' to them, nor could it know 'the state of their discipline and numbers'.[46] Yet the government had to be assured of both before it could send its Regular Army overseas against the enemy.

Many of the inspection reports of the Inspecting Field Officers on the much discouraged Volunteers made dismal reading. Their numbers for one thing had fallen by over 90,000, from 330,116 in 1805 to '240,000 under arms at the last inspections' of 1807.[47] Castlereagh, therefore, planned a new force, to be called the Supplementary Militia, (or, later, Local Militia) and to be recruited, where necessary, by ballot. Balloted men were to be compelled to serve by a fine, and, as fines were now so much discredited, by the alternative of a prison sentence too. They were to have 28 days' training a year and to serve for four years, during which time, and for two years after, they were to be free from being balloted for the regular Militia. The maximum whom Castlereagh's act permitted the government to call out was up to 308,934 men – or more than half as many again as Windham's Training Act. Unlike Windham's '200,000 men . . . drawn out in splendid array under a few constables and drill sergeants',[48] Castlereagh's Local Militia were to be formed into battalions; and each battalion was to have its own full complement of officers and a regimental staff on permanent pay.

The number of Local Militia called out was intended to make good the shortage of the diminished Volunteers. But Castlereagh's aim was to amalgamate the two forces. He began at the start in 1808 by offering a bounty of two guineas a man to all Volunteer units which would transfer bodily into the new force; and this plan had the merit of bringing into the Local Militia the Volunteer officers who now had up to five years of military training behind them. Steps were also taken to disband Volunteer units which the Inspecting Field Officers found inefficient.

In March 1809, after a year's experience with them, Castlereagh brought a bill into the House to improve the Local Militia still further. This bill allowed Local Militia units to be filled at any time by voluntary enlistment or the ballot. It abolished the two guinea bounty originally used to encourage Volunteers to transfer to the new force. Further, it permitted Local Militiamen to volunteer for the Regulars at any time except during the annual training period. In June 1809 Castlereagh also warned the Volunteers that the government would give them no more grants for clothing; and this encouraged more Volunteers to transfer to the Local Militia. Then, of course, in September Portland's ministry

---

[46] Londonderry, *Castlereagh's Correspondence*, VIII, 51–2.

[47] Fortescue, *County Lieutenancies and the Army*, 209.

[48] As George Canning described them in the House: *Parliamentary Debates*, 5 July 1806, 914.

broke up and Castlereagh resigned his office after his duel with Canning.

His place was taken in Perceval's new cabinet by that fair-minded, level-headed man, Lord Liverpool; and when Liverpool became premier after Perceval's death, Lord Bathurst succeeded him as Secretary of State for War and Colonies. Neither was an innovator in any great degree; instead each followed the trail Castlereagh had blazed, and it was a good trail. But one new portent did appear in September, 1809; that was the emergence of the twenty-five year old Lord Palmerston as Secretary-at-War.

The job Palmerston undertook was then more important than is sometimes suggested. When the Secretary of State for War and Colonies was in the House of Lords, the Secretary-at-War became the government's spokesmen on all military matters, from finance and law to strategy and manpower, in the House of Commons. In the crisis of a great war that was a very responsible job and Palmerston flung himself into it with characteristic energy. Though he was, as ever, abrasive and inconsiderate of others,[49] it was good for the country to have such a vigorous administrator take over the War Office which had been left too long in the hands of less than second-rate men;[50] and it must also have been good for Palmerston, as a future Foreign Minister and Prime Minister, to serve his apprenticeship in a post that forced him to study the military facts of life in a warlike world.

In this post one of Palmerston's tasks was to introduce in 1811 the war's last major recruiting legislation. In that year he, first, took steps to secure another 11,453 volunteers for the Regular Army from the Militia, and, second, made this sort of volunteering a permanent feature of British recruiting with an act enabling 10,000 men every year to transfer from the Militia to the Regulars. Thus amended, Castlereagh's system remained in force until the end of the war; and, between them, the men raised by ordinary regimental recruiting parties, supplemented by those who volunteered from the Local Militia under Castlereagh's act of 1809 and those who volunteered from the old, or Regular, Militia under Palmerston's legislation of 1811, were enough to meet Britain's needs in the field down to the end of the fighting in 1814.

This is a result which would seem to reflect much credit on the authors of the system, but it did not satisfy Sir John Fortescue. That great pioneer in British military history insisted that these sources would not have produced enough men for much longer. 'Another twelve months of war', he wrote, 'would have seen the entire recruiting machinery of the Army broken down. And break down it will and must in any long

---

[49] E.g. the feud he picked with Field Marshal Sir David Dundas, who had recently replaced the Duke of York as commander-in-chief.

[50] On which, see Glover, *Peninsular Preparation*, p. 36.

and serious war, unless it is founded upon compulsory National Training.'[51] There is no need to dispute Fortescue's prophecy that another twelve months of war would have seen the breakdown of the army's recruiting machinery, or the view that defence in a great war must rest on some effective form of compulsion – a fact Britons have recognised twice over in the present century. But one must object, first, that it is the habit of governments to cross bridges when they come to them; and that in fact the recruiting system of Castlereagh and Palmerston did last out the war. It gave Wellington the men he needed to storm the Spanish border fortresses, Ciudad Rodrigo and Badajoz, and launch the campaign of Salamanca that freed Andalusia in 1812, to win Vitoria and invade France in 1813 and conquer still more French territory in 1814. It also maintained Britain's other expeditionary army, which began as the garrison of Sicily, campaigned in Eastern Spain in 1812 and helped liberate Italy in 1814. Likewise, it furnished the troops with which Graham invaded Holland in December 1813, the small Regular component in the forces that defended Canada in 1812–14, and also garrisons for Britain's other colonies, including her conquests from France and Holland. In short, the Castlereagh policy, as amended by Palmerston, did what was required of it; and nothing of which that can be said is a failure. Second, one cannot share Fortescue's belief that 'compulsory National Training' would ever be sufficient foundation for defence. Canada adopted that policy in the Hitler War; it left her in 1944–5 unable to find enough reinforcements for her five depleted divisions of volunteers fighting in Europe, at a time when her camps at home were filled with thousands of young, fit and healthy, but unusable, soldiers, whom the law compelled to receive training, arms, clothing, food and pay at public expense in Canada, but not to employ their training by serving overseas against their country's enemies; therefore, *pace* Sir John, one must insist that any new compulsion that became necessary in 1815 would have had to be compulsion actually to serve in any theatre of war where men might be wanted. Third, a weakness must be noticed in Palmerston's legislation of 1811. When he permitted an annual draft of 10,000 men every year to transfer from the old Militia to the Regulars, he also revived Windham's unhappy precedent of denying the Militia the right to refill its ranks with the ballot. So he took compulsion out of training men even for Britain's principal home defence force and left the Militia dependent on voluntary recruiting. Yet compulsory training for home defence, though inadequate, is not useless. As we have seen, there could be no offensive overseas unless the homeland was secure; also, many balloted men, who had originally no wish for a military life, were glad to volunteer for the Regular Army after the Militia had once introduced them to

[51] *History of the British Army*, X, 185.

soldiering; and one cannot tell how many potential Rifleman Harrises or Private Wheelers were denied to the army by Palmerston's reversion to Windham's policy. But for this step the system of Castlereagh and Palmerston might have worked still better.

It is now time to sum up the nation's manpower policies.

Outside the colonial world, where Grinfield's victories in the West Indies and Wellington's in India either won bargaining counters that would help secure a good peace or permanently extended British rule, Addington had no opportunity to take the offensive. But he devised a very practical method of strengthening the Regular Army; his organisation of the Volunteers, though not the best imaginable, was effective, and added much to Britain's strength at home. Pitt did not improve on Addington's policies for raising men; he marred them, so far as the Regular Army goes. But he did improve the discipline of the Volunteers; and, imperfect as his recruiting policy was, he still was able to send General Craig with 6,000 men to the Mediterranean. In his premiership, too, the nation had men enough to make an invasion of north Germany whose total strength was intended to 'exceed 70,000 rank and file'.[52] It failed, in part because it was organised too late and because Bonaparte struck down the Austrians too soon; also, in part, because Frederick William III of Prussia was too cautious to seize the opportunity the Third Coalition offered for delivering Europe from French domination. But still a Britain which was ready to put 70,000 men in the field in Germany, as well as ruling the sea, was once again a significant land power abroad, while at home she was strong enough to make the success of a French invasion doubtful, even if there had been no Third Coalition to prevent Bonaparte from attempting it.

The All-the-Talents ministry had wit enough, and troops enough, at least to garrison Sicily; and it must be given credit for that, if for little else. As for this government's failings in other theatres, I suspect that in Windham it got the War Minister it deserved. It had indeed one very able soldier in its Master General of the Ordnance, Lord Moira; but his advice, if proffered, did little to improve Windham's recruiting policies or to divert the cabinet from its futile strategies in Egypt and South America.

In 1807–9 Castlereagh did more than any other man since the Seven Years War to enable Britain to fulfil the role of a great power in a continental war. On his return to the war ministry he contrived to make the nation once more both strong for defence at home and formidable abroad. His work on recruiting, as supplemented by Palmerston, and his strategy, which his successors maintained, first paved the way to victory, and then enabled him to 'negotiate from strength' when, as Foreign Secretary, he helped decide the future of Europe at the Allied

[52] Londonderry, *Castlereagh's Correspondence*, II, 25–9.

headquarters in 1813 and at the Congress of Vienna in 1814–15. In
short, his policies at the war department as well as the Foreign Office
contributed to securing that balance of power through which the
Treaty of Vienna was to preserve international peace among its signa-
tories for longer than any other great treaty before or since. All that
Castlereagh did to bring lasting peace to Europe also added to the
security of Britain; and with the fall of Bonaparte, to which his policies
contributed so much, the years in which Britain stood at bay were ended.

DOCUMENTS

1. Questions to Admiral Lord Keith, commanding the North Sea Fleet, from H.R.H. the Duke of York, Commander-in-Chief of the Army, 18 October 1803
FROM: P[ublic] R[ecord] O[ffice], WO/30/75

My Lord,

I shall feel myself much indebted to your Lordship for the communication of your sentiments upon the following points which I feel to be of much importance, should a question arise upon the propriety of moving troops from the interior of the Country in the instance of more than one attempt at Invasion being made at the same time.

1st. What are the Ports from whence it is apprehended an Enemy may make his attempt in undecked vessels or boats of shallow draught of water, without very much endangering his own safety from the effects of weather upon a lengthened vogage?

2nd. Is it supposed that vessels of the description alluded to can pass over the sands which cover the Downs upon the coast of Kent, and the mouth of the Blackwater, the Wallet and Hollesley Bay upon the coast of Essex?

3rd. Should it be the intention of the Enemy to invade at the same time the different parts of our Coast hereafter enumerated from the corresponding parts opposed to him, what are the most favourable points for the wind to proceed from to carry into effect such combined operations:

Supposed Landings

a. From the Isle of Wight inclusive to the Westward of Plymouth.
b. From Selsea Island to Whitstable Bay in the mouth of the Thames.
c. The Coasts of Essex, Suffolk and Norfolk.
d. The Humber and Newcastle.
e. The Firth of Forth.

I should next ask your Lordship's opinion in respect to what you might consider the probable allotment of the Enemy's force as supposed to be placed in the Ports of France, Flanders and Holland, and intended to be employed against the different lines of Coast which have been enumerated assuming the policy of an Enemy in the present state of his Navy to seek the shortest voyage.

Lastly – What are the Winds required by an Enemy to make his Passage good in the different probable cases which shall have been thus determined: in order that a judgement may be formed as far as the case will permit of what proportion of his force can be brought to bear upon our coast, according to the Points from whence the wind may blow. . . .

2. Lord Keith's Answer, *Monarch*, off Broadstairs, 21 October
1803
FROM: P.R.O. WO/30/75

Sir;

I was yesterday honoured with Your Royal Highness's letter of the
18th Instant requiring a communication of my sentiments upon the
several queries therein proposed respecting the Ports on the Enemy's
coast from where it is most probable that he may make this attempt to
invade this Country in small vessels or craft.

Brest has been watched by great officers and in general extremely
meritoriously; but it is impossible to prevent an Enemy slipping out a
force from a place which is defended by Rocks and has three passages.
Through the Passage du Four they could go with S.E. winds to Cornwall
and Devon; and likewise from Morlaise and St Malo – With certain
winds there are many places on which to land on the West Coast. –
At St Ives with East Winds; and at Mousehole with a West Wind; but
there is no anchorage that could protect the Enemy's ships from our
fleet.

I think that Plymouth will be defended by the constant resort of the
Fleet, the troops which compose the garrison etc., and the great number
of Artificers and Labourers employed by the public all of whom should
be trained to Arms.

Torbay an excellent Roadstead the whole coast of which is fit to be
landed on with West or North West Winds is so well known it cannot
have escaped the notice of Government. In Portland and Weymouth
Roads Naval force seems more important because the anchorage is safe
and such a force would serve to cover those places and the Coast up to
the Needles during the prevalence of Westerly Winds, and to Torbay
with Easterly winds – from St Aldans Head to Chichester there is a fair
landing with west Winds, particularly at Sandwich or Swannage as it is
commonly called.

I hardly think an Enemy will land on an Island like the Wight unless
they had the superiority by Sea because it would not be easy to get
off it to the Main, if we take the common precautions. Besides there are
at all times a great number of ships, frigates and other vessels of war at
Spithead and a stationary force at St Helens.

All the coast from Weymouth to Dover can be invaded by vessels
from Cherbourg, Havre de Grace and Boulogne with winds from S.E.
to S.W. but it is to be observed that Southerly winds must make a surf
upon all that shore that, in bad weather, it is impossible to land; and that
in good weather our squadrons will be off their ports; we have also an
increasing naval force upon our own Coast and the armed boats and

vessels, (their Crews being strengthened by the Sea Fencibles) will form a third line of defence for opposing any attempts to land off Selsey Island – in the Park there are two sloops of war. There is a considerable squadron off Havre de Grace; another off Dungeness and a third before Boulogne which will anchor off that place when the weather will admit of putting off to sea in boats

The Landing Places along the Coast are:—

All the Beach near Brighton in certain Winds:

Seaford Bay in East Winds, very good:

The East side of Beachy Head; in Pevensy Bay; and Rye Bay with Westerly Winds:

The West side of Dungeness with easterly Winds:

The Opposite side and in Hythe Bay with Westerly Winds:

A small portion of Wear Bay near Folkestone:

I think that the Downs are secure unless the enemy be superior by sea, and that Pegwell Bay is too difficult except accidently and that it is protected by being in the immediate vicinity of the Downs.

Ramsgate Pier at High Water might be forced. It is large and would yield shelter to a great number of boats – four large carronades, six 8 pounders or Howitzers on the piers and a Boom would render it secure.

The Coast of the Isle of Thanet is generally high cliffs and rocky off them – but if the Gates are attended to and defended, it will be very difficult to land there.

From Margate to Bishopstown Cliff is all good landing and attracts naval attention. The vessels and boats that have lately been armed at Margate will add much to its security.

The Coast from Bishopstown to Whitstable is good for landing upon but the Water is shallow. Boats of small draft, however, may in good weather, land at half flood; although at the time of the Tide it is shallow to a great distance from the Shore.

On the Isles of Shippey and Grain I think the Enemy would not land for the same reasons that I have assigned to the Isle of Wight. There is a great flotilla ordered at Sheerness: and I think it is proper here to observe that the signal post, erected at Prittlewell Church in Essex, furnishes good means of communication with Kent from whence it could be conveyed to London by the telegraph established at Sheerness – the necessity of crossing Troops from one side to the opposite, both at Sheerness and Gravesend I have no doubt will be held in view. It may always be accomplished at the latter place and frequently at the former.

I have put a strong ship to defend the Black and Barrow Deeps so that with the provision already made I consider the mouths of the Thames security against Vessels of Size – of Boats I shall speak hereafter.

The Maplin and Buxy Sands secure the Burnham, Malden and Colne Waters against Vessels but not against boats; for at times the latter can cross the sands, although it is attended with danger – the entrances of the rivers are intricate and easily defended – there are vessels of War in each; but I am of opinion the craft of this Country should be armed to a certain extent for their better protection, as has been done on the coast of Kent, and that they should be manned from the Sea Fencibles.

The whole of the Wallet is a harbour and most of its coast is fit to land upon; but the Water is so deep as to admit of Ships sailing near the shore all over it. The accesses to it are pretty well defended.

Harwich is a gerat feature defended by Landguard Fort and a Battery on the Tower side: I have proposed a gun vessel off the Altar sand, and I think that the Country vessels should be armed here as before mentioned. They are very numerous and fit for the purpose and the Men are skilful Pilots for that part of the Coast.

From Harwich to Bawdsey the Beach is good and within Bawdsey Sand may be landed upon, but in Horsley [Hollesley] Bay and towards Orfordness I doubt it because I was there in fair weather with the wind off the land, and yet there was a wash on the Beach; besides it is a long peninsula of Shingle running up to Orford Castle. There are Ships in Horsely Bay [=Hollesley] and if they can remain there all Winter, it is a good situation for covering the coast up to the Wallet and also to the Northward as far as Lowestoff.

From Oxfordness [=Orfordness] to Yarmouth I have not examined; but it is an open Coast, – and I think that landing there would be exposed and uncertain.

North of Yarmouth towards Clay and Blakeney the Beach is good, but it is also exposed; and any landing must be made in Vessels of a larger Class, consequently they would not be able to approach the shore like open boats.

With Lynn Deeps I am unacquainted; but I am informed that the navigation of them and the contiguous Coast is very difficult and dangerous.

The Humber is an object of much consequence and will have a ship of the line and at least one Frigate stationed in it. I should recommend the country vessels to be armed there, as at other places before mentioned, for cooperating in the general defence.

Part of the coast in the vicinity of Bridlington, Filey Bridge and Robin Hood's Bay is fit to land upon with winds off the shore, that is from the West – at Scarborough there is a pier, but it is extremely easy to defend it, and I doubt not that provision has been made for that purpose.

Newcastle Bar is so dangerous and so well defended by Tinmouth [sic] that I think the river safe unless the Enemy should land on the

South side in fine weather in which case he would command the River; but the length of voyage gives reasonable hope that our Ships would be on the Coast before him.

The Firth of Forth is not easily defended. The first shelter for Ships of War is in Leith Road which is a very indifferent anchorage. In summer months it is true they can anchor in Aberlaidie Bay and off Musselburgh sands. The enemy may land anywhere within and on the Bays, on the southside with South or West Winds and on the coast of Fife with North or North West winds; but as the voyage is long from any part of the Enemy's Coast it is hoped our fleet would be in the mouth of the Forth as soon as he could reach it. – Besides it is intended that there is to be an Admiral with an adequate force in Leith Road, and certainly there as at other places, the small Vessels of the country may be armed with excellent effect and at small expence – I shall therefore here for the present stop for Your Royal Highness's further commands and take a short view of the ports of equipment on the Enemy's coast: Reports of the force within them: The nature of the Winds which will be favourable for bringing the enemy to our shores: the naval means employed for watching and defeating their attempts: and the possibility of their Vessels passing over the sands.

Havre de Grace and other ports in the Seine is the quarter from where I should most expect an embarkation intended for England to come; because any number of Vessels even of a considerable size can be assembled there without their being subject to our view and because they can quit the River with a fair wind at any time of tide, and the troops and stores can be embarked unperceived.

At Boulogne there is not above five hours tide out of twelve to depart with and the troops must be seen embarking or marching for that purpose to the Shore.

The Harbour of Dunkirk has advantage in point of size and in being covered with sands and Banks yet before a great Force can sail from thence it must be seen collecting, and can only quit the Port at certain times of tide.

Ostend has fewer hours of tide still than Dunkirk to embark and sail with. It is hardly possible for a great armament to put to sea in any one tide from that place.

Flushing is by far the most considerable Port on that side – From thence small vessels may come with fair winds – the rivers and harbours are capable of containing any number of vessels and its is difficult to watch this port on account of the surrounding sands.

It is not easy for large Ships to get out of Helvoet, and it can be watched by ships of war with better effect than Flushing.

Any material attack upon Scotland or the North of England will probably proceed from the Texel. But at present I do not understand that much preparation is making there, and the season of the year is fast approaching when all the Dutch ports will be shut up for some time by Ice.

With respect to the probable allotment of the Enemy's Force in the different Ports of France, Flanders and Holland, for the purpose of Invasion, it is impossible for me to give Your Royal Highness any satisfactory information as the accounts of their present numbers differ so much but all of them lead to a persuasion that there is a great army on the Coast. That part of it that is in Holland is said to be sickly. I was lately very close off Calais and Boulogne – at the former place I observed very large Barracks but saw no considerable number of Troops. At the latter place there are two very extensive Camps of Huts which I think might contain 16,000 men.—They seemed full of Troops and then there were also small camps at all the Batteries along the Shore and Soldiers in the towns – There were about 55 rowboats in the harbour and two Brigs, two Schooners and one Galliot all armed; at Ostend I hear that there are in readiness 40 Fishing Boats drawing 5 feet and many open vessels of a smaller description – 12,000 men are said to be about the place – 29 decked boats of some size, with two Guns each, are said to have left Rotterdam for the purpose of proceeding by the inland navigation to Dunkirk where there are no doubt many other vessels of various descriptions.

With East and South East Winds the Enemy may sail from Brest, L'Orient, Basque Roads, and generally from all the Ports in the Bay of Biscay, as well as from Morlaise to the Coast of Ireland.

From Morlaise and St Malo, with winds from South South West to South South East the Enemy may proceed to any part of the western coast of England unless interrupted by the Jersey squadron.

Southerly Winds will carry the Enemy from Cherbourg, Havre de Grace and Boulogne to the coast of Hampshire, Sussex or Kent; but nothing can come out of Boulogne with a west wind which blows in.

From Dunkirk, Ostend, Flushing and the Dutch Ports, South and East Winds will serve to carry Ships to most parts of our Coast to the North East of the North Foreland, but if the wind be fresh a surf will be produced on the Shores.

Although I have no doubt that Your Royal Highness is already acquainted with the disposition of the Force under my orders, made by direction of the Admiralty for obstructing the departure of the Enemy's embarkation from their Ports on that part of their Coast which is within the limits of my command, it is so much connected with the subject of this Letter that I think it right to include it in my report.

For watching Havre de Grace the western extremity of the Command, a squadron is appointed consisting of 3 Frigates, 3 sloops and 2 Cutters and two sloops of war are anchored within the [word illegible].

For the protection of our Coast off Dungeness and for attending the Enemy's motions at Boulogne there is a squadron of one Ship of 2 Decks, 4 Frigates, 3 Sloops, 1 Bomb vessel, 3 Gun Vessels and 2 Cutters.

In the Downs a force consisting of 2 Ships of the Line, 3 Frigates, 5 Sloops, 2 Bomb Vessels and 10 or 12 smaller Vessels at least, will rendezvous for the protection of that Anchorage and for detaching Squadrons off Calais, Dunkirk and Ostend to check the Enemy's movements on that line of their Coast. A Line of Battle Ship may also be expected to range along the Coast of Sussex and Kent.

One Ship of 50 Guns, 3 Frigates, 3 Sloops and 2 Cutters are ordered to maintain a station before Flushing and the mouth of the Scheldt to prevent the sailing of any embarkation from thence.

Three Frigates, 2 Sloops and some smaller Vessels are ordered off Helvoet for the like purpose.

For the service of the Texel I have appointed 3 Ships of the Line, 2 Frigates, 2 Sloops, 2 Gun Vessels and 2 Cutters.

And for the blockade of the Rivers Elbe and Weser, 3 Frigates, 1 Sloop and 2 Cutters.

The Officers in charge of these several duties are directed respectively to maintain communications with the Squadrons on their Right and Left; and the senior Captain off Havre de Grace will hold occasional intercourse with the Ships under the orders of Rear Admiral Sir James Saumarez off Cherbourg. It is to be understood that all these squadrons are independent of the Stationary Force appointed for the defence of the entrance to the Thames, Humber and Firth of Forth; but in laying this statement before Your Royal Highness it is proper that I should acquaint you that some of the Vessels of which the squadrons are to consist are not yet in readiness, or at my disposal; but they will soon be so; and I have reason to believe that the Lords Commissioners of the Admiralty will as soon as possible increase the number of ships under my command, because occasional accidents and calls for Convoy and for Vessels to protect the Commerce upon the Coast will naturally prevent the possibility of keeping the squadrons at any time quite compleat.

It is extremely difficult to speak with certainty of the sands upon the Coast of Essex and Kent. – Many of them are very little known; some of them are dry at low water and at an early time of the tide; but most of them can be crossed at High Water in Boats or small Vessels when the Weather is fine; but it requires skill for if the wind and tide are in contrary directions it must be hazardous; and after bad weather it is also dangerous because it requires some time for the swell to subside.

In considering a subject of this important nature it is fair to look at it from every point of view. I therefore hazard a possible, although not a very probable, conjecture which is that a Fleet or Squadron may get out of Brest unperceived and watch an opportunity for running up the Downs or Margate Road, in which case it might be superior to our squadron long enough to cover the landing of any extent of Force from the opposite coast; and might then escape through the North Sea or run off the Dutch Ports, and from thence protect an Embarkation of Troops to Scotland.

        I have etc.

               (signed)

                    Keith

3. Duties of the Ordnance Department
FROM: *The 12th Report of the Commissioners of Public Accounts*

The Office of Ordnance is governed by a MASTER GENERAL, and a BOARD under him, all appointed by separate Letters Patent. The Board consists of five principal Officers; the Lieutenant General, the Surveyor General, the Clerk of the Ordnance, the Storekeeper, and the Clerk of the Deliveries; any three of whom form a Board. The Master General and Lieutenant General are each, by virtue of their offices, in two capacities; the one Military, the other Civil. In the first, the Master General is Commander in Chief, and the Lieutenant General is second in Command, over the Artillery and Engineers. In his Civil capacity, the Master General is entrusted with the entire management of, and controul over, the whole Ordnance Department; for he can alone do any act which, if he does not interfere, may be done by the Board; and the whole patronage of the Ordnance, Civil and Military, with the exception of the Clerks acting immediately under the respective Board Officers, is in the Master General. The Lieutenant General, in his Civil capacity, is first in rank amongst the Members of the Board; and his signature is considered as essential to certain instruments, to warrant the payment of them by the Treasurer; but he has no other distinct duties in this capacity. The other four principal Officers have, each of them, independent of his being a Member of the Board, a separate and distinct branch of business committed to his management.

The Board are subordinate to the Master General; but if he does not interfere, they are competent of themselves to carry on all the official business. They can make Contracts and Agreements for the purchase of Stores, and performance of Services, and direct the Issue of Money; and, during the absence of the Master General, or vacancy of the Office, the whole executive power devolves on the Board. . . .

4. Intelligence: Bonaparte's Methods. Bonaparte to Marshal Berthier, 28 August 1805.
FROM: *Correspondance de Napoleon Ier*, No. 9148

My Cousin, I desire that you have made two portable boxes, divided into compartments; one for me, and the other for you. They should be designed in such a manner that at a glance one can tell, with the help of entry cards, the movements of all Austrian troops, regiment by regiment, battalion by battalion, and even the movements of fairly considerable detachments. You will divide them into as many armies as there are Austrian armies, and you will reserve spaces for the troops which the Emperor of Germany has in Hungary, in Bohemia or in the interior of his States. Every fifteen days you will send me a statement of the changes which have taken place in the preceding fortnight, using all the means which you will get not only from the German and Italian gazettes but also from the various reports which should come to you as well as to my Minister for foreign affairs, with whom you will collaborate for this purpose. The same person should work on the cards in the box and prepare the situation report on the Austrian army each fortnight.

Napoleon.

It is necessary to entrust this responsibility to a man who works on it all the time, who knows German well, who receives all the gazettes from Germany and would make all the changes necessary.

5. Intelligence: the Opportunities of Smugglers. Sir John Moore
reports to the Home Office, 17 February 1804
FROM: P.R.O., HO/50/396

I have enquired about Butcher. His history is that of a hundred others
in Folkestone.

There are four brothers – one a Blacksmith in Folkestone; the other
three – *Tom* lives at Flushing, *Henry* in Scotland at Aberdeen on the
East Coast, *James* goes to sea – the three last are Smugglers.

Henry was at Folkestone not long since, James no doubt takes his
cargoes sometimes to Scotland, sometimes lands them on this Coast,
– it is difficult to trace him.

The Mayor, to whom I communicated confidentially, will let me
know if he discovers anything of confidence respecting him. There is a
constant communication with this coast and that of Holland. I take for
granted that the Government know this and that both Countries find
their advantage in it. – There are vessels launched daily both here and at
Folkestone which it is well known are for no other purpose but to
smuggle from the coast of Holland. – Flushing was open to them some
time back, now it is *Browers Haven*, *Campveer* and *Zederikzea*.

When an attempt is made against this Country no doubt as many of
these vessels as can be seized will be stopt by the Enemy and Captains
and Crews employed as Pilots.

There is hardly a family in Folkestone which has not Relatives settled
at Flushing and there is a constant intercourse.

6. Intelligence: News from Deserters, Atlantic Theatre.
D'Auvergne to J. W. Croker, Jersey, 11 September 1811
FROM: P.R.O., ADM/1/226

Three French Sailors and one Spaniard, the Frenchmen natives of
Nantz and the neighbourhood of St Maloes, deserted a week since from
the *Eylau*, the Flag Ship at L'Orient bearing Allemand's flag. They were
furnished with a boat near St Maloes by their connections there, with
which they yesterday came to this place to offer to serve in Merchant
vessels, representing they were not paid for serving in the French
ships of war and [were] very ill treated. The following information,
which is corroborated by neutrals lately arrived at Guernsey from those
ports, has been obtained from them.

One of them (very intelligent) left Rochefort in the last week of
August, says there were 10 Line of Battle Ships, one of which was a
Three-Decker, ready for sea in the Charrente . . . that the two following
were just finished on the Stocks at Rochefort, and to be launched about
this time:

> The *Jenna* [*sic*]
> The *Ville de Vienne*.

At L'Orient the following ships were ready for Sea, Stored and
Provisioned under the Orders of Admiral Allemand and understood
to be destined for Brest for which Port they had embarked their
Pilots:

> The *Eylau*,   80 – bearing Allemand's flag.
> The *Veteran* ⎫
> The *Marengo* ⎬ 74s
> The *Golimin* ⎭
> The *Echo*,   18 – Corvette

They are pretty well manned, having from 7 to 800 men each, though
principally conscripts.

There are on the stocks at L'Orient nearly finished:
> 3 Ships of 74 Guns each
> 2 Frigates of 40 Guns each

The *Diligente* Corvette undergoing a through repair . . . The Three
Frigates building at St. Maloes are finishing up with great diligence,
one of them, ready for launching; [it is] to be put afloat in the approaching equinoctial tides, and, her stores and materials being ready,
she is directed to be equipped for sea with every possible activity.

7. Intelligence: Report on the Basque Roads from an escaped Prisoner of War
FROM: P.R.O., ADM/1/224

Declaration of Ralph Dunlop, Seaman, who was on board the *Foud-royant* in Basque Roads, on the day of the Action of the 12th of April last, and who escaped from Rochefort in a Neutral Vessel, on the 1st of August last (1809).

He declares that having been taken prisoner about six years ago, he had been detained at Givet till the 10th of last November, when wearied with cruel and harsh treatment, into an almost hopeless state, he with several others agreed to engage in the French Service, in the hopes of being brought to the Coasts, to find an oportunity to escape; that they were forced on board the *Foudroyant* in December last, at Brest, from whence they got to Rochefort in the French squadron; that on the day they were ordered out to Basque Roads, the Ship *Jean Bart*, of 74 Guns, ran aground and was wrecked, and most of the stores saved; that on the 12th of April the four following Ships were destroyed by the English fleet, viz,.

La Ville de Varsovie	80 Guns
Le Tonnerre ⎫	
L'Aquilon ⎬	74 Guns
Le Calcutta ⎭	

and the Frigate *L'Indienne*, burnt by the French.

The Triomphant of 74 Guns	
La Hortense	Frigate
La Pallas	idem
L'Elbe	idem, were in the Charente, with a Corvette

from Bordeaux, name not known, and *L'Epervier* Brig of 18 Guns.

La Dragonne, Brig, . . . was attacked by the Boats of the English Fleet, in which attempt, it was reported at Rochefort, two Boats were lost; there were two English seamen killed, and the Lieut. who Commanded was severely wounded in the thigh and with fifteen or 16 Men taken.

There remained at Rochefort on the 1st of August

(Ship's Name)	Guns	(Ship's Name)	Guns	
L'Ocean	120 ⎫			These escaped up
Le Foudroyant	74 ⎪	*Le Patriote*	74 ⎫	the Charente after
Le Cassart	74 ⎬	*Le Jemappe*	74 ⎬	the Action of the
Le Regulus	74 ⎭	*Le Tourville*	74 ⎭	12th of April

Le Triomphant   74 Guns and the three Frigates above.

The *Regulus* and *Cassart* have been docked and the others are to be docked in succession; all the Crews have been sent to Toulon, that of the *Cassart* excepted that are fitting out the *Triomphant* for Admiral Gourdon's Flag, who has succeeded M. L'Allemand, who is gone to Toulon.

The *Regulus*, *Tourville* and *Patriote* were most damaged; they with the *Ocean*, *Foudroyant* and *Jemappe*, are laying alongside old *Hulks*, waiting to be docked.

These are for the defence of the Charente, on the establishment of that Port as follows vizt

36 Lug-rigged Gun Vessels, with a 24-Pounder in the Bow, six Swivels and thirty two men.

12 Pinnaces, built like Ships of War Launches to row, and their masts to be struck; Armed with one 36 or 24-Pounder Howitzer and six swivels and thirty four Men.

12 Caiques, Vessels of the same description as the preceding, but heavier and stronger, with a long 24 Pounder aft and a 36-Pounder Howitzer forward and thirty four Men.

2 Armed Schooners No. 9 and 10, called Ballahoes attending the insular Forts.

There are now building in the Arsenal 2 Three-decked Ships of the largest Class called

Le *Jenna*
La *Ville de Varsovie*

These two are getting forward in their planking. One Frigate on the Stocks by then, *La Salle* of 48 Guns.

The 66th. Regiment of the Line Infantry is all the Garrison of Rochefort; and it is stated that the garrison of the Ile d'Aix consists of 700 Men.

8. Intelligence: Checking an Agent's Story. D'Auvergne to J. W. Croker, Jersey, 23 October 1811
FROM: P.R.O., ADM/1/226

The part [of the report] relating to the movement of Troops in the interior may, perhaps, be correct, but the details relating to the oyster vessels I have every reason to judge not so . . . neither has there been, or is there, one single vessel employed on what is called a Whiting Fishery, [which is] absolutely unknown in that district, all of that fish caught, and that in small quantity on the coast of Normandy or Bretagne, being taken in wares [i.e. weirs, or traps of basketry] staked on the flat sands, in which no marine craft of any description is employed. With respect to the small armed vessels employed on convoy between Cherbourg and Morlaix, the 'o' may safely be taken off the 4o or 5o. There is certainly not more than 6 or 7 Gun Vessels at the most so employed . . . the principal part of the Armed [vessels] consist of 14 or 16 Privateers from St Maloes and 2 or 3 from each of the harbours and Rivers of Binic, Brehat and Treguir. This I have from different channels corroborating each other and I am confident is nearer the truth than the very exagerated report exhibited to their Lordships. Indeed there is scarcely any Trade whatever stirring along shore, all seafaring Persons even to the very River Fishermen having been all included in the forced conscription sent to the North.

9. Intelligence: Reading the Enemy's Semaphore Signals. (Collingwood learns of General Sir John Stuart's attack on the islands in the Bay of Naples.) Collingwood to W. W. Pole, *Ville de Paris*, off Toulon, 20 July 1809
FROM: P.R.O., ADM/1/415

Yesterday the French Signal Posts telegraphed that a Fleet of Transports were anchored to the southward of Port Especia and Transports landed – the Ships of War standing into the Bay.

The *Scout* is in sight, when she joins I shall know the truth of this report.

I have not heard from Admiral Martin & Lieutenant General Sir John Stuart that they were about to make this movement.

Monthly Return of the State of the Enemy's Ships and Preparati
Channel Fleet, under the Command of Admiral the Right Honble

Name of Port, Place or Roadstead	Number of Ships in a State of Readiness for Sea				
	Date of Intelligence and by whom communicated	3 Deck-ers	2 Deck-ers	Fri-gates	C v
Brest roads....	Oct. 24th From Men taken in a lugger privateer captured by the Brilliant	1	8	3	
harbour..	Do	1	»	»	
L'Orient......	Sept. 18 Reconnoitred by the Gibraltar	»	3	5	
Concarneau ...	No late account	»	»	»	
River Loire....	Sept. 21. From men taken by the Narcissus boats in Quiberon Bay	»	»	2	
Rochefort	Octo. 14. From Captn. Percy of La Nymphe	»	»	»	
at Isle D'Aix	Octo. 19 From Captn. Ball of the Gibraltar	»	2	»	
Bourdeaux	Augt. 20 By Captn Rodd of the Indefatigable from the Officers of L'Adele Privateer captured	»	»	1	

Remarks
Names of the Enemy's ships in Brest, as obtained by Captain Smyth of the Brilli
from the crew of a French lugger privateer captured

		Guns	Men	
in the roads	L'Ocean	130	1650	
	Foudroyant........................	80	1200	
	Caesar	74	1000	
	Tonnière..........................	74	1000	
	Regulus...........................	74	1100	
	Ulysse	74	600	
	Aquilon...........................	74	700	
	Tourville..........................	74	1000	
	Jean Bart..........................	74	1000	Bad conditi unfit for se
in the harbour	Republican	130	none fitting	
	Invincible	130	complete fit	
	Wattigny..........................	74	— unfit for sea	

Caledonia *at Sea, 1ˢᵗ Novʳ, 1808*

fferent Parts of the Coast comprehended within the Station of *the*
ier &c &c

	Number of Ships fitting for Sea				Number of Ships building or repairing in Dock (those building in bold type) and when expected to be afloat				
e of Intelli-ace and by 1om com-unicated	3 Deck-ers	2 Deck-ers	Fri-gates	Cor-vettes	Date of Intelli-gence and by whom com-municated	3 Deck-ers	2 Deck-ers	Fri-gates	Cor-vettes
————	»	»	»	»	————	»	»	»	»
————	1	»	»	»	....*Unfit for Sea*	»	1	»	»
21 By men captured by the Eclair					....	»	2	»	»
————	»	»	»	»	*The* Veteran *laid up*	»	1	»	»
Nazaire	»	»	»	»	*ready for launch-ing on the Stocks*			2 3	at Pairs boeuf
oon be ready a..........	{13}				————	»	»	»	»
————	»	»	»	»	————	»	»	»	»
————	»	»	»	»	————	»	»	»	»

(signed) Gambier

11. Intelligence: a Local Commander's Monthly Report, Mediterranean Theatre.

(a) Admiral Pellew, Commander-in-Chief, Mediterranean Fleet, to J. W. Croker, Secretary to the Admiralty, 5 October 1812, with enclosures

FROM: P.R.O., ADM/1/424

Sir,

I have the honour to enclose the copy of the latest despatch from Rear Admiral Fremantle, stating the situation of affairs in the Adriatick, and the proposed arrangements he intended to make in consequence of my orders that he should remain in charge of the Services of that station.

Rear Admiral Laugharne has been directed to forward supplies for his division from Malta.

I have the honour to be,
Sir,
Your very obedient Servant,
(signed)   Ed. Pellew

(b) Rear Admiral Fremantle's General Reoprt of 27 September 1812, on the Adriatic State of the Enemy's preparations in the Adriatick, and Disposition of the British Squadron

	State of the Enemy's Force	Disposition of the British Squadron
Venice	Vide the information transmitted in my letter No. 46; in addition to the above Captain Rowley's report of the 15th [?5th] Instant states a Line of Battle Ship in the Arsenal with Top Gallant Masts fidded, top masts struck and Topsail yards across; and another Ship with her lower masts in.	Eagle – now at Lissa Achille Bacchante
Chiozza	Vide Account above referred to	
Trieste	Do. Captain Rowley reconnoitred Trieste on the 12th Instant and found the Report of the Danae's being blown up true, having seen a number of dead bodies floating and having picked up a piece of her figure head.	
Ancona	Vide the Account above referred to	Alcmene
Corfu	One Frigate (Guard Ship)	Apollo Cerberus Kingfisher – now at Lissa Weazle – Ordered to join me at Lissa Imogene St. George's harbour, Lissa, 27th September, 1812 (signed) Thos Fras Fremantle, Rear Admiral

(c) Copy of Intelligence received from a Deserter on 17 August 1812
Information obtained from Sig[re.] Nicholas Richitelli (late Pilot of the *Principessa
di Bolognia* at Chiozza) who deserted her with the Guard Boat and Crew on the
17th August, 1812, to H.M. Ship *Orlando* N.B. This Man was in the Arsenal on
the 16th of August, on which day the *Real Italiano* and *Piave* were launched.

	VENICE	
4	Line of Battle Ships launched; their Names are as follows:	

Ship's names		Admirals and Captains Na[mes]	Situation of Ship
	Guns		
San Bernado	74	Contre Ammiral[io] Dupéré	At the Malamocca quite ready for Sea
Il Regeneratore	74	Capt[no] Pasqualligio	
Castilone Francese	74	Late Capt. Frig. at Trieste	
Real Italiano	74	None appointed	In the Arsenal
Piave	44	None appointed	

9	Ships of the Line building – Vide annexed plan
3	Frigates building ... D⁰ ...
1	Corvette quite ready for Sea, but not manned
4	Brigs ready for Sea, called *L'Eridano*, *Principessa di Agusta*, *Mamalucco*, *Lieno*
1	... D⁰ ... in the Arsenal, quite new, name not known
4	Schooners manned and ready for Sea
60	Gun Boats or thereabouts
1	Brig building on a new construction (110 feet long)
	There is an abundance of all kinds of Stores for Ship Building in the Arsenal. All the Workmen employed in the Dock Yard are formed into a Regiment; the Engineer's name in Salvini, a Man of Science and information; he has engaged to the French government to build 13 sail of the Line in a year.

	CHIOZZA
1	Frigate manned and ready for Sea called the *Prin[a] di Bologna*, 325 Men, 44 Guns, Captain Ajchard

	TRIESTE
1	Frigate, the *Danae*

	ANCONA
1	Frigate, *L'Uranie*

Milford, St. George's harbour, Lissa, 10 September, 1812
(signed) Thomas Fra[s] Fremantle

(d) Report of a Reconnaissance made on 4 September 1812

A List of the Enemy's Ships at Venice and Chiozza, as Reconnoitred by His Majesty's Ship *Eagle*, Charles Rowley, Esqr·, Captain, on the 4th September, 1812, commencing at the point of Lido, Viz^t:

1	A Telegraph
2	A Man of War Brig ⎫ Ready for Sea
3	A Man of War Brig ⎭
4	A Gun Boat
5	A Gun Boat
6	A Man of War Brig – ready for Sea
7	The three lower Masts of a Line of Battle Ship, with her Top Masts pointed through (the Fore and Mizen ones Rigged while we were reconnoitering) supposed to be the Castiglione
8	A Man of War Brig
9	Three lower Masts, with Tops over, of a small Ship which appears to be in ordinary – Supposed to be the *Carolina*
10	Three lower Masts of a Ship: Fore and Mizen Masts rigged and Mainmast rigging. Not quite satisfied whether it is the *Royal Italian* or *Piave*
11	The Sheers
12	The Hulk, with a jury Main and Maintop mast
13	A Man of War Brig refitting
14	Several Merchantmen, two of which are Polacre Ships
15	The Camels laying at Povia, near the town of Malamocca
16	A Man of War Schooner
17	A Man of War Schooner
18	A Man of War Schooner
19	The Admiral's Ship ⎱ Seventy-fours – both ready for Sea with
20	The *Regenitore* ⎰ Royal Yards across and all Sails bent

CHIOZZA

21	The Frigate laying farther in than before
22	A Man of War Schooner
23	A Man of War Schooner
24	A Merchant Ship
	N.B. Besides the above there appears to be a Flotilla of Gunboats & Row Boats

Signed – C. Rowley, Captain

(e) Information obtained from the Trabaccola, Madona Rosario, Nicola Lazzari, Master, from Venice bound to Malta, boarded by His Majesty's Ship, Eagle, Charles Rowley, Esqr, Captain, on the 4th of September, 1812, Viz^t:—

The *Castiglione* 74 and *Piave* 44 laying at the Arsenal. The *Castiglione* has her lower Masts and Bowsprits in, Tops on and the Crews belonging to the Men of War Brigs are fitting her out; and she is expected to go down the Malamocca in twelve days. The *Real Italiano* lies under the Sheers and is getting her upper Decks in and Caulking.

No French Troops at Venice but all Italian and are from seven to eight thousand strong. All kinds of Provisions are cheap. The new Governour had not arrived.

They had the same report at Venice some time since about the Action with the Russians, as we heard, and that the Germans had all deserted over to the Russians.

Signed
C. Rowley

(f) Information received by Capt. C. Rowley,

His Majesty's Ship Eagle,
Off the Coast of Istria, 11 September 1812

Sir,

I have the honour of acquainting you I have been informed from undoubted authority that the Danae French Frigate laying at Trieste blew up on the night of the 5th Instant and that every Officer and Man on board perished; but it has not been ascertained whether it happened by accident, or was done wilfully . . .

I have the honour to &c.
Signed
C. Rowley, Captain

Rear Admiral Fremantle

12. Intelligence: the Enemy's Coasting Trade, Atlantic Theatre. Rear Admiral Keats to Admiral Lord St Vincent, from 'off Chasseron, 31 March 1807'
FROM: P.R.O., ADM/1/133

It appears by a Register kept on board the *Stationaire* (sloop of war) at the mouth of the Garonne, taken by Lord Cochrane, whose business it is to board all *Coasting Vessels*.

That in the space of something less than Ten Months no less than 1,231 Vessels from 10 to 400 Tons Burthen – of which the Tonnage amounted to 65,602 Tons, and the Cargoes to 59,189, navigated by 5,817 men – clear'd out and sail'd from the Garonne to the *Northward* – with cargoes consisting of Brandy, Wine, Rosen, some Oil and Naval Stores.

The names of some of the Vessels appear in the Register Twice or Thrice, according, as it should seem, to the number of Trips they made – consequently it reduces in the same proportion the number of seamen employed in the Trade.

13. Intelligence: the Enemy's Coasting Trade; Methods in Atlantic Theatre. Report from Capt. Lord Aemilius Beauclerk, of the *Saturn*, 16 December 1808
FROM: P.R.O., ADM/1/139

There are now in Crac and Morbian upwards of 60 sail of vessels, from 50 to 200 tons burden, laden chiefly with Timber and Provisions for L'Orient.

With respect ... to the supplying the Arsenals at L'Orient and Brest, it is invariably collected either in Morbian or Crac, from whence they go in a strong northerly wind to Sauzon in Belle Isle, waiting there till the wind comes to the South West, from whence they push for L'Orient, from whence the provisions etc. are sent chiefly by land or in small Boats coastways to Brest; in a South West Wind in Winter our Cruizers cannot with any degree of safety remain in the South East entrance of L'Orient, in order to intercept them.

14. Bonaparte's Naval Planning, 1805
(a) to Villeneuve, 14 April
FROM: *Correspondance de Napoleon 1er*, No. 8583

Monsieur le Vice-Amiral Villeneuve, you should by now have arrived at our island of Martinique with 12 of our ships of the line and at least 6 of the King of Spain's ships; contre-amiral Magon is taking you two more. Our intention is that if, thirty five days after the arrival of contre-amiral Magon, you have no news of Admiral Ganteaume, whom you must suppose to have been delayed by circumstances and the enemy's blockade, you will come back, directly and by the shortest route, to Ferrol. There you will find 15 French and Spanish ships of the line, which will increase your squadron to 35 ships. With that force you will appear before Brest, there you will join the 21 ships of the line which Admiral Ganteaume commands, and without entering the port, you will come up the Channel with that force and appear before Boulogne. In these circumstances our intention is that you should have the command of the whole naval force.

(b) to Decrès, 18 May
FROM: *Correspondance de Napoleon 1er*, No. 8699

... On 29 June, and not later, Villeneuve must sail and arrive like an arrow before Ferrol. As for Ganteaume, if he has not gone [from Brest] by 20 May, my intention is that he should not sail but that he should remain, always embarked, always ready, always provisioned. You will let him know the plan of campaign; but, in order that he may be still more on his guard, you will tell him that Villeneuve should appear before Brest between the 9th and 19th of July. I think that it would be very useful if you had a statement inserted in the Dutch newspapers that a new squadron of 3 line of battleships and 4 frigates has sailed from Rochefort, under Admiral Magon's orders, and has on board that officer whom Lauriston should bring forward, whom you will name, and who is said to have been a prisoner so long at St Helena. To sum up I hold invariably to this program: Ganteaume must sail, if he can, at any time up to mid-night on 20 May. From the moment of sunrise on 21 May, however many opportunities of sailing he may have, he will stand firm at Brest and not go. Admiral Villeneuve will be informed of these arrangements by the *Topaze*; he will have the order to leave [the West Indies] on 29 June; the *Président* will sail from Lorient on 21 May; she will inform Villeneuve that he is not to lose another hour, that he is useless if he waits. For this purpose you will order Ganteaume that, if he has not sailed by mid-night on 20 May, he is to send a courier to the commander of the *Président* to make him sail forthwith. By these means we shall gain many days. The packet [of instructions to give to Villeneuve] will have been sent in advance to the commander of the *Président*. On 14 July I shall be on the [Channel] coast and up to 29 July I shall wait for the return of my squadrons.

(c) to Villeneuve, 16 July; Orders to sail for the Straits of Dover
FROM: *Correspondance de Napoleon Ier*, No. 8985

Monsieur le Vice-Amiral,

You have made your junction with the squadrons in Ferrol and you will take steps to make yourself master of the Straits of Dover, even if it is only for four or five days. That can be done by uniting under your command our squadrons in Rochefort and in Brest, or either our squadron in Brest or our squadron in Rochefort, and sailing round Ireland and Scotland with that force in order to join up with the Dutch squadron in the Texel.

Our Minister of the Marine will inform you of the strength of our squadrons and the different combinations which have seemed to us most likely. We rely entirely, for their success, on your experience and on your zeal for the glory of our arms.

If as a result of combats in which you have engaged, the separation of ships from your fleet or other events which we have not foreseen, your situation should be seriously changed we do not wish your force under any circumstances to enter Ferrol; in that case, which with God's help will not occur, we wish you, after releasing our squadrons in Rochefort and Ferrol, to anchor in the port of Cadiz. Europe is on

tenterhooks waiting for the great event which we are preparing. All our trust is in your bravery and skill. . . .
Napoleon

(d) to Ganteaume, 20 July
FROM: *Correspondance de Napoleon 1ᵉʳ*, No. 8998

Monsieur le Général Ganteaume, Commander of our naval forces at Brest, our minister will let you know the news which we have just received, through England, of our squadron under Admiral Villeneuve. He will also inform you that the English squadron has lifted the blockade, which has enabled our squadron there to sail on 17 July.

Your dispatches over the telegraph have likewise informed me that for several days the English fleet has not been reported off your anchorage.

We have already given you the order to go out and chase off the enemy's frigates and discover where the enemy has gone.

If you find him on the open seas off Brest, with fewer than 16 ships of the line, it is our positive intention that you attack him with your 21 ships. We are justified in hoping for a victory.

If, on the contrary, the enemy is not in sight, and has gone either to Ferrol or further out to sea to meet Admiral Villeneuve, our intention is that you should enter the Channel and come to Boulogne where everything is ready and where, if you command the sea for three days, you will put an end to the destinies of England.

If the enemy has a considerable squadron before Brest, but not too strong for you to fight, and if that squadron retreats from you, you will make a point of chasing him, if that is possible and putting yourself in a position to aid Admiral Villeneuve and joining up with him the moment he appears before Brest; and if you are led to consider that the squadron opposed to you has been weakened in order to strengthen the one at Ferrol and confront Admiral Villeneuve, we authorise you to chase the enemy off Brest and then evade him and come by a misleading route to Ferrol, to surprise the enemy and pick up our combined squadron there which has 15 line of battle ships; then pick up our squadron at Rochefort, commanded by Captain Allemand, whose station the minister of marine will point out to you. After disconcerting the operations of the English admiralty in this way, you will swiftly enter the Channel.

(e) Statement of Invasion Craft ready 8 August

FROM: E. Desbrière, *Projets et Tentatives de Débarquements aux Iles Britanniques* (Paris, 1902), Vol. IV, Pt. II, facing p. 465

THE NATIONAL FLOTILLA

State showing the number of Invasion Craft of each type in Bonaparte's flotilla existing in the ports of assembly on 8 August, 1805

NATIONAL FLOTILLA

WARSHIPS

PORTS	Prames Number			Bomb Ketches Number			Packet Boats Number			Sloops of War Number			Gun Brigs Number			Gun Boats Number		
	of vessels	men which can carry	horses which can carry	of vessels	men which can carry	horses which can carry	of vessels	men which can carry	horses which can carry	of vessels	men which can carry	horses which can carry	of vessels	men which can carry	horses which can carry	of vessels	men which can carry	horses which can carry
Étaples	»	»	»	»	»	»	1	20	2	»	»	»	36	4,680	»	108	10,800	216
Boulogne	14	1,680	690	3	150	»	9	360	54	2	260	»	187	24,310	»	221	22,385	426
Wimereux	»	»	»	»	»	»	»	»	»	4	520	»	32	4,160	»	36	3,620	72
Ambleteuse (c)	3	270	150	»	»	»	»	»	»	»	»	»	»	»	»	»	»	»
Calais (c)	1	90	50	»	»	»	»	»	»	»	»	»	»	»	»	»	»	»
Dunkerque	»	»	»	»	»	»	»	»	»	»	»	»	10	1,300	»	»	»	»
Ostende	»	»	»	»	»	»	»	»	»	»	»	»	»	»	»	»	»	»
Crews on French Transports	»	»	»	»	»	»	»	»	»	»	»	»	»	»	»	»	»	»
TOTALS	18	2,040	890	3	150	»	10	380	56	6	780	»	265	34,450	»	365	36,805	714

THE NATIONAL FLOTILLA (*continued*)

PORTS	WARSHIPS				NATIONAL FLOTILLA			TRANSPORTS											
	Pinnaces Number		Caiques Number		Number			Horse Transports Number			Artillery Number			Staff Officers & army baggage number			Unclassified Boats Number		
	of pinnaces	of men they can carry	of caiques	of men whom they can carry	of vessels	which can carry men	which can carry horses	of vessels	which can carry men	which can carry horses	of vessels	which can carry men	which can carry horses	of vessels	which can carry men	which can carry horses	of vessels	which can carry men	which can carry horses
Étaples	(a) {72 / 25}	4,884	»	»	»	»	»	72	5,663	1,200	18	270	»	36	540	72	»	»	»
Boulogne	(b) {154 / 85}	10,692	19	570	»	»	»	44	8,537	2,070	36	540	»	72	1,080	144	23	345	»
Wimereux	72	4,752	»	»	»	»	»	56	3,286	667	14	210	»	15	235	30	»	»	»
Ambleteuse	(c) {3 / 1}	264	»	»	»	»	»	(c) 17	309	309	(c) 4	80	»	(c) 10	200	»	»	»	»
Calais	(c) {3 / 22}	1,650	»	»	81	8,349	233	81	5,800	1,800	»	»	»	(c) 5	100	»	»	»	»
Dunkerque	(c) 12	792	»	»	»	»	»	(c) 15	280	280	5	100	»	(c) 6	120	»	»	»	»
Ostende	»	»	»	»	»	»	»	(c) 20	370	370	(c) 3	60	»	(c) 2	40	»	»	»	»
Crews on French Transports	»	»	»	»	»	»	»	»	»	»	»	»	»	»	»	»	»	»	»
TOTALS	349	23,034	19	570	81	8,349	233	405	24,245	6,596	80	1,260	»	246	2,315	246	23	345	»

THE NATIONAL FLOTILLA (continued)

PORT	BOATS				DUTCH FLOTILLA						Total of vessels assembled in each port Number		
	Newfoundland Number		Whalers Number		Gun Brigs Number			Gun Boats Number					
	of vessels	of men whom they can carry	of boats	of men whom they can carry	of vessels	men	horses	of vessels	men	horses	of vessels	men	horses
						which can carry			which can carry			which can carry	
Étaples	20	240	»	»	»	»	»	»	»	»	365	27,097	1,390
Boulogne........	73	876	188	1,216	»	»	»	»	»	»	1,153	73,001	3,384
Wimereux........	6	72	2	14	»	»	»	»	»	»	237	16,869	769
Ambleteuse.......	3	36	»	»	25	3,250	»	107	10,700	214	173	15,109	673
Calais	»	»	19	133	11	1,430	»	»	»	»	223	17,552	2,083
Dunkerque	»	»	»	»	19	2,470	»	100	10,000	200	157	13,762	480
Ostende.........	»	»	»	»	»	»	»	»	»	»	35	1,770	370
Crews on French Transports	»	»	»	»	»	»	»	»	»	»	»	2,430	»
TOTALS	102	1,224	209	1,363	55	7,150	»	207	20,700	414	2,343	167,590	9,149

(a) Pinnaces detailed to serve Marshal Ney and Rear-Admiral Courand, commanding the left at Etaples.
(b) Pinnaces detailed to serve Bonaparte himself, his minister Berthier, Marshal Soult, Rear-Admiral La Crosse, commander-in-chief of the flotilla, and Rear-Admiral Savary, commanding the centre, and chief of the general staff of the flotilla.
(c) Vessels forming part of the Dutch flotilla.

Boulogne, le 20 thermidor an XIII de la République française.
Le Chef de l'état-major de la flotille nationale,
LAFOND.

15. Bonaparte's Planning after 1805: a Proposal of March 1808.
FROM: *Correspondance de Napoleon Ier*, No. 13,708

The Boulogne flotilla is too large. It is established that it could not leave its roadstead all in one body. This project of centralising [the flotilla] would be good only if there were a fine and good roadstead. In this situation of affairs it is necessary to pick a larger place.

1st. The Texel invasion fleet ought to be restored to its condition during General Marmont's command there [in 1804] and be capable of carrying 15,000 men in large transports.

2nd. A second invasion fleet ought to be assembled at Flushing. It ought to be escorted by the 8 ships of the line I have there; it ought to be able to carry 20,000 men. In the month of November, when the weather is good, a camp would be set up at Flushing; and at all times this squadron, composed of 10 ships of the line (another 2 can be added between now and November), and about 40 transports, should be ready to sail. I think it is also necessary to concentrate the whole Dutch flotilla at Flushing. The gun-brigs would be useful in the game our ships have to play. One could also assemble there the transports which at this moment are assembled at Calais, so that the 20 or 25,000 men could be easily transported from Flushing in Holland.

3rd. The camp at Boulogne will be so organised that 80,000 men could disembark on the enemy coast.

The squadron at Flushing will also be reinforced every year.

The difficulties of this system are: to find sailors to man the 10 ships of the line and 30 or 40 transports. For that men must be conscripted at Hamburg, Bremen, Lubeck and in Denmark.

We can very well have 10 ships of the line at Flushing, in the month of November, which will carry 6000 men [besides their crews]. It is necessary to provide 20 large 'flutes' each carrying 1000 men; which will make more than 26,000 men. The whole Dutch flotilla, and gun-brigs, are needed, as much to assist in the disembarkation as to confuse the English over our true destination, since it is obvious to the English that gun-brigs can only be intended for the coast of England. The gun-brigs would likewise be useful for the whole movement from the coast and the protection of the convoy.

The English would then have to maintain all summer a flotilla against our flotilla and a squadron against our squadron, a kind of war which will keep them very busy.

At the same time in Corfu, Taranto and Naples I will make preparations for an expedition against Sicily or Egypt.

I will have an invasion fleet prepared at Cadiz.

Supposing everything succeeds I can have 16 French and 8 Spanish line of battle ships on the port of Toulon by the month of November. I will make them set out as if for Sicily and I will send them to Cadiz where they will join 8 French and 8 Spanish ships of the line which I have there; that will give me 26 French line of battle ships, or at least 24, and 12 Spaniards [sic] total, 36 ships of the line. I shall either send them to Lisbon, where they will join 2 French and 10 Russian ships;[1] or, if there is nothing to be gained by that operation, I will have them sail up the Channel, to come before Boulogne, to enter Cherbourg or to go to Flushing.

It will be so evident that we are aiming at Sicily and Egypt – preparations to be made at Constantinople will point to the same conclusion – that the English cannot help being deceived.

[1] The 2 ships of the Line in Lisbon, which Bonaparte here calls 'French', can only be those Portuguese ships which had been unfit to sail to Brazil before Junot occupied Lisdon in the preceding November.

16. Bonaparte's Planning after 1805: a Draft Plan for 1812.
Bonaparte to Decrès, 17 September 1810
FROM: *Correspondance de Napoleon Ier*, No. 16,916

Monsieur le Comte Decrès, I have informed you that I wish to have at
Cherbourg a concentration of force large enough to threaten the Channel
Islands and to compel the enemy to keep troops there. The arrival of a
division [of French troops] at Cherbourg has already had a good effect.
But I wish the two large 'flutes' at Le Havre to be manned without
delay and to be sent as soon as possible to Cherbourg. These transports,
with the frigate and two ships of the line now in that harbour would
make the enemy afraid of having from 6 to 8000 men descend on his
islands. Likewise, these ships, being at Cherbourg, would be ready for
any expedition. The English would be compelled to blockade this
force all winter and that would keep several ships busy for them. . . .
I want to know when these transports and the frigate will be ready at
Cherbourg.

By my decree of 15 July last I have ordered a transport flotilla in the
Mediterranean. I wish to know where that flotilla is and what it can
carry. When, for example, shall I have the means of carrying to Egypt
five divisions of troops of the line, each composed of eight battalions,
or 6,000 men, making 30,000 infantry, with 4,000 gunners and engineers
and 6,000 cavalry, total 40,000 men, with five hundred artillery waggons
and 2000 horses for the artillery and cavalry?

Let me know what sort of boats can be built at Dordrecht; I would
like to build there a flotilla capable of carrying to Ireland or Scotland a
force of four divisions, each of ten battalions or 8000 men, making
32,000 infantry, 4000 gunners and engineers and 6000 cavalrymen,
total 42,000 men, with 3000 horses for the artillery and cavalry, and
120 field guns, for a total of 700 vehicles [i.e. including the ammunition
waggons of the artillery]. I suppose that the boats should be loaded to a
point just within the margin of safety. Bring me a report on this expedition at next Friday's council, on the type of ships and their tonnage (the
smaller their number the better) and on the construction of the horse
transports, likewise calculated to total as few ships as possible.

I wish you to make me another report on the position in which we
can hope to find ourselves in 1812. Everything leads me to believe that
before that date our prisoners should be exchanged [i.e. Decrès is to
reckon on having by then French sailors who in September 1810 were
still prisoners of war in England]. I think that in the month of August,
1812, I shall have, in the Texel anchorage, nine ships of the line at the
Texel, six in the estuary of the Maas; twenty six in the estuary of the
Scheldt, six at Cherbourg, including the *Ulysse*, total fifty one; eight

ships of the line at Lorient, ten at Rochefort (my intention is to try during this winter and next winter to concentrate the ships at Lorient and Rochefort in Brest, which would make twenty two in this last port and recreate this squadron), twenty four ships at Toulon; this, with the three which the King of Naples will have at Naples, and the eight which France and the Kingdom of Italy will have at Ancona or Pola, will make one hundred and four ships of the line.

If these one hundred and four ships are backed by a fleet of transports in the Scheldt carrying 42,000 men, composed as above, by a fleet of transports in the Mediterranean carrying 40,000 men, by the flotilla of Boulogne able to carry 60,000 men, by a flotilla opposite Sicily [held by a British garrison] able to carry 20,000 men, by a transport fleet in Cherbourg able to carry 12,000 men, and also by transport ships taken from Holland and escorted by the Texel and Maas squadrons, which would total 200,000 men, the English would find themselves in a position very different from the one they occupy today.

That is my plan of campaign for 1812. I shall await the report which you will bring me at the next council. One must never lose sight of the aim which is to be achieved.

I also wish to build a transport fleet in the Scheldt, and one at Havre for the expedition for Cherbourg; to have one in the Mediterranean, and at the same time to reduce my flotilla at Boulogne in such a way that it becomes a means of diversion and an accessory which need no longer operate alone and can threaten a landing of 60,000 men on the enemy's territory at a time when he would be occupied elsewhere.

                                                        Napoleon

17. Bonaparte's Planning after 1805: Choice of a Port of Assembly.
Bonaparte to Decrès, 16 August 1811
FROM: *Correspondance de Napoleon 1ᵉʳ*, No. 18,039

Monsieur le Comte Decrès, which is the port which should be preferred
for assembling my squadron of the [Atlantic] Ocean? I see only two
possible choices: Cherbourg or Brest. Which of these ports offers me
the most opportunities for a landing in England or Ireland? Which
offers me the most opportunities for sailing to America and the Indies?
Could ten ships of the line assembled at Cherbourg sail out every day
and play at helmsmanship with a superior squadron, as the one at
Toulon does?[1] The squadron which I would assemble there would
be composed of five ships of the line from Lorient (for that purpose I
would want one of the ships being built there to be launched and ready
to sail before January), two ships from Brest (and, likewise, I would
wish an order to be given in that port for the *Orion* to be launched as
soon as possible), also the four ships at Cherbourg, including those
which are still on the stocks; that would make a squadron of eleven
warships, which could easily be concentrated at either Brest or Cherbourg. As the equinox is coming, the necessary orders should be given.
I wish you to make me a report on this important question.

It is also necessary to see how many frigates can be drawn from
Nantes, Brest, St. Malo, Cherbourg, le Havre, etc. to add to this
squadron.

[1] This is just about what the Toulon squadron was constantly doing, thanks
to the local winds; see, for example, Henry Raikes, *Memoir of the Life and
Services of Vice-Admiral Sir Jahleel Brenton, Bart., K.C.B.*, (London, 1846),
321, 328, 336, and especially Admiral Thornborough's letter (320–1) warning
Brenton: 'I dread particularly the treacherous calms off Cape Sicie whilst the
ships in the outer roads of Toulon have a fresh breeze off the land, which might
bring them alongside you in a few minutes'. The calm further out combined
with shore breezes closer in enabled the Toulon squadron to exercise out of
harbour without the main blockading fleet being able to interfere.

18. Bonaparte's Naval Programme: a reminder to the Minister of Marine. Bonaparte to Decrès, 17 September 1810
FROM: *Correspondance de Napoleon 1er*, No. 16,915

Why has the building of the *Impérial*, the *Tibre* and the *Romulus* not yet been started at Toulon? Another ship must be begun in place of the *Sceptre*. I would wish to have four more ships of the line at Toulon, the *Impérial*, the one which will be put on the stocks vacated by the *Sceptre*, the *Tibre*, the *Trident* and the *Romulus*. No progress is being made on the *Agamemnon* at Genoa. By the end of 1812 I want to have twenty five ships of the line at Toulon.

19. Bonaparte's Naval Programme: Exposé of 29 June 1811
FROM: *The Times* (London), 11 July 1811

[This document contains passages from Bonaparte's *exposé* of 29 June 1811, which deal with the war at sea. Note the attention paid to his ports, including the Channel ports, the great size of the fleet for which he was preparing anchorages in the Scheldt and the large overall total of ships of the line which he intended to build.]

PARIS, July 1

EXPOSITION OF THE STATE OF THE EMPIRE PRE-SENTED TO THE LEGISLATIVE BODY AT ITS SITTING OF JUNE 29, BY HIS EXCELLENCY COUNT MONTALIVET, MINISTER FOR THE INTERIOR...

... FORTIFICATIONS

... (Here several works in the Texel, at Antwerp, Cadzand etc. are enumerated.)

In 1810 and 1811 more than eight millions were expended on the forts on the Scheldt; it was natural to bestow great labour on a point which will ever be the object of the jealousy and fears of our natural enemies.

(The Report then proceeds to enumerate other works at Ostend, Boulogne, Cherbourg and Havre...)

PORTS

At our ports the labours go on with the same activity. At Antwerp since the end of last year they have removed the dam from the bason. Eighteen ships of the line, even three deckers, can enter and go out fully equipped. In the beginning of this year two 80-gun ships have been coppered and refitted there. The work continues with great activity. Before the end of next September the bason will be able to hold thirty ships.

Ships of the line can only enter the bason of Flushing without their guns. The sluice is now dried and insulated and they are busied in lowering it so that twenty ships will be able to enter it with their guns. The quays which the English damaged are now restored. They are labouring now at reconstructing the magazine and making it bombproof.

The ground has already been chosen for the bason of Terneuse; its foundations are now laying. Twenty ships of the line, fully equipped, will be able to leave this bason on one tide. It will be able to hold forty.[1]

---

[1] In fact the basin at Terneuse was a failure, as the soil there was unequal to supporting its foundations.

The sluice of the race of Ostend is finished; it has been of the great service to the fort[2]; that of Dunkirk will be finished by the end of the year. Great advantages are expected from the deepening of the Channel. The sluice at Havre is finished and has been of great advantage.

At Cherbourg the expences of the road[3] are of two sorts. The first operation is to raise the dyke above the low water mark, and this will be accomplished in the course of the present year; the second is to construct forts at the extremities of the dyke to defend the road; the fort of the centre is just finished. The road being in this manner secured it remained to dig the port of this great work; nine tenths are executed. Thirdly, ships of the line will be able to lie in the port and bason; already a vessel which had received damage at sea has entered the bason and been refitted here. The *avant-port* and bason will be finished in 1812. The building docks and frames already exist. The works at Cherbourg alone require more than three millions yearly . . .

MARINE

Since the annexation of Holland[4] that country has furnished me with 10,000 seamen and thirteen ships of the line. We have considerable fleets in the Scheldt and at Toulon. Squadrons of ships of the line more or less strong are in the different ports and fifteen ships are on the stocks at Antwerp. Everything is so arranged as to add every year a great number of ships of war to our squadron in the Scheldt.

Two ships of the line are building at Cherbourg; and the magazines of timber, and other materials of every kind, are there so considerable that we may put five on the stocks before the close of 1811.

L'Orient, Rochefort and Toulon have all their frames occupied. Numerous ships are constructing at Venice.[5]

Naples ought in pursuance of treaties to have this year six ships of the line and six frigates. That kingdom has them not, but its government will be convinced of the necessity of repairing this negligence.

Our resources [and] our interior navigation are[6] sufficient to advance the *material* part of our marine to the same point as our enemies.

The experiments made of a maritime conscription have succeeded. Young men of 18, 19 and 20 sent on board our ships display the best inclination and are rapidly forming . . .

[2] 'Fort' is printed; 'port' seems clearly intended.
[3] Meaning, of course, the sort of 'road' in which ships 'ride' at anchor.
[4] On 1 July 1810.
[5] For reports on the dockyards of Venice a year later, see Doc. 11.
[6] Meaning canal systems, since water transport was then the only way to move bulky oak timber any distance.

We shall be able to make peace with safety when we shall have 150[7] ships of the line; and, in spite of the obstacles of war, such is the state of the empire that we shall have that number of vessels. Thus the guarantee of our fleet, and that of an English administration founded on principles different from those of the existing Cabinet, can alone give peace to the universe.

[7] This number would give France a numerical superiority of nearly 50 per cent over the total of 107 line of battle ships which the Royal Navy had in commission in the course of 1811.

20. Bonaparte's Naval Programme: Tasks ordered for 1813-14.
Bonaparte to Decrès, 23 January 1813
FROM: *Correspondance de Napoleon Ier*, No. 19,488

I can by no means agree to reducing my naval armaments; I am not in a
position to balance 12 or 15 million francs against the reaction which
this reduction would produce on the morale of my sailors and my
enemies. The only thing to which I can consent is not to increase my armaments in Holland and on the Scheldt; but my intention is to increase
those in Toulon, Rochefort, Brest and Cherbourg as much as possible.

I wish to have at the Texel a squadron equal to the one I had there
last year; I consent only to refraining from equipping a ship of 64 guns
and instead to equip the two new frigates, for I am very impatient to
have two frigates armed in the French pattern at the Texel. I see no
inconvenience in disarming the *Hollandais*, if she is a Dutch ship, but I
cannot consent to disarming the *Illustre*, the *Anversois*, the *Duguesclin*,
the *César*, the *Ville-de-Berlin*, the *Commerce-de-Lyon* and the *Danzig*.
There is no objection to disarming the *Tromp* and the *Chatham*. You
see that I consent to disarming only Dutch ships which I wish to keep
as good 'flutes' in the basin at Antwerp, for service at the moment when
I am in a position to start operations at sea.

I by no means wish the *Castiglione* to be disarmed at Venice; that
would have the worst effect.

Besides the *Weser*, the *Trave*, the *Montenotte*, the *Zélandais*, etc.
I want a ship equipped at Brest. My intention is that the building
programme should be carried on with the same activity in 1813; but I
agree that, instead of launching ships of the line and working to arm
them, we should start work on a good number of vessels and make progress, of such a kind that I can launch a score of them in a single year,
when I am in a position to undertake naval operations.

During 1812 I had eight ships of the line and five frigates at the
Texel. I consent to not equipping the *Aurora* and the *Maria*, which
strike me as bad frigates, and to equipping only the *Meuse*, the *Yssel*,
the *Trave* and the *Weser*. If it is necessary, we can, as I said, disarm
one of the ships of 64 guns.

I need to train sailors; the Texel has been pointed out to me as the
place which is most suitable for that.

At Amsterdam little progress has been made on the *Couronne* and the
Audacieux; the *Polypheme* has not even been started. I wish work on
all three to be pressed on in such a manner that they could be launched
in 1814, if that was necessary. I consent to not launching the *Pitheen*
and the *Amstel* in 1813; but enough progress must be made on these
ships to enable them to be launched in March, 1814.

I have fourteen ships on the stocks at Antwerp. Three of these ships, the *Monarque*, the *Hymen* and the *Superbe*, were to have been ready for launching in 1813; they must be carried on in such a way that we can launch them in March, 1814, if that is suitable. Of the eleven others, you will make progress enough to enable them to be launched in March, April and June, 1814; and progress enough on the five others to enable them easily to be launched in 1815.

If you send out the two frigates which are at Dunkirk, they should be given a free hand, for, with the English waiting to see them go to Flushing, they would perhaps enter Brest or Cherbourg more easily, provided they were equipped to keep the sea for some months.

At Cherbourg work on the *Jupiter*, the *Centaure* and the *Inflexible* must be carried on in a way that will enable them to be launched in 1814. The *Zelandais* and the *Duguay-Truin* are finished. That will give me seven ships at Cherbourg, counting the two I have there already.

I wish the *Orion* to be launched as soon as possible at Brest and that at Lorient work on the *Brabançon*, the *Magnifique*, the *Algésiras* and the *Jean-Bart* should be carried on so that they can be launched, the first in 1814, and the three others in 1815.

It would be proper to start building an 84-gun ship at Rochefort, which would give me six ships that I could have there in 1814 and 1815.

At Toulon I wish the building programme to be carried on as vigorously as possible. I do not see why you should not wish to launch a ship in 1813. It is necessary to launch the *Héros*, to start building a 118-gun ship and to press on with the work so that the *Colosse* and the *Kremlin* can be launched in 1814.

At Genoa work on the *Scipion* and the *Brilliant* should be pushed on so that they can be launched in 1814.

As for Venice, the work there must not be reduced at all. The Kingdom of Italy could not pay me 30 million francs, above all at a moment when it is stripped of troops, if I did not help it by making payments there. Suggest to me how that sum could be best laid out. It is desirable to launch the *Duquesne* and the *Montenotte* immediately at Venice, also the *Amphitrite*. Work on the _____ [1] should be pushed on so as to enable her to be launched in 1814. With the two ships that I now have in Venice, and with the three ships belonging to the Kingdom of Italy, I shall have a fleet of eight ships there.

As for the levies of 1813, take the conscripts who belong to you; my intention is not to reduce my state of preparedness at sea, and if you should lose a year, it would be irremediable.

Prepare your budget on these bases and make it surpass the expenses of 1812. You had reported much more work than you have done. I see

---

[1] There is a gap here in the original.

that you have launched only one single ship, which is the *Montebello*.

In the month of September, 1814, I wish to have at Toulon seven ships of three decks, two 80-gun and seventeen 74-gun ships, total, twenty six; at Venice, five; which will give me thirty one ships in the Mediterranean; and with the three Italian and two Neapolitan ships, thirty six ships of the line; at Rochefort, eleven ships, four of them to be three-deckers; at Lorient, three ships; at Brest, seven, one of them to be a three-decker; at Cherbourg, seven, one a three-decker; that would give me on the [Atlantic] Ocean twenty-eight ships including six of three-decks. Then, for the Scheldt, thirty ships, including two three-deckers, and ten for the Texel; a total of one hundred and four ships.

Then, after establishing a system of complements and gunners for the sea service, and with a good number of trained sailors, we shall have a fleet capable of imposing on the enemy.

In your budget you will show as an economy the provisions and other things of that kind which would no longer be issued to men who have left the marine service.

21. The Fortification of England's South Coast: the Martello Towers.
(a) The First Proposal. Report of Captain Reynolds, 7 April 1798
FROM: P.R.O., WO/30/62.

My Lord,
Sensible as I am that we have no time to lose in providing every means that may ensure the safety of the Kingdom and especially of the Capital I cannot forbear again offering some Opinions on the Defence of the Coasts of the Eastern and Southern Districts, in addition to those I have already had the honor of laying before your Lordship

In the course of my rides along the coasts in question I have observed with regret that neither the Situation nor construction of most of the batteries established for its Defence will allow us to place much dependence on their Efficacy. In whatever way I regard them, they appear to me as more calculated to promote the views of the Enemy when landed than to resist their Descent; it was a sense of the Inefficacy of Open Batteries that made me so cautious in proposing their adoption; and whenever I made choice of a situation for a Work of this Description it will be seen by a Reference to my Reports that I have always had an Eye to its Security against Assault. But the points of the coast which require defence are so many and the natural advantages to which I allude so few, that it behoves us to consider of some other means of Resistance, more calculated to produce the Effect desired; viz. of preventing the Enemy from settling in any Bay, Harbour, or Roadsted; or at least to oblige him to abandon his craft when landed. Now there are no Works that appear to me so likely to Effect this great Object, as a Simple Tower of Brickwork defended by a Handful of Resolute Men. . . .

The walls being perfectly round, 6 feet thick at the Base and three feet thick at the top, ought to be sufficiently strong to resist a well directed fire of Heavy Ordnance for some days, especially as I propose to fill up the vacuum below the Cisterns and Magazine with the Earth dug out for the Foundation. Marshal Saxe in his Reflexions observes that he has frequently seen Brick Towers, Hollow and very weakly constructed, that have sustained the Fire of 20 pieces of Large Cannon for three or four entire days and that at a distance of 400 Paces without having been destroyed.

Should the Tower be built on a Chalk Cliff or Rock then as no other foundation, will be necessary the whole vacuum may be filled up with an entire Map of Brickwork.

The Height of the Tower being 33 feet in the clear reckining [sic] from the Surface of the Ground renders it scarcely liable to an Escalade but is a further Security against Assault. I would recommend a Fraize of

Iron Work or of Oak if the former should be found too Expensive to be planted round the lower part of the Parapet with the Points rather depressed.

The Roof which ought to be arched and made Bombproof should also consist of BrickWork and project sufficiently over the Walls of the Tower to allow for Horizontal loopholes and a Parapet of Proper solidity.

The Tower has only one Circular Chamber about 15 feet in diameter, lighted by 12 small loopholes, and a window three feet in diameter at which it is proposed the Garrison shall enter by means of a Ladder near 30 feet long. This ladder should be jointed to admit of its being secured within the Tower when an Attack takes place. The Window ought to be placed on the Side least exposed to the Fire of land Batteries, therefore unless Ships of War can lay within Musquet Shot of the Tower, it will be best to have it look toward the Sea.

The Principal Defence might consist of one Heavy Piece of Ordnance of large Calibre, mounted En-Barbette a sliding Carriage, constructed so as to give it the greatest Angle of Depression possible. A spare Gun and Carriage with the means of mounting it might also be kept in Reserve; and further to annoy the Enemy should he have made a Lodgement within the fire of the Great Gun, an Apparatus may be prepared for mounting Swivels on the parapet. These together with 20 or 30 Musquets and Pikes will be all the Arms that are requisite.

It is evident that a tower of this construction can only be destroyed by Cannon or the Miner, to effect what in either case must be a Work of Time.

If built on a height that commands the Country on every side, the Enemy cannot effectually elevate his Guns to make any Impression of consequence; and if it should be erected on a Shingly Beach or Rocky Ground, which will frequently occur the Miner will meet with great impediments in his Operations.

I am not in the habit of Estimating the Expense of Military Works . . . [but he thinks cost would equal £2000 each]. . . .

It may be objected that the Tower will not be ready for the Attack meditated by the Enemy; this I will admit, but I look to a period more distant than the present, for that crisis which is to determine the fate of the Kingdom, I allude to a period when by a Combination of the Marine Powers of Europe and the Efforts of our implacable Enemy we may find it necessary to collect the whole of our Naval Strength to a point, and leave for a time the Coast of England to the protection of Military Force only, in which case a Cordon of these Towers will be found of the utmost Importance.

(b) The Approved Model. Committee's Report to Lt Gen. Morse, 14 October 1804

FROM: P.R.O., WO/30/78

Sir,

We beg leave to submit the following description of a Project we have formed of a Bomb Proof Tower for the defence of the Coast, without waiting untill the Drawings for it are finished, which are now in hand.

The interior Circle of the Tower has a diameter of 26 Feet, and the area at the top is calculated to receive one 24 Pounder Gun, and two Cannondades of the same Calibre, all mounted on traversing Platforms, to fire over a high Parapet, the Crest of which is about 33 Feet from the Foundation.

The Ground Floor to contain a Powder Magazine and Cistern with rooms for Provisions, Fuel and other Stores.

The Middle Floor to lodge a Garrison of One Officer and 24 Men, having an Entrance placed ten feet above the exterior Ground.

In this Project the centre Pillar is solid and a Stone Stair Case is contrived in the Exterior Wall which at that part is so increased in thickness as to render it every where equally strong.

After weighing all the propositions of this Construction, we can recommend it as preferable to any of those we have submitted before to your consideration. . . .

We have &c.

SIGNED ⎱ N. D'Aubant
⎰ Wm. Twiss
⎰ Thomas Nepean

22. The Fortification of England's South Coast: Romney Marsh.
(a) Original Plans for Flooding the Marsh. General Sir Charles
Grey to the Duke of York, 30 April 1798
FROM: Huskisson Papers, B.M. Addit. MSS

Sir

My excursion to Brighton and since my return having been fully
employed on business that could not be put off has prevented my
obeying Your Royal Highness's commands which I was honored with
on the 5th Instant – and hope you will excuse. – I have now the honor
to lay before Your Royal Highness Lieutenant Colonel Twiss's report
in a letter to Lord Cornwallis with an estimate of expense calculated to
attend the inundating Romney Marsh, the Country bordering on the
River Rother, Pevensey Level, making dams for the purpose and erecting works to protect the sluices and to request your commands for
carrying the same into Effect which will very greatly strengthen the
position of those parts, and how the money is to be paid, as also, when
done, the pay of the people appointed to attend the sluices et cetera,
and opening Dimchurch walls to render the plan effectual on the actual
landing of an enemy. I have it not yet in my power to send Your Royal
Highness a sketch of the position from Uckfield to Orleston, on the
Clayhills but you shall have it very shortly.

(b) Proposal of the Royal Military Canal. Gen. Sir D. Dundas and
Lt Col. J. Brown to the Duke of York, 19 September 1804
FROM: P.R.O., WO/30/78

Lt Col. John Brown writes:—

It is proposed to make a Cut from
Shorncliffe Battery, passing in front of
Hythe, under Lynn Heights to West
Hythe following nearby the dotted
line C.D. This Canal or Cut should be
Sixty feet wide at the Top, Forty at
Bottom, and Nine Feet Deep, which
would always ensure from 7 to 8 Feet
of Water, and being everywhere within Musket Shot of the Heights; under
such circumstances it might be
deemed impregnable. This would
only form part of a greater Plan which
might be advantageously extended on
the same scale along the rear of Romney Marsh, under Lynn and Alding-
ton Heights, by Hurst, Balington,
Ruckinge, Wearhorn, Appledore,

Gen. Sir David Dundas comments:—

The Ditch or Canal proposed, of
the Dimensions and to the extent
pointed out would most effectually
Bar the entry into the Country out
of Romney Marsh. On the West End
it is strongly flanked by Rye, Playdon
Heights and the Isle of Oxney, as it is
at the East End by the Lynn and the
Hythe Heights and other defences.
Did such an obstacle present itself the
attempt upon Romney Marsh would
probably not enter an Enemy's contemplation, and he would be thrown
beyond the Reach of an attack by
small Vessels.

Such a Ditch or Canal would not
be totally unproductive and [would]
be of use for commercial and Hus-

N*

Lt Col. John Brown writes:—

under the Heights of Oxney Isle, and join the River Rother above Boons-bridge, thus in a manner cutting off Romney Marsh from the Country, opening a short and easy communication between Kent and Sussex, but above all rendering unnecessary the doubtful and destructive measure of laying so large a Portion of the Country Waste by Inundation. The whole length of this Canal would not exceed Nineteen Miles and it covers near 30 Miles of assailable Coast. On the Interior side of this Cut a great Military Road would be conducted its whole length, and by throwing the excavation all on the interior side, the Road would be raised and covered by a Sort of Rampart, thus:—

[Neat sketch of section occurs here]

The following rough Estimate will demonstrate that this plan is not of such Magnitude as may at first appear and that it is practicable even in a short period.

Sixty feet at Top, forty at Bottom and Nine feet deep gives for every yard in length Fifty Cube Yards to excavate. One Good Labourer will dig and remove to a moderate distance 12 Cube Yards per day, but allowing ten Yards to each man, One Labourer will excavate in five days [pencilled correction 'six'] a Yard in length of this Canal; consequently if 1760 Men were employed on it, they would complete one Mile of it every five [pencilled correction 'six'] days. The general expence of such works is about 6^d p. Cube Yard, amounting in this Case to £2,200 Per Mile, or on the whole length of 19 Miles to £41,800. As the Road would not be made till after the Canal was navigable, it would then be done at no great expence. I believe it is certain that this Canal may be carried on one level without a Lock or Sluice except one (if the latter) at its junction with the Rother by which it would have a communication at Rye Harbour with the Sea.

Gen. Sir David Dundas comments:—

bandry purposes. Floating Defences would be moveable and manageable, and contribute much to its Strength and the quick movement of Troops. Partial inundation would bar its approach, and Temporary Bridges on all Passages leading out of the Marsh would afford quick Passage for the Inhabitants and Cattle, and when necessary leave the Interior a desert for the Enemy.

Supposing a Breadth of 120 Feet necessary for the Ditch, Parapet and Road about 320 Acres of Ground would be required to be purchased, suppose at £50 per Acre – £16,000. In addition to the Excavation, this would be the principal expense and £80,000 seems a full allowance to put it in a complete State.

At any rate the Excavation of the part recommended in the Neighbourhood of Hythe is essential and within a very moderate Expence.

Lt Col. John Brown writes:—

Without pursuing this Idea further at present, it seems essential that something of this sort should be adopted, perhaps on a lesser scale about 30 feet wide at the top, 20 at bottom and 6 or 7 feet in front of Hythe and I am persuaded will prove the readiest in execution, the most effectual in Defence and the least expensive Plan that can be resorted to, to place this part of the Coast in a state of perfect Security; it would even be greatly advantageous to carry it for the present only as far as Lynn Heights, where a work might be placed at E to flank the end of it at F.

23. The Fortification of Eastern England: the Problem of Landguard Fort. Memoir of Gen. Sir James Craig, 11 July 1804
FROM: P.R.O. WO/30/78

[Craig points out that an invasion from the ports of Holland can only
come in the sort of easterly winds that would blow Britain's blockading
squadrons off their stations; but such a wind would raise too dangerous
a surf on the East Anglian coasts for a landing on open beaches to
be practicable. Therefore the enemy must 'make for a Harbour in
which they may land in smooth water and in which they may take
measures for the future security of their vessels'. Craig then continues
as below].

Harwich is the only Harbour on the Coast of the Eastern District
that comes in any way under this description and I own that I have all
along been particularly anxious that something further should be
done for its security. All the other Harbours on the Coast of Suffolk
are small and difficult of access . . . Yarmouth (in Norfolk) is indeed of
another description from these . . . and will be considered separately.

At present the Defence of Harwich rests almost entirely on Landguard Fort. The Batteries here are all well placed; though some of them
are a little out of repair they form, a good line of Sea Defence. Unfortunately the great breadth of the Entrance of the Harbour prevents
its being so entirely under the Command of them, as it should be, for
the purpose of compleat security. The Channel for Ships, or Vessels of
any size, lies very near the Fort, but Boats of small draft of Water may
pass it at almost any part of the entrance. The Tide is from 14 to 18
Feet, and I have never yet seen any of Shoals dry, at the lowest Tide
at which I have happened to be there. This I consider as a sufficient
answer to those who would persuade me that Vessels cannot pass
anywhere but in the Channel that runs near the Fort.

The defects of the Fort at Landguard are well known; we have done
what could be done to it in its present state, but I by no means consider
it as secure against a Coup de main; on the contrary, I think a resolute
Enemy would carry it by escalade – at any rate it is certain that it would
not stand two Days if any Enemy having passed with his boats should
have landed and should be desirous of its Possession, in order to be
complete masters of the Harbour.

The consideration of what could be done at Landguard Fort to
render it tenable against an attack by Land does not perhaps strictly
fall within the scope of what is required [in this report]. It is, however,
so much connected with the consideration of the defence of Harwich
that I may be excused for referring to it. I fear nothing short of pulling
it down and erecting a new one of larger dimensions in all its parts

would be effectual, and that I apprehend is scarcely to be undertaken at this Moment. While, however, the opposite Coasts of Flanders and Holland continue hostile to us, Harwich will in my mind be the most important point of the whole extent of Coast from the Thames to the Forth and the money would be well laid out that may be expended on its security. In the meantime I think it should be submitted to the consideration of some of our ablest Engineers whether anything short of reconstruction could be undertaken at Landguard Fort. Possibly half moons before the Curtains and Counterguards before the Bastions, with a good covered way, instead of the present miserable one, might be constructed at a less expence than a New Fort. They must, however, contain lodging for a more considerable Garrison than can be couped up in the confined area of the present Fort.

[Yarmouth Road is so difficult to enter that Craig will trust defence there to the Navy who can remove buoys.]

24. British Manpower: the Royal Navy and the Problem of Sham Americans.
(a) Capt. M. Western to Admiral Lord St Vincent, 3 May 1806, with Enclosures (i) and (ii)
FROM: P.R.O., ADM/1/130

My Lord,
    I beg leave to represent to your Lordship that on examining into the qualifications of the Crew of His

Thos. Brown   Majesty's Ship *Hibernia* under my command, I find the two men named in the margin have passed for American Citizens, and had Protections as such; Altho' by the

Rt. Clark   enclosed statements, made by themselves, your Lordship will observe that one is a native of Falmouth in Cornwall, the other of Edinburgh in Scotland, and subjects of His Majesty.

I have the honor to be,
Your Lordships
Most obedient humble servant
M. Western.

Enclosure (*i*)

I, Thomas Brown, do hereby certify that I am a native of Falmouth in Cornwall and that about six years ago I went to New York in the *Princess Amelia* Packet, where I left her and lived about three years[1] working as a rigger and that a woman I then lived with named Deborah Ann went with me to the Custom house at New York and swore she knew me to be an American, in consequence of which the Custom House gave me a Certificate, as an American Seaman, without asking me any questions.

I then shipped on board the American ship *General Davy*, bound to Falmouth for orders but put into Kingsale in distress – where I was impressed – and sent my protection to the American consul in London about a year ago but have heard nothing of it since.

Dated on board H.M. Ship *Hibernia*
at Sea, May 2, 1806
his
Thomas X Brown

Signed in the Presence of   mark
M. Western Captain ⎱
Ed. Fairfax Master ⎰ H.M. Ship *Hibernia*

[1] That is a period of time too short by two years for Brown to seek naturalisation as an American, even under the Federal act of 1802.

Enclosure (ii)

I, Robert Clark, do hereby Certify that I was born at Edinburgh in Scotland and that I shipped on board the Merchant Ship, *Pitt*, at Greenock sometime in the Month of June, 1803, and went in her to New York where I shipped on board the American Schooner, *Fancy*, belonging and bound to New Orleans. On my arrival there I left her and shipped on board the *Eliza*, a ship belonging to a Frenchman, and bound to Bourdeaux under American Colours, the Captain of which Ship informed me the Customhouse would not clear him out unless all the crew had American protections. He therefore took me and another man to the Office of a Notary Public which man swore he knew me to be an American born, but as I told the Captain I did not like to take a false oath he said there was a writing book laying by the bible, and I might put my hand on that for it was only a matter of form, which I did. The Captain paid 4 dollars to the Notary and I paid a quarter of a dollar to the Customhouse for getting it stamped. The *Eliza* instead of going direct to Bourdeaux went to New York where all her crew was discharged and the Cargo landed and reshipped.

I then shipped on board the *Mary Ann* Schooner and went in her to Havannah and then shipped on board the *Nicholson Guinea* bound for Liverpool from which I was impressed.

Dated on board His Majesty's Ship
Hibernia at Sea –

Signed in the Presence of: –   2 May, 1806
M. Western Captain ⎫   Robert Clark.
Edw. Fairfax Master ⎭   H.M. Ship *Hibernia*

(b) Gambier to W. W. Pole, 11 July, 1808 with Enclosures (i) and (ii)

FROM: P.R.O., ADM/1/138

Sir,

I herewith transmit Captain Quash of His Majesty's Sloop Eclair's report upon cases of four men named in the margin belonging to that sloop and said to be Americans, in conformity to the directions of the Lords Commissioners of the Admiralty signified to me in your letter of 8th. Ultimo accompanied with a document purporting to be the protection of Charles Johnson. I also enclose a paper transmitted at the same time by Captain Quash, signed by Mr Leyman the American Consul to which I particularly beg leave to request their Lordships'

attention, as it is a convincing proof of the irregularity of these documents and the extensive deceit which they are calculated to shield.

I have the honour to be
Sir
Your most obedient
humble Servant
Gambier.

The Honble. W. W. Pole
&c &c &c
Admiralty Office. London.

Docket reads: – 16th July.

Acqt Mr Lyman that no doubt rem[s] of these men being British
Subjects they cannot be discharged.

Enclosure (i)

My Lord,

In obedience to your commands I have to acquaint you that John
Bakeman and Charles Johnson were impressed from the American
Ship *Neptune*, – Osgood Master, in consequence of my conviction that
they were English subjects. Johnson's protection which I herewith
enclose was easily obtained in Charleston at the low price of $\frac{1}{4}$ Dollar.[1]

John Bakeman, whose real name is Edward Thorp,[2] by birth a Welsh-
man, gave himself up as a Deserter (from H.M. Ship *Greyhound* nine
years ago) immediately after the American ship parted company his
protection, similar to Johnson's, has been lost since he was impressed.

Jacob Blasdell and Samuel Brackett are two of four Prisoners who got
on board the *Neptune* at Algesiras, they were in no wise a part of the
Neptune's Ships Company. It is my belief from their dialect that one is
Irish, the other a native of Cornwall. Under this impression little show
of conviction in my mind (*sic*) I caused them to be impressed. As they
are now absent in a Prize I cannot have the satisfaction to forward any

[1] This price is just what Robert Clark paid the New Orleans Customs House
for stamping his protection, and hence this protection was perhaps issued by the
Charleston Customs House, like the one which Thomas Brown got in New York.

[2] Note the *alias*. A deserter would naturally take a false name as one means of
covering his tracks, and any protection he got later would be made out in the
false name. These facts may lie behind Dr Zimmerman's observation 'Lyman
charged the British with making it a rule to impress seamen under different
names so that when applications were made for their release they could reply
that they had no one by that name'. (*Impressment of American Seamen*, p. 142).
Note, then, that here the alias is supplied by the seaman who had the crime of
desertion to cover up, and the British officer gives both his names, the true and
the false.

documents they may possess, nor have I any belonging to them in my possession.

I beg leave to state to your Lordship that the information of my having taken their certificates of Citizenship from them is willfully incorrect. Enclosed I have the honour to transmit a paper that will prove Mr. Lyman is not over scrupulous in *granting* papers for the protection of Deserters and others, however delicate he may be on the subject of withholding such documents.

I have the honor to be Your Lordships obediant humble
servant
C. H. Quash.

Rt. Hon.
Lord Gambier,
Commander in Chief.

Enclosure (ii) [printed overleaf]

(c) Capt. John Gore to Sir Charles Cotton, 15 September 1808
FROM: P.R.O., ADM/1/138

The Facillity with which American Protections and Certificates are Obtained in London is too notorious to need animadversion from me – but I trust the following Circumstances will not be deemed Irrelevant or Improper from me upon this Subject, as His Majesty's Navy has lost many hundreds of its most valuable Seamen by similar Frauds.

William Williams a Seaman lately sent from *San Joseph* to this ship told me when I was mustering him that he was an American – He had been under my command in the *Triton* and then called himself an Englishman. I consequently enquired – what circumstance had made him so and where was His Protection and Certificate of Birth. He replied that when he heard where he was coming and who was his Captain, knowing they would avail him nothing, he had thrown them overboard, for that he could any Day get others as he had them, *for half a Crown in London.*

Enclosure (ii) [to Gambier's letter of 11 July, 1808]

ROLL

Roll of the Officers and Seamen on board the American *ship* Called *Wareham* of *New York* whereof *Richard Chadwick* is Master, bound from the Port of *London*, to the Port of *Tangiers*

Names	Stations	Native of	Residence	Description			Hair	Complexion
				Age	Height			
					Feet	Inches		

AMERICAN CONSULATE AND AGENCY
London

THESE may certify that *Richard Chadwick* Master of the above named *Ship Wareham* Personally appeared before me, and made Oath, That the above Roll contains the Names of all Officers and Crew of the said Ship, together with their Places of Birth and Residence, as far as he is able to ascertain the same

GIVEN under my Hand and Consular Seal, this *Eleventh* DAY OF *March* in the Year of our Lord One Thousand, eight Hundred and *Eight* and of the Independence of the United States the Thirty Second

Wm. Lyman

Consular
Seal

[*Note*. Italics indicate words written in by hand].

25. British Manpower: Report on the Royal Artillery, 1803.
Lord Chatham to the Duke of York, 7 July, with Enclosure
FROM: P.R.O., WO/30/76

St James's Square.
7 July, 1803

Sir,

I was honoured with Your Royal Highness's Letter of the 24th of
June recommending to me (the) . . . carrying into immediate effect the
full extent of Ordnance preparation, which Your Royal Highness
considers as necessary within the principal Military Districts and at
the same time detailing not only the Number of pieces of which the
Brigades should be composed, but also the several Natures of Ordnance
which Your Royal Highness wishes should be introduced into the
Field Service.

Having given the subject a very full and minute consideration I shall
proceed to offer Your Royal Highness such observations as the Duty of
my Situation indispensably requires and to submit to Your Royal
Highness such a proportion of Ordnance for the Field Train and such a
Disposition of it as I should conceive under all circumstances to be most
for the good of His Majesty's Service.

I have in the first place the satisfaction of being able to state to Your
Royal Highness that there would be no difficulty in complying with the
full extent of Your Royal Highness's requisition, as far as concerns the
several Pieces of Ordnance demanded together with an ample supply
of Ammunition; also that the additional Number of Horses probably
might, by great exertions, be obtained at no very distant Period; and
it would be in Your Royal Highness's power to direct the appropriation
of 1,500 Men of the Army of Reserve of serve as Gunner Drivers, as it
would be impossible at this time for the Contractor to obtain a sufficient
number of Men either fit for the purpose or that could be depended
upon.

So far, therefore, there does not appear to be much difficulty in
complying with Your Royal Highness's demand, but what I feel it
my duty to press most earnestly upon Your Royal Highness is the
consideration that the strength of the Royal Regiment of Artillery at
Home is totally unequal to so large an Equipment and that although
Your Royal Highness is pleased to propose the furnishing any Number
of Men as additional Gunners from the Militia (Over and above those
Corps already placed at the disposal of the Ordnance) I do not conceive
they would in any respect supply the deficiency under which we labour.
I know that *good will* and *numbers* will sometimes supply the quality of
Troops, but I take it that the reverse is true with respect to Artillery, at
least for the Field Service; that it is only formidable in as much as it is

efficient and that a numerous Field Train, with all its appendages, unless conducted and served by Officers of experience and Science together with a due Proportion of trained Artillerists and expert Drivers, is so far from being useful, in comparison to the enormous expence, that it is on the contary in itself a serious evil and a dangerous encumbrance upon every movement of the Army. It is in this view that I must beg leave to differ from Your Royal Highness's Proposal of making the several Brigades consist of Eight Guns, and upon this principle, that though one Captain may direct 6 guns, it would be necessary to attach Two Captains to a Brigade of Eight Guns, unless an increased proportion of Subalterns could be given; whereas so far from that being in our power, there will actually be one Subaltern less than there ought to be, to the Brigades of the present number of pieces, if composed, as intended, in part of Howitzers.

The Number of Field Brigades which I conceive may be furnished as really efficient are detailed in a paper which I have the honor to enclose, and I have calculated them according to the Strength of the Royal Artillery, which either are or can be sent into the several Districts together with the Militia Corps attached to the Artillery Service.

This proposition would, I trust, be deemed sufficient to be brought forward, at least as yet, and that the *Reserve*, destined principally for the Service of the Eastern and Southern Districts and to man which would require the whole effective Force remaining at Woolwich, including all the Recruits now at Drill, might be suffered to remain there till some moment of emergency should require the whole, or any part of it, to move to a more forward position. For unless a certain portion of Artillery is suffered to remain at Woolwich, there would not only result the greatest possible inconvenience and Danger to the Establishment itself, but there would be an end to all further exertion, and to the hope of bringing forward, in the event of obtaining Recruits from the Army of Reserve, such a respectable increased force as may be applicable to any Service either at Home or Abroad.

The Additional Brigades, which I propose bringing into the Field, together with the Reserve, and other general Services called for, will cause a large addition of Horses, and I should therefore hope that Your Royal Highness will have the goodness to order not less than 1000 Soldiers of the Army of Reserve to act as Gunner Drivers. Detachments from the several Regiments of Militia will be wanted for the Coast Batteries, unless an arrangement can be made by the General Commanding in the District for their being manned either by the Sea Fencibles or Volunteers.

With respect to Your Royal Highness's demand for Horse Artillery, I perceive it extends to Seven Troops, which is one more than at present in England. I should also hope that Your Royal Highness would consider the necessity there is for keeping one Troop at Woolwich, not only for the Security of the Capital, but that it is essential with a view to a progressive increase of this Force, and, since the establishment of the ferry and road to Ilford, it can be considered as applicable to the service of the Eastern District.

Orders have been given for increasing the Troop in Ireland to Eight Guns and it is my intention to add as soon as possible a like number to the Troops in England; this augmentation will more than give what Your Royal Highness asks, and as the troops of Horse Artillery have by their Establishments two Captains, they may be occasionally distributed to act as half troops.

I am inclined to think that the Spherical Cannon Shot,[1] to which Your Royal Highness alludes, may be brought into Service with great advantage, and with most natures of Ordnance, but to what extent and under what circumstances it should be used requires further consideration. I have directed a large supply of Shells suited to its purpose to be prepared. . . .

Your Royal Highness, I believe, knows the uniform anxiety I have felt to be enabled to bring the Establishment of the Royal Artillery to a Scale more adequate to the numerous and various demands upon it than it has been the policy of this Country for many years past to place it upon; but Your Royal Highness at the same time knows that in a Profession as scientific as that of Artillery, the increase can only be to a certain degree gradual, without the risk of rendering it inefficient.

[1] So WO/30/76 reads; but 'Spherical *Case* Shot' (meaning Shrapnel) is almost certainly intended.

Field Train etc. of Artillery in England. 8th July 1803

| | 12 Pounders | | 6 Pounders | Howitzers | | General Totals |
	Medium	Heavy	Light	8 Inch	5½ Inch	Pieces Of Artillery
Southern District						
2 Heavy Brigades	8	„	„	„	4	
2 Do Do	„	8	„	„	4	
4 Light Do	„	„	16	„	8	
Battn. Guns for 13 Regr·Regts	„	„	26	„		— 92
3 Troops of Rl. Horse Artillery	„	„	12	„	6	
Eastern District						
4 Heavy Brgds as above	8	8	„	„	8	
4 Light Do Do	„	„	16	„	8	
Battn Guns for 9 Regr·Regts.	„	„	18	„	„	— 72
1 Troop Rl. Horse Artillery	„	„	4	„	2	
South West District including the Isle of Wight						
1 Heavy Brigade	4	„	„	„	2	
2 Heavy Brigades	„	„	8	„	4	— 24
1 Troop Horse Artillery	„	„	4	„	2	
Western District						
1 Heavy Brigade	4	„	„	„	2	— 18
2 Light Brigades	„	„	8	„	4	
Yorkshire District						
1 Brigade	„	„	4	„	2	— 6
Northern District						
2 Brigades	4	4	„	„	4	— 12
Reserve at Woolwich						
Park of Artillery*	12	18	38	12	„	
1 Troop of Horse Artillery	„	„	4	„	2	— 86
	40	38	156	12	62	310[1]

* A Light Brigade according to a project of Major General Congreve is also forming under his direction.[2]

[1] The figures do not add up correctly but are given as they stand on folio 188 of WO/30/76.

[2] The 'project of Major General Congreve' on which a Light Brigade was being formed is almost certainly an oblique reference to his newly invented and highly secret 'Congreve Rockets'.

26. British Manpower: the Progress of the Volunteers.
(a) Lt Col. Maxwell, to Lt General His Royal Highness Prince
William Frederick, 25 February 1804
FROM: P.R.O., HO/50/397

Sir,

I beg to represent that having, agreable to Your Royal Highness's
Command, inspected the different Volunteer Corps in Manchester and
its Neighborhood – I have found the Arms in possession of the 1st.
Manchester and Seaford[1] Regiment, commanded by Lt. Colonel J. L.
Phillips, received from the Government Store in Chester, in so very bad
a state as in my opinion to be entirely unfit for Service, except the
Flank Companies which have been provided with new Arms of Superior
quality from the Funds of the Regiment – I have the pleasure to assure
Your Royal Highness that this Corps is deserving of good Arms –
being highly disciplined and in every other respect fit for immediate
Service.

I have been informed also by the Commanding Officer that an
allowance for Accountrements of 4/6d to 5/– per Set has been promised
by Government, but not yet paid; they are provided, however, at the
Expence of the Town. They also claim Knapsacks, Havresacks, Canteens
and Great Coats from Government.

The Second Manchester and Salford Regiment, commanded by
Lt. Colonel Silvester, have been provided with 841 Stand of new,
excellent Arms, but are yet deficient in 239, with which they are very
anxious to be supplied, as also Knapsacks, Havresacks, Canteens and
Great Coats – and I cannot do otherwise than Report this Regiment
as equally fit for immediate Service.

The Oldham Volunteers, commanded by Lt. Colonel Lees, have
received 180 Stand of Arms in very bad condition – they are old Dutch
Pieces, but may be repaired; the remainder, to the number of 300 are
provided by the Corps and are remarkably good.

The Ashton-under-Line Volunteers, commanded by Lt. Colonel
Wood, have been provided with very good arms complete, but have not
received any accoutrements; – both these Corps are also perfectly fit
for immediate Service. . . .

I have the honor &c.
(signed) H. Maxwell,
I.F.O.

[1] So says the text in HO/50/397; but the text is a copy made in the Quarter
Master General's Office and this is certainly an error for 'Manchester and
Salford'.

(b) Gen. H. E. Fox to Major Gen. H. Calvert, 14 March 1804
FROM: P.R.O., HO/50/397

Sir,

I have the honor to enclose the Reports of the Inspecting Field
Officers of the Yeomanry and Volunteers in the Home District.

Having seen a considerable proportion of these Corps myself in each
County of the District I have satisfaction in observing that there
appears without exception a general zeal and order for the Public
Service, although for a variety of circumstances some are infinitely
more forward than others; but the majority of them (both Cavalry and
Infantry) are in my opinion fit to be joined to Regular Troops; indeed,
much more so than many new raised Corps and bodies of Recruits I
have frequently seen join an Army on Service and who have upon
joining almost immediately been opposed to the Enemy and have
behaved well.

In many Corps it is certainly to be wished that the Officers (Gentlemen of Education and Abilities) would attend themselves more to the
Instruction of the Privates who are frequently left to much to hired
Drills (many of whom are discharged Serjeants not of the best
character. . . .)

All the Corps I have seen are well clothed but several want Great
Coats and I am well informed by their Commanders that there are no
possible means of obtaining a Fund sufficient to procure them – in
some instances it is conceived that money has been thrown away in
useless ornaments and appointments, which might have procured
comforts, and, if I may presume to give my opinion I should think that
the Volunteers ought to be discouraged as much as possible in indulging
in useless and ornamental dress.

In the countries of Berks and Hertford the Volunteers are by no
means completely armed and I have everywhere found a great repug-
nance to receiving Pikes and very few Corps have been able themselves
to supply the deficiency of Arms from their own Funds.

I think it however my duty to say that considering all circumstances
they have improved to a surprising degree and I repeat that I think the
majority of them which I have seen are fit to join the Regular Corps if
the emergency of circumstances require it. . . .

I am &c &c.

H. E. Fox.

27. British Manpower: Marching Orders for the Volunteers.
Duke of York to Generals Commanding Districts, 27 March 1804
FROM: P.R.O., WO/30/76
Confidential

Sir,

Circumstances requiring that arrangements for the Assembly of the
Volunteer Force should forthwith take place throughout the Kingdom,
with a view to its being brought into activity in support of the Military
Operations in which His Majesty's forces may be engaged – I have to
acquaint you that the principle, upon which this Disposition proceeds,
is the allotment of the Volunteers of the Coast Districts most exposed
to Invasion, for their immediate Defence; in which case the Force is
from the beginning left at the disposal of the Generals in Command
who are to direct the Assembly and march of the Corps according to the
extent of danger against which they are individually called upon to
provide.

In some Districts of less easy approach to the Enemy a part only of
the Volunteers are left at the disposal of the General in Command.

In the Inland Districts Places of Assembly are given upon such
centrical Points as are conceived to be most convenient for the primary
Assembly of Large Bodies, with a view to the force being afterwards
directed for the support of whatever Districts may have become the
Theatre of War.

The Volunteers of the Metropolis, forming in themselves a considerable   [blank in orig.] will be called upon to detach according
to the circumstances of the moment.

The numbers given are from the January Inspection Returns –
which, although they do not in every instance afford the complete
information required, are such as to enable me to determine a general
outline to be the guidance of every General Officer in Command,
should the Troops be called into the Field upon any sudden emergency.

This Disposition may hereafter undergo such alterations as experience
and a further knowledge of the circumstances may render expedient.

[The list is printed overleaf]

Where the Force of any County is to be divided, you will immediately
determine upon the Corps which are to remain and those which are to
march, and the latter to be notified by you to the General for whose
district they are intended.

Previous to its being possible to determine the Numbers which can
actually march, it is necessary that you should ascertain how far a
measure recommended to Lords Lieutenant of Counties by the
Secretary of State in a Letter dated the 8th November, 1803, [?Decem-
ber intended?] has been carried into Effect – namely, to provide for the

General Disposition of the Volunteer Force

1st Head	2nd Head
Consisting of the Force left at the disposal of the General in Command.	Volunteer Force whose places of General Assembly are ordered as follows.

Northern District

Northumberland
Cumberland
Westmoreland
Durham
}

Cavalry　Infantry
1050　　13076

Yorkshire District

	Cav.	Inf.		Cav.	Inf.	
East Riding } York North Riding }	655	8802	York West } Riding	1408	12,803	} To assemble at Wakefield
Lincolnshire	661	6720				

Eastern District

Norfolk
Suffolk
Cambridge
Huntingdon
Essex part within
the district
}

Cavalry　Infantry
2961　　18,600

Southern District

Kent part within
the District
Cinque Ports
Sussex
}

Cavalry　Infantry
1521　　10,257

South West District

	Cavalry	Inf.		Wilts	Cav.	Inf.	
Hants } Dorset	1475	10296			745	4,299	} at Salisbury

Isle of Wight

Isle of Wight　Cav.　　Inf.
　　　　　　　98　　1772

Western District

Devonshire
Cornwall
Somerset part
within the
District
}

Cavalry　Infantry
2797　　23,246

1st Head   2nd Head

Severn District

	Cav.	Inf.		Cav.	Inf.	
Monmouth			Somerset			
Brecon			part			
Cardigan	Cav.	Inf.	within the	427	3943	
Carmarthen	—	7,945	district			Gloster
Glamorgan			Gloucestershire	381	3742	
Pembroke			Worcestershire	520	3191	at
Radnor			Herefordshire	„	2865	Bristol

North West District

	Cav.	Inf.		Cav.	Inf.	
Anglesea			Shropshire	900	4975	At
Carnarvon						Gloucester
Denbigh	Cav.	Inf.	Cheshire	200	2000	Chester
Flint	797	9009		461	2568	Litchfield
Merioneth			Lancashire	287	3000	Liverpool
Montgomery				300	9626	Litchfield

North Inland District

	Cav.	Inf.	
Derbyshire	314	5093	
Notts	452	3416	Litchfield
Staffordshire	847	6063	
Leicestershire	487	3024	
Warwickshire	486	3752	Northampton
Rutland	172	332	

South Inland District

	Cav.	Inf.	
Oxfordshire	499	2643	Reading
Bedordshire	186	2401	
Northampton	927	2688	Aylesbury
Bucks	1125	2356	

London District

	Cav.	Inf.	
London	1403	26880	To assemble in the Metropolis
Part of Middx.	34	6765	
Part of Essex	138	1063	Brentwood
Hertfordshire	567	2172	
Part of Surrey	622	4934	Dorking
Part of Kent	192	1551	Bletchingley
Berkshire	539	2886	Reading

RECAPITULATION OF THE VOLUNTEER FORCE IN RESERVE

		Cavalry	Infantry
At	Wakefield	1480	12,823
	Salisbury	743	4,299
	Bristol	805	7,690
	Gloucester	1420	11,031
	Chester	200	2,000
	Liverpool	287	3,000
	Litchfield	2374	26,766
	Northampton	1139	7,108
	Reading	1038	5,528
	Aylesbury	2238	7,445
	Brentwood	738	9,999
Considered	Dorking	622	4,934
as One	Bletchingley	192	1,551
Station	Metropolis	1403	26,880

Internal Good Order and tranquillity of the County by the appointment of Special Constables from among the Trusty House Holders not included in the Volunteer Corps, to take charge of the Police in the Absence of Armed Force.

Should His Majesty's Lieutenants be of opinion that this measure has not been either so generally or systematically adopted as to Justify a perfect reliance being placed in all cases upon the complete efficacy of this arrangement – you are in conjunction with the said Lords Lieutenant to direct such portion of the Volunteer Infantry to be allotted for the Garrison of the Large Towns, and also such portion of the Yeomanry for Patrolling the Great Roads as will ensure Public tranquillity and the security of all Provisions and Cattle which are travelling to supply the Markets either of the Chief Towns in the Particular Country or in the Capital.

Bridges, commanding principal communications in the County, are in like manner to be guarded by an armed Force.

For these purposes (whenever the Lord Lieutenant should deem the Number of Special Constables insufficient) you will take immediate measures in conjunction with the Lieutenants for determining what Number of the Volunteer and Yeomanry Force it is absolutely necessary to leave behind in each County.

You will then cause an Inspection to be made of the Volunteer Corps by the Inspecting Field Officers, at which a Deputy Lieutenant of the District [query – slip for 'County'] should be invited to attend, when Detachments of each Corps are to be selected for the Home Duty from amongst the individuals least fit for active Service and those burdened with the Largest Families.

Previous to this you will have determined the Numbers each Corps is thus to allot, having reference to its Numbers compared with the

Total wanted, to remain from the whole Cavalry and Infantry of the County.

These precautionary measures are to be immediately arranged.

As I have reason to conclude that the Number calculated upon in the foregoing Disposition falls short of the real effective force within your District, I shall assume that every deficiency of Non-Effectives for Field Service will be made good by the Surplus Numbers not returned by the Inspecting Field Officers upon the 1st January, and I shall therefore direct the formation of Military and Commissariat Depots at each Station, adequate to the Scale pointed out in that General Distribution.

I must further call your immediate attention to other preparatory measures required to give effect to this General Arrangement: –

– To issue March Routes to the Inspecting Field Officers for the march of the different Corps from the place of their Regimental Assembly to the Boundary of your District towards the principal station pointed out for them;

– the General into whose District the Corps are ordered to be informed, that He may make arrangements for their proceeding to the points determined upon;

– the Inspecting Field Officers to have a discretionary power to give those Routes in charge of Commanding Officers of Corps situated so as not to admit of their being speedily sent to.

– Upon the general Signal of Alarm being given the Corps are immediately to Assemble and commence their march, the Inspecting Field Officer attaching himself to the Largest Body collected under his Orders.

– The Commanding Officer upon the march to apprize the General at the Station of General Assembly upon which the Troops are moving of the time when they may be expected to arrive by detaching an Officer for that purpose.

Commanding Officers where there is a deficiency of Arms will direct those belonging to the Non Effectives, or such as remain for the Police, to be made over to the Men of their Corps who march. Measures will be taken for supplying the Men who may still remain deficient, before they are brought into Actual Service, but None on account of want of Arms are to remain behind.

Quartering and Supplying Corps upon their March must sometimes be discretionally [?]. It will however be the duty of the Inspecting Field Officer, or in his absence, of the Commanding Officer of the Corps to make such arrangements as will tend least to the inconvenience of the inhabitants.

Copies of the enclosed Marching Instructions are to be generally circulated by you to the Corps under your command.

Another object to which I am to call your attention is the allotment of proper and connected Cantonments for the Force appointed to assemble at the principal Station named in the Disposition . . . which is within your Command.

This dislocation of Quarters is to be made in reference to the State of things at the only time when they can be required, namely, when the presence of an Enemy demands every consideration is to yield to the Public Service in Quartering troops.

That this inconvenience may be as little felt as possible, Quartering troops upon Individuals is not to be resorted to, until Public Buildings of every description have been set apart, after which the remaining Force must be equally distributed amongst the House Holders according to the capacity of the Dwellings.

You will communicate with the Civil power in regard to the least inconvenient mode of immediately ascertaining the extent of Quarters required for the Numbers stated to assemble at any point within your District. Stabling and Barns of every description must be set apart for the Cavalry and other Horses attached to the Army.

It is also required of you to determine the Situations in which the Carriages attached to the different Corps *are to be parked*. The Ground least intersected with enclosures and having the best communications to the Principal Roads is to be chosen for this purpose.

The Carriages belonging to each Corps are to be conducted to the Park on their arrival, the Horses are to be tied to the Carriages to which they respectively belong, and the Drivers are to remain with them. The same Regulation holds as to the Commissariat or other Waggons of the Army.

The Waggons of the Park are to be guarded by Pickets of Cavalry, and none suffered to depart without an Order from the General Staff.

Of the Waggons and Carts provided in pursuance to the Secretary of State's Letter, dated the 16th of January, the Carts only are to be permanently attached to the Corps. The Waggons carrying Men ordered in support of a Point attacked will continue with them until the Corps come into the Vicinity of the Enemy, or longer should you judge it expedient.

Where the Troops are to march upon a place of General Assembly, you will send their Waggons back upon the arrival of the Corps at that Station.

Lastly, where you are of opinion from the Nature of the Communications that greater inconvenience will arise to the Service (by encumbering the Roads) than can be compensated by the benefit look'd to from the more speedy arrival of the Troops you may order the Corps to move without this assistance.

When the Troops again march from such Place of General [Assembly] they may be expedited by Water Conveyance or by Relays from the Waggons of the Country through which they march, as the case will admit.

Upon the first Alarm, your Head Quarters are to be taken at the principal Station for the Assembly of Troops within your District, where your Staff will be assisted by the Inspecting Field Officer attached to the Volunteers.

Upon the arrival of each Corps, and before it is *dismissed to quarters*, an Inspection is to be made by yourself, or some Officer of confidence; and the following Return is to be filled up and dispatched the same Day to The Adjutant General, Horse Guards.

—— Head Quarters

Inspection Report of the Cavalry and Infantry which arrived
this   Day of   , 1804.

Names of Corps.	Numbers fit for active service	Numbers fit for Garrison Duty	Numbers Armed	Numbers wanting Arms

The 2nd and 3rd Columns are descriptive of the Bodily Strength of the Men whether they are armed or not. The Arms of the Men pronounced fit for Garrison are to be then taken to make good any existing deficiency of Arms within the *same Corps only*.

According to the circumstances of the moment the different Corps may remain some time at the Station under your Orders, or you may be required to direct their march without delay upon a given Point. In the former Case the whole must parade twice each Day for Inspection and Exercise and you will class them into Brigades of nearly 3,000 each.

In the event of there being no Principal Station as yet named in Your District for the Assembly of Volunteer or Other Force, you will please consider the foregoing Instructions in regard to Quartering and Marching as the Rule of your Conduct, should such an Assembly be hereafter ordered, or should you be called upon to detach any part of Your Volunteer Force into a Neighbouring District.

I am, Sir, Yours,

(signed) Frederick, Commander-in-Chief.

28. British Manpower: Brigade Organisation for the Volunteers. Duke of York to Generals Commanding Districts, 12 May 1804.* FROM: P.R.O., WO/30/76

Sir,

Notwithstanding any former directions I have to desire that you will immediately make an arrangement for my approbation for Brigading the Yeomanry and Volunteer Force within the District under your Command.

It is desirable that the Brigades of Cavalry should not be less in Number than 1500 men each nor exceeding 2000, and that the Brigades of Infantry should not be less than 3000 or exceed 4000 men each.

You will also point out the Plans of Assembly for the different Brigades, governing yourself by the local Situation of Corps, and bearing in view that several Brigades are to be Canton'd in the first Instance.

When this arrangement is finally determined upon, Officers of sufficient Rank will be appointed to the different Brigades, and who, according to [the] circumstances of [the] Invasion, will march with them from the Places of Primary Assembly either to a district which has been attacked or to one of the Points of Assembly specified in my letter of the 27th of March.

I am,
Sir,
Yours
/signed/ Frederick

* This date is significant. Pitt had just succeeded Addington as prime minister. This letter appears to mark a change of policy, with the new government approving the Duke's plans which Addington had vetoed earlier.

29. British Manpower: Recruiting the Regular Army.
(a) The Sergeant's Problems
FROM: 'Recruiting the Army' by 'a Practical Recruiter', *United Service Magazine* (1837), III, 433 ff.

Few parties newly sent out are successful at first, for recruiting is a trade, which, like all others requires experience, and many an unfortunate sergeant has been the victim of incautious zeal in his first essay. There are in every town a considerable number of young men who have previously been rejected as unfit to serve, owing to physical defects, imperceptible perhaps to the eye of any other than an experienced medical practitioner. These men gladly avail themselves of the sergeant's anxiety to procure recruits, take his enlistment money, and put him to the expense of supporting them till brought up for medical inspection, when of course they are discharged. As this loss has to be borne by [the sergeant] himself, a few such mistakes teach him to be cautious, and he then finds candidates for enlistment become comparatively scarce, though perhaps, other parties longer in the town, can procure them for their corps without any difficulty. . .
He soon finds that all the martial strains of the 'spirit-stirring drum and ear-piercing fife' – if perchance he has such auxiliaries at his command – are of little avail, and that he might bawl himself hoarse in proclaiming the merits of his corps without adding a single recruit to its ranks; he therefore changes his mode of attack, and wisely determines to follow the example of those who have had longer experience in the service. Finding nothing is to be done without an intensive acquaintance in the town, he visits the public houses and places of amusement frequented by the tradesmen during their idle hours, where he generally spends his evenings, and furnishes many a tale of campaigns he has never served, and foreign adventures he has never witnessed, to his gaping auditors . . .
By such arts as these our recruiter gradually acquires the confidence of his youthful acquaintances – they become pleased with the careless freedom of military life, and readily contrast it with the constant toil by which they have hitherto earned their subsistence . . . and on the first stagnation of employment, family quarrel, or temporary embarrassment in which they find themselves involved, they readily avail themselves of the opportunity of enlisting, and in general constitute the very best class of our recruits, whom none but parties some time domiciled in a town can readily obtain.
Another class consists of workmen who are . . . on the tramp in search of employment; and of these too the sergeant who is most acquainted with the town has obviously the best chance – for as he

takes care to be on intimate terms with the landlord of the house they
frequent he has generally a hint given him of the arrival of any who are
likely to answer his purpose. He drops in, as if by accident, shares with
them his evening potation, hears the detail of their wants and difficulties,
and suggests the expedient of enlistment, which at such a time they are
readily disposed to adopt.

These, however, are dangerous customers, and require to be sharply
watched, for, as it is difficult to trace them, it not infrequently happens
that they change their mind in the course of the night and start off,
leaving the sergeant *minus* the expences he has incurred on their
account. Among this class, too, it necessarily happens that there are
often the very worst of characters: deserters from other corps, or men
who have deemed it prudent to leave home in consequence of the
commission of some serious offence.

A third class is composed of the sturdiest of our yeomen, who, having
increased the population of their parish without permission of the
clergy, are glad to escape the consequences by sheltering themselves
under the licence of the camp. These once constituted the great mass of
recruits from the country districts, where military ardour seems by no
means so readily excited as among the crowded population of towns
[but Poor Law care of bastards has largely cut off this supply].

[The Medical Inspection. (Ibid.)]

The sergeant or person who brings the recruit is of course anxious he
should pass, and not unfrequently gives him some hints how to appear
the proper height; if there is any doubt on the subject. A common
plan . . . is to keep the recruit in bed up to the hour when he is brought
to the subdivision officer to be measured; for, strange as it may appear
to those who are not versed in such matters, most men are taller by at
least $\frac{1}{4}$ inch when newly risen than after walking about for a few
hours.

(b) The Sergeant's Methods
FROM: James Donaldson *Recollections of an Eventful Life, passed
chiefly in the Army,* by a soldier (Glasgow, 1825), 167–72

[He is visited in hospital by a sergeant from Glasgow, who] had been
long on the recruiting service and was considered a first-rate hand at
it . . . (I) expressed my surprise that he should have been so much
more (successful) than others who had been on the same service. He
replied, 'No wonder at it – no wonder at all. I knew Glasgow well. It
was my own place – knew the minds of the young fellows better than
they did themselves – for I had been a weaver myself, and a lazy one

too. I knew how I used to feel . . . The trouble is, you could scarcely ever catch a weaver contented. They are always complaining. Therefore you would never have much troubling enticing them to enlist, if you knew how to go about it . . . for whenever they got lazy, they came up and lounged about the Cross. You could not manage them, however, the same as a bumpkin. They were too knowing for that. The best way was to make up to the individual you had in your eye, and, after bidding him the time of day, ask him what sort of a web he had in. You might be sure it was a bad one for when a weaver turns lazy, his web is always bad; ask him how a clever handsome-looking fellow like him could waste his time hanging see-saw between heaven and hell, in a damp unwholesome shop, no better than one of the dripping vaults in St. Mungo's church, when he could breathe the pure air of heaven, and have little or nothing to do, if he enlisted for a soldier; that weaving was going to ruin, and he had better get into some berth, or he might soon be starved. This was generally enough for a weaver, but the ploughboys had to be hooked in a different way. When you go into conversation with them, tell how many recruits had been made sergeants – when they enlisted – how many were now officers. If you saw an officer pass while you were speaking, no matter whether you knew him or not, tell him that he was only a recruit a year ago; but now he's so proud he won't speak to you; but you hope he won't be so when he gets a commission. If this won't do, don't give up the chase – keep to him – tell him that in the place where your *gallant honourable* regiment is lying, everything may be had almost for nothing – that the pigs and fowls are lying in the streets ready roasted, with knives and forks in them, for soldiers to eat whenever they please. As you find him have stomach, strengthen the dose, and he must be overcome at last. But you must then proceed quickly to work before his high notions evaporate. You must keep him drinking – don't let him go to the door, without one of your party with him, until he is passed the doctor and attested' . . .

. . . 'Your sentimental chaps are the easiest caught of all. You had only to get into heroics, and spout a great deal about glory, honour, laurels, drums, trumpets, applauding world, deathless fame, immortality and all that, and you had him safe as a mouse in a trap.
But if all these methods failed . . . your last resource was to get him drunk, and then slip a shilling into his pocket, get him home to your billet, swear he enlisted, bring all your party to prove it, get him persuaded to pass the doctor, as it will save the *smart* should be he rejected. If he passes you must try every means in your power to get him to drink, blow him up with a fine story, get him inveigled to the magistrate in some shape or other, and get him attested; but by no means let him out of your hands . . .

As for the magistrates, we knew who to go to on these occasions. You
know, it was all for the good of the service . . .
Perhaps we were not ordered to do all we did; but we were black-
guarded if we didn't get men, and that was the same thing; and what's
the use of a man if he can't take a hint?'

(c) Experiences of a new Recruit
FROM: 'Reminiscences of a Light Dragoon', *United Service
Magazine* (1840), II, 455–6

I enlisted in London; and, marching to Maidstone, underwent the
customary examinations, – after which I was attested before a magistrate, and had my bounty paid with strict exactitude. Unfortunately
for me, however, the party into which I was thrown bore no resemblance
at all to a well-regulated regiment. The barracks were filled with small
detachments from a countless variety of corps, and the sergeants and
corporals, on whom the discipline both of regiments and depôts
mainly depends, seem to me at this distance of time to have been
selected from the very scum of the earth. Like a band of harpies they
pounced upon us recruits, and never let us loose from their talons till
they had thoroughly pigeoned us. We were invited to their rooms of an
evening – introduced to their wives who made much of us – praised,
favoured, screened and cajoled, till our funds began to run low, and
then they would have nothing more to say to us. Under these circumstances, we were sufficiently pleased when the order came to join the
regiment . . . being put in charge of one Corporal Gorman.
An admirable specimen was Corporal Gorman of the sort of land-
sharks out of which the staff of the recruiting department used to be
formed. His first step was to extract from each of us, in the shape of a
loan, whatever happened to remain of our bounty. His next was to
defraud us of the better half of our marching money . . . Like bad men
in general, however, . . . he committed the mistake . . . of overshooting
his mark and we, having been much irritated by his tyrannical behaviour,
reported him, when at Lichfield to a magistrate. It appeared that he
was not now about to form his first acquaintance with that functionary.
His worship knew him well; and by a threat of bringing the case before
the General commanding the district, soon forced the knave to pay back
the money which we in our simplicity had lent him. The arrears of our
marching money, on the other hand we never succeeded in recovering.

(d) Bounty Jumping
FROM: *Recollections of Rifleman Harris*, ed. by Henry Curling, with
an introduction by Sir John Fortescue (London, 1928), 3

A private of the 70th Regiment had deserted from that corps, and afterwards enlisted into several other regiments; indeed I was told at the time (tho' I cannot answer for so great a number) that sixteen different times he had received the bounty, and then stolen off. Being, however, caught at last, he was brought to trail at Portsmouth, and sentenced by general court martial to be shot.

30. British Manpower: the Commander-in-Chief on Recruiting.
Duke of York to Rt. Hon. William Windham, Secretary of State
for War and Colonies, 18 March 1806
FROM: George III's MSS, Windsor 12407–18

[Acknowledges Windham's letter of 8th] desiring that I should state
to you for the information of His Majesty's Ministers My Opinion as
to 'the Force which should be maintained, in His Majesty's Dominions,
for the several purposes of Home Defence, Colonial Service and possible
Offensive Operations'.

The advantage of maintaining strong Corps in preference to a larger
number of smaller Establishments is obvious in many points of view,
both as to the efficiency of the Corps themselves and the Economy of
this measure.

[This rule especially applicable to Cavalry – hence practice of last 12
years of augmenting old Corps.]

[Increased importance of Cavalry and Artillery] – the proportion of
Cavalry in all Continental armies is never less than $\frac{1}{6}$ and in some
amounts to $\frac{1}{4}$ of their whole force; whereas in the British army it never
has been above $\frac{1}{8}$, and now if complete to its present Establishment,
would not exceed $\frac{1}{10}$ of the Force required for the Defence of this
Country!

. . . On the Continent where there is comparatively speaking little or
no trade or manufactures and consequently little means for the Employment of the Population otherwise than in agriculture, the Pay and
advantages of a soldier are equal if not superior to that of the Handicraftsman and therefore is a sufficient inducement for a man to enlist;
besides which in most of the Continental Powers the Plan upon which
their Armies are formed by giving a Property to the Captain in their
respective companies and obliging them under pecuniary Risk to keep
them constantly complete makes it both an Object and Credit to them
to use every exertion upon the Recruiting Service:– But in this Country
where all Labor is so exceedingly high and where such inducements
are held out to the Lower Class of the People either to engage in manufactures or to be employed at Sea, and where no temptation whatsoever
is offered to the Officer to exert himself on the Recruiting Service, but
on the contrary he finds himself exposed to great pecuniary risk and
responsibility, that branch of the Service must be materially impeded,
and the continual drain which is unavoidably occasioned by the common
casualties of the Army, particularly in Our Colonial Possessions, causes
such an Annual deficiency, as has as yet at least never been supplied by
ordinary recruiting . . .

Many different Schemes have been proposed and resorted to for facilitating the Recruiting of the Army such as New Levies, raising draftable Corps and raising men for Rank etc., all of which except the latter have more or less failed; as, in the first instance, many of the proposed New Corps to be raised, have never been completed, and many of those that were have proved very inefficient, and at best, have required an enormous time to render them fit for any Service, while the raising of draftable Corps opened a door to all kind of peculation, and brought with it a great many circumstances very disadvantageous and disgraceful to the Service.

The only Plan therefore which has certainly to a degree succeeded has been to permit Officers, under certain restrictions, to raise Men for Rank, allowing them to receive the usual Bounty, which though liable to some Objections has undoubtedly procured a large proportion of men, it being their interest to use their utmost exertions.

Some little advantage has also been gained by receiving Recruits generally from any person who would bring them and therefore it is not improbable that an extension of that Plan by engaging the permanent Non-Commissioned Officers in the Volunteers in that Service might afford some assistance to the general Recruiting of the Army.

[The Duke hopes that Pitt's Armed Defence Bill may be maintained. It is useful for filling second battalions, in which] the men, when raised by the respective Counties, were solely to be placed in the first instance, and from whence, if they could be induced to extend their services generally, they could be removed to the first battalion, thereby making the second a nursery for the first, a system which has been so far crowned with success, as may be seen not only by the actual strength of the first battalions of those Corps, but by the number of men in the second battalions who are already enlisted for General Serivce, and who from the complete state of their first battalions are not yet able to be placed in them. Sensible therefore of the success of this measure, I cannot but regret the intention of giving it up, unless His Majesty's ministers have formed some other plan which they think will be equally productive.

[Proportion of Officers and non-Commissioned Officers is much lower in Britain than in 'any Service on the Continent' and yet in Britain Staff Officers are taken out of Regiments, and vacancy not filled up as on the Continent. To officers thus absent on Staff appointments] must be added the number of Officers who must necessarily be absent constantly on the Recruiting Service, and it will be found that upon an average there is scarcely ever more than $\frac{2}{3}$ of the officers of a Regiment of Cavalry, or of a Regiment of Infantry of one battalion actually effective and doing duty with his Corps, which proportion I am certain every Military Man will agree with me is as small as can be allowed.

[If Armed Defence Bill scrapped (a) second Battalions can go BUT
(b) what is done with general Service
men for whom first Battalion lacks Room? And
(c) what can be done with Limited

Service Men] – as it will be equally impossible to mix them with their first Battalions from the different terms of their enlistment, and it will therefore be necessary to incorporate them into separate Corps, which cannot but create a considerable additional expence, as each of them must, of course, be placed upon the footing of a new Regiment.

[The Duke can make no decision about the Staff of the Army] without being informed what is intended to be proposed to His Majesty concerning the Volunteers. The present staff was formed under the impression of the whole Volunteer Force being held in readiness to take the field at a moment's notice.

[In reckoning force needed to defend Britain Duke of York has] never taken the Volunteer force into consideration, which, however, must upon all occasions be considered though by no means upon the same footing as the rest of the troops.

INDEX